29-1818   H62   91-6941 MARC
Whyte, William Foote. **Social theory for action: how individuals and organizations learn to change.** Sage, 1991 301p bibl index ISBN 0-8039-4166-8, $36.00

Whyte presents insights from 50 years of industrial relations and of fieldwork and community studies of agricultural development in Latin America. These essays challenge mainstream academic sociological theory and research, calling for a revitalization of sociology through ethnography. In Whyte's experience, abstract-formal theories in economics, management, and sociology falter when applied to cultural and historical settings. Whyte argues that theories must be grounded in the specificities of actual cultural settings, in the meanings, intentions, and interests of the groups under investigation. He calls this "participatory action research [PAR]," a variety of applied and advocacy sociology that incorporates the intellectual contributions of ordinary people and endeavors to promote their interests while increasing organizational efficiency. Chapters on the Green Revolution in Latin America, worker's cooperatives in Spain, employee involvement and the "new manufacturing organization" in Japan, the US, and Scandinavia offer fascinating case studies of how grounded theory sensitized to the expertise of ordinary workers and farmers overcomes the deficiencies of formal theory. Yet, Whyte departs from his agenda by attempting a formal theory of action that seems at cross-purposes to PAR. Only future study will determine whether, as Whyte maintains, social scientists can simultaneously achieve new theoretical insights through PAR, improve the technical efficiency of agriculture or industrial organizations, and empower new groups. This book is the summation of a life in the field by a sociological pioneer whose plea for the revitalization of sociology through PAR merits careful consideration. Upper-division undergraduates and above.—*J. H. Rubin, Saint Joseph College*

SOCIAL THEORY FOR ACTION

SOCIAL THEORY FOR ACTION

HOW INDIVIDUALS AND ORGANIZATIONS
LEARN TO CHANGE

WILLIAM FOOTE WHYTE

SAGE PUBLICATIONS
The International Professional Publishers
Newbury Park   London   New Delhi

For information address:

SAGE Publications, Inc.
2455 Teller Road
Newbury Park, California 91320

SAGE Publications Ltd.
6 Bonhill Street
London EC2A 4PU
United Kingdom

SAGE Publications India Pvt. Ltd.
M-32 Market
Greater Kailash I
New Delhi 110 048 India

Printed in the United States of America

Library of Congress Cataloging-in-Publication Data

Whyte, William Foote, 1914-
   Social theory for action: how individuals and organizations learn
to change / William Foote Whyte.
        p.   cm.
   Includes bibliographical references and index.
   ISBN 0-8039-4166-8
   1. Action research.   2. Social participation.   3. Management—
Employee participation.   4. Organizational behavior.
   5. Organizational change.   6. Agriculture—Research.   I. Title.
   H62.W457   1991
   302.3'5—dc20   91-6941
                                                            CIP

FIRST PRINTING, 1991

Sage Production Editor: Michelle R. Starika

Contents

Acknowledgments

For helpful criticisms and suggestions on an earlier draft of this book, I am indebted to Craig Lundberg and Jim Thomas. Davydd J. Greenwood proposed major structural changes in that draft, thus costing me substantial additional work but, I believe, greatly improving the value of the book. His contribution is described in Chapter 21.

For permission to reprint copyrighted material, I am indebted to the *New York Times* and *Business Week*. I am also grateful to the University of California Press for allowing me to print a paragraph from Robert Cole in *Strategies for Learning: Small Group Activities in American, Japanese, and Swedish Industry* (1989). Permission for reprinting quoted material has been received from the International Potato Center and the International Service for National Agricultural Research, from the American Sociological Association and Robert Guest, and from the Cornell University Press for use of a diagram in my book *Higher Yielding Human Systems for Agriculture* (1983, coedited by Damon Boynton).

Over a period of many months, Helen Champlin provided invaluable secretarial assistance. I am indebted to Carol Foster for drafting camera-ready figures.

—William Foote Whyte

1. Introduction

What is this book about? I am presenting a description and interpretation of the evolution of participatory structures and processes in agricultural research and development and in industrial relations. Because I have found striking parallels between the processes developed in such extremely different social and economic settings, I assume that these similarities must have important scientific and practical implications. I aim to explore those implications.

WHY WRITE SUCH A BOOK?

As far as I can interpret my own motivation, I am responding to several driving forces. In the first place, I acknowledge a value commitment to improving the lot of society's underdogs in agriculture, industry, or wherever they are. I learned in my first field study on the street corners of Boston (Whyte, 1943) the weaknesses of paternalistic programs designed to do things *for* poor people and began casting about for ways in which underdogs could participate in improving their own conditions. When I began studying industry, I always was happy to discover cases in which workers had information and ideas, unknown to

1

management, that had the potential of improving efficiency. Years later, when I began studying agricultural research and development in Latin America, I got the same satisfaction from discovering what small farmers knew that agricultural professionals did not know.

Such experiences naturally led me to wonder how the intellectual contributions of underdogs could be incorporated into the work process in ways that would improve the underdog's lot as well as increase organizational efficiency. This book presents my response to that quest.

This book is an opportunity—and a challenge—for me to pull together and spell out what I have learned about social structure and social processes since 1936, when I set out on fifty-odd years of social exploration. As fieldwork has taken me into community studies from Boston to Peru, into industrial studies from the United States to Canada, Venezuela, Peru, and Spain, and into studies of the agricultural research and development process in various Latin American countries, critics (friendly or otherwise) naturally find it difficult to place me and my work in any familiar academic category. I can be described favorably as a very wide-ranging field researcher who comes up with interesting ideas, or, unfavorably, as someone never able to decide what he wanted to concentrate on. At least for my own satisfaction, I feel a need to report what I now see as the central themes of this long quest.

Those central themes lead me here to set forth the theoretical and practical implications of what I have learned through the study of participatory structures and processes in industry and in agricultural research and development.

ON THE RELATIONS BETWEEN
BASIC AND APPLIED RESEARCH

I also have a political objective, in terms of academic politics. I hope to persuade some of my colleagues who are not yet irrevocably committed to mainstream styles of research that it is not only scientifically legitimate to do applied research but that scientific progress requires more integration of theory and practice than has been customary in the academic establishment.

It has taken me many years to arrive at my own resolution of the tension between the commitment to the pursuit of scientific knowledge and the urge to advance human welfare. When I began my first study on the street corners of Boston's North End, as a member of Harvard University's Society of Fellows, I found myself in an academic culture glorifying the values of "pure" or basic science. The chairman of the society, Lawrence J. Henderson, was a distinguished biochemist whose encounter with the works of Vilfredo Pareto had interested him in sociology and led him to teach a seminar on the Italian social theorist and also a course on "Concrete Sociology" focusing on the analysis of cases. A staunch conservative himself, Henderson especially appreciated the way in which Pareto sought to demonstrate that the views of various liberal or radical writers were devoid of rational foundations. Henderson was constantly on guard against any young sociologist who might let his social values or political ideology shape the conclusions he drew from his research.

In this period, I accepted intellectually the separation between basic research and practical applications, but I could not accept it emotionally. I set out to write *Street Corner Society* as a scientific contribution, with only the vague hope that sometime somewhere that book might be used to improve the lot of poor people such as I was studying. I sought to avoid action roles, but my values led me into them on at least two occasions. I could justify one such intervention on scientific grounds: I persuaded a setlement house director to appoint as director of one of three storefront recreation centers a man who had demonstrated his leadership skills on the North End street corners. When Doc, the man I recommended, was able to run a very successful program while the two trained social workers were unable to handle the young corner boys and had to shut down within two weeks of opening, I took this as evidence that I had figured something out.

My other intervention had no such justification. I organized a march on City Hall to protest the lack of towels and hot water in the district's public bathhouse and other cases of neglect in public service to the North End. (The protest march did provoke the city to take some immediate corrective actions but had no long-term effects.) From that experience I learned something about protest marches and their relation to longer-run change programs, but those topics were remote from the main lines of my research. I recognized even then that I was responding to my values rather than to science.

When I moved away from Henderson and Harvard, I gradually abandoned the notion that science and practice should be kept in two separate compartments, but it was not until the 1980s that I was able to combine them in a way that was satisfying to me both intellectually and emotionally. In the years between 1940 and 1980, when I did venture into action research, I was acting out what I now call the *professional expert* model. I would gain entry into an organization, do my fieldwork, figure out the action implications of what I had learned, and then try to persuade the decision makers to follow my recommedations. It was perhaps fortunate that I did not have much success with this model, since that led me to recognize the limitations, beyond my personal lack of social skills, of the model for dealing with cases involving major organizational changes. As I see it now, the skillful professional expert can move people to change their behavior so as to solve or ease current problems, but this role may simply serve to make the organization dependent on the outside consultant rather than contribute to organizational learning.

Beginning with my first field study in 1936 and in many field explorations in later years, I was encountering individuals I liked and also respected for the information and ideas they could give me regarding their own social world. I found I was not using them simply as passive informants to be pumped for my data. In my North End years, Ernest Pecci (Doc) was not only my guide and principal interpreter of the local scene; he read and cogently criticized first drafts of everything I wrote on this project. And I got $100 from Harvard to hire a younger corner-boy leader, Angelo Ralph Orlandella, to collaborate with me on further studies of corner gangs. (This may have been the first time that Harvard had employed a high school dropout as a research assistant.) Later I collaborated in joint publications with practitioners: a union leader in Chicago (Whyte and Garfield, 1950/51) and a management consultant in Peru (Whyte and Braun, 1968).

By my definition, in those projects I was engaged in *participatory research* as my collaborators were not simply providing me with information I requested. They were providing vital ideas and, in the Chicago and Peru cases, they contributed also to writing the research reports. My practitioner collaborators may have gained some satisfaction from the sense of contributing to knowledge that someday and somehow might be useful to society, but I had not yet visualized the possibility of establishing more direct linkages between participatory research and action.

There are various ways of achieving such integration, but I will attempt no comprehensive discussion of these ways. Instead, I will concentrate on one strategy that is little known so far but that seems to have the potential of producing breakthroughs in knowledge while yielding important practical results. I am referring to what I call *partic-ipatory action research* (PAR), a strategy in which professional social researchers go beyond treating members of the organization studied as gatekeepers and passive informants in order to involve some of them as *active* participants in the research process. That means involving them in all stages of the research process—from research design to data gathering, data analysis, and report writing—as well as seeking to apply the implications of the research findings, to the extent to which practi-tioners wish to assume such joint responsibilities.

Those committed to the further development and utilization of PAR continue to explore the various ways in which it can be structured. Some of those ways are illustrated by contributors to a recent book (Whyte, 1990) and in this book. I conclude my treatment of this issue in Chap-ter 21 with a general discussion of the theory and practice of PAR.

DOES SOCIOLOGY NEED REVITALIZATION?

This combination of aims leads me to one more objective. Like many of my colleagues, I have become unhappy with the current state of sociology and with what I conceive to be its mainstream styles of research. I would like to do whatever I can to move my field toward what I see as more promising lines of theory and practice.

One of my aims is to make a contribution to the revitalization of sociology. Does sociology need such help? Although sociologists differ in their diagnoses, there is a surprising consensus among critics regard-ing the unsatisfactory state of our discipline.

After interviewing a number of his colleagues, Alex Inkeles (1986) rendered this judgment:

> The dominant mood today is one of discouragement—a feeling that re-searchers go around in circles, that conceptual clarity is lacking, that theory is uninformed by empirical findings, that blind empiricism is rampant, that knowledge fails to accumulate, and that the former consensus about the core of the discipline has broken down.

After noting the stinging criticisms of our discipline by several of his colleagues, Richard Berk (1988) came to this conclusion:

In short, whether the target is sociology's stance toward the empirical world or its quantitative apparatus, some of the discipline's major figures are now suggesting that as currently undertaken, the enterprise is probably bankrupt. . . . A prima facie case exists that mainstream sociology is in serious, and perhaps unprecedented, trouble.

Without undertaking my own comprehensive review of the state of sociology, let me offer my own diagnosis, focusing on what I see as the chief weaknesses of my discipline as it has been practiced in recent years.

Concentration on subjective states. Years ago I offered this critique of the works of Talcott Parsons, then considered sociology's leading theorist (Whyte, 1959):

Parsons expresses a great interest in "action", and indeed the word is in the title of three of his books. This would lead one to think that Parsons was interested in the actions of people—in what they actually do. In this case, the appearance is deceptive. Parsons is instead concerned with "the orientation of the actor to the situation." In the world of Talcott Parsons, actors are constantly orienting themselves to situations and rarely, if ever, acting. The show is constantly in rehearsal, but the curtain never goes up. Parsons focuses on the process whereby the individual sizes up his social environment and makes up his mind about what he might do. At this point he stops. It is precisely at this point that some of us wish to focus our attention.

Was Parsons an extreme case? And, if not in his day, has sociology changed in this regard in the last quarter century? To be sure, any sociology professor will tell his students that knowledge of the actor's attitudes provides a very imperfect guide to predicting his actions. Nevertheless, with advances in survey methodology and in data processing technology, it has become so easy to amass enormous amounts of data on subjective states and to perform highly sophisticated statistical analyses of the data that many sociologists have been unable to escape from the subjective.

I am not directing my critique at surveys or even at sociological interest in subjective states. Although early in my career I had no use for the survey, since the 1950s I have made increasing use of that instrument, particularly where I think it serves best: in combination with observational and interview data on the actions of the people being studied. Similarly, I find subjective data valuable when linked with behavioral data. (See Whyte, 1984, and Whyte and Alberti 1976, for discussion of the integration of research methods.)

I grant that it is more difficult to deal scientifically with observational and interviewing data on how people act, but I believe we must get on with the job. In this book, I aim to provide some illustrations of how that job can be done.

The gulf separating basic from applied sociology. Not only is there a barrier between the "pure" and the applied, there is also a marked status difference. In the culture of academic sociology, those in the mainstream, doing basic sociology, have high status, whereas those doing applied sociology are thought to be on the fringes of the discipline.

Evidence for this conclusion comes to us neatly packaged in *Contemporary Sociology* (Vol. 18, no. 4, 1989) in reviews of Neil J. Smelser's (1988) monumental *Handbook of Sociology.* Those essays also indicate that there has been no change in the relation between the pure and the applied in the mainstream view over the last quarter century.

In comparing the Smelser volume with Robert E.L. Faris's (1964) *Handbook of Modern Sociology,* James F. Short (1989) writes as follows:

> Faris (1964, pp. 3,34) viewed the social sciences as "the best, and probably the only, basis of hope for control over the modern threats to human survival," but he clearly favored a discipline oriented toward the pursuit of "fundamental knowledge wherever it leads and without reference to early application"; and he expressed confidence that sociology had entered a new cumulative phase in which research-based findings would release investigators "from any special responsibility for making immediate contributions to human welfare."

Consistent with this stance, Faris did not include any chapters on applied sociology in his *Handbook.* Still, he implied that sociology should be able to contribute to human welfare in the long run.

About a quarter century later when Smelser published his *Handbook,* had that long run arrived? Not according to Smelser. In the 824 pages of his opus, he found no place for even a single chapter on applied sociology.

In his review essay, Kai Erickson (1989) offers this dissenting opinion:

Smelser clearly feels that the pressure to be "useful" can endanger the integrity of sociology and that the field itself reached a new level of maturity when it managed a clean break with social work. Most sociologists would agree with that view, I suspect, and would also agree that to assign chapters in a handbook of this kind on what sociology has to say about human problems would be a bit inappropriate. So those who want to argue with that sense of what sociology is and ought to be—as I do—have to recognize that their quarrel is less with Smelser and the authors he has assembled here than with the moral center of gravity, so to speak, of the field they are describing.

Erickson concludes with this observation on "outsiders" who might question this neglect of practical applications:

Those well-meaning outsiders may recognize that a handbook like this is addressed to members of the profession and is not meant as a public display of our wares. But, even so, they may very well conclude that the main subject matter of sociology is sociology.

In other words, if you are concerned with carrying on a well-informed and intelligent dialogue with fellow sociologists, Smelser's *Handbook* is an indispensable resource. If you are concerned with developing a useful dialogue with practitioners, you will get no help here. Even if you simply want to communicate with fellow sociologists regarding how sociological knowledge gets applied in practice, you must look elsewhere.

To be sure, this mainstream view of sociology reflected in the Smelser *Handbook* has been challenged by some prominent members of the profession, and in recent years the executive office of the American Sociological Association (ASA) has been making major efforts to promote applied sociology. However, such promotional efforts can be justified simply in terms of service to current or potential ASA members. Because academia does not provide enough jobs to employ all sociologists, it is important for the association to expand opportunities for employment of sociologists outside of the academy. In that outside world sociologists will not be hired simply on the promise that their research will have practical payoffs in the long run.

While accepting the employment justification for promoting applied sociology, in this book I am emphasizing a different argument: that scientific advances in sociology depend on progress in applied sociology and on the integration of applied sociology into the mainstream of our discipline.

From card shuffling to tape spinning. Many years ago, I was shocked to learn that a Cornell student had been encouraged by the chair of his doctoral committee to do his thesis with a secondary analysis of a deck of computer cards punched with survey data from an earlier field project. All he had to do was figure out several hypotheses not already tested on these data, run the statistical analysis, and then write up what the numbers told him.

Attempting to discourage what I considered a perversion of graduate education, I wrote for *Human Organization* an editorial titled "The Card Shuffling Method of Graduate Education" (Whyte, 1960-61). Today, to adapt the message to technological advances, I would need a new title: "The Tape Spinning Method of Graduate Education," but otherwise the message would be unchanged.

When I wrote the editorial, I was hoping that this method was not becoming common practice, but apparently it has—at least in some universities. In 1981 a colleague in a major university with a highly regarded sociology department told me that tape spinning had become the most common route to the Ph.D. thesis in his department. With so many tapes available from previous studies at this university or from other research centers, it seemed hard for students to resist this fast and easy track to professional status, and those who did resist were regarded by some professors and students as deviants.

When I told that story at a regional sociological meeting, a professor from Penn State came up to tell me of his recent experience in recruiting for a tenure-track position in his department. Nine candidates were invited to visit and present to faculty and students reports on their doctoral thesis research. Eight of those nine were tape spinners. When they were asked what might be going on in the community or organization surveyed that might help to explain the findings, the tape spinners were not only unable to answer the questions but also seemed to feel that the questions were illegitimate. It was as if they were thinking, "If I have the numbers, what else can you expect of me?"

Are our universities now producing sociology Ph.D.'s who have never gone out into the field to gather their own data? If so, must we give up hope that sociologists will be able to communicate with people outside of the academy so as to understand their problems and help them to solve those problems?

MY GUIDE TO RESEARCH AND PRACTICE

I reject the sharp separation between methodology and theory, as often reflected in the academic literature. To a considerable extent, the way I go about gathering research data shapes the theorizing I am able to do with those data. And, as new ideas occur to me, they influence the next steps in methodology.

The data I use are drawn predominantly from my own fieldwork and from the work of those with whom I share major intellectual interests. This poses an obvious limitation: I forgo the comprehensive coverage of the research literature that is expected of the proper scholar. It does give me the advantage of dealing with materials familiar to me and about which I can claim some systematic knowledge.

I study cases. As I go from case to case, I ask myself these questions: In what ways do cases A and B resemble each other? In what ways do they differ from each other? When I think I am beginning to perceive a common pattern characterizing a number of cases, I then begin to look for deviant cases—those that do not fit the pattern. This leads me toward modifying the pattern or reinforcing that pattern, with more detailed definitions of structures and processes.

I am basically interested in understanding organizational behavior, but that requires me to operate at several different levels. I am interested in individual motivation, the relations of the individual to the group, group processes, interorganizational relations, and the relations between technologies and formal structures as they shape organizational behavior—both in industry and in agriculture. With such a wide-ranging focus, it would be impossible to make a comprehensive review of the research literature on all of these topics and still get on with writing this book. I have therefore opted to interpret the data simply in terms of the theoretical ideas that have seemed most helpful to me. I am assuming that I am on the right track so that critics who know segments of the literature better than I do will be able to strengthen the analysis rather than undermine it.

This form of presentation is especially suitable for revealing both how I go about my research and how I think about what I and my colleagues are learning in our field studies. Readers will then be in a position to judge whether some aspects of this way of working and thinking could be useful to them.

PLAN OF THIS BOOK

This book focuses on participatory structures and processes in work organizations. First, I need to define what I mean by participation. I have been studying participation in decision making by those of low formal position and social status as it affects their own work situation and livelihood. I distinguish between the following two forms of participation:

> *Delegation:* Those at the bottom have the right (and the responsibility) to make their own decisions regarding the organization of their work and the work methods used.
>
> *Upward initiation of action:* Those at the bottom make demands, proposals, criticisms, and suggestions to their superiors, and the superiors respond by taking actions in line with those initiatives.

These two forms are acted out somewhat differently in industry and in small-farmer agriculture. In industry, workers may have little opportunity to make their own decisions unless management delegates that right to them. (As we shall see, there is a strong trend toward such delegation in modern manufacturing.) Independent small farmers are generally free to make their own work decisions—except where others have gained control over the resources they need. In such cases, those others can unilaterally make major decisions for them—unless the small farmers are able to engage in upward initiation of action.

Part I of this book focuses on the development of participatory processes in agricultural research and development. Part II applies the same focus to industrial relations. In both fields I start with a chapter on "discovering what ain't so," reporting how some researchers discovered some of the fallacies in then popular theories of how the world worked.

That discovery, however, may have little or no effect on current practices for it does not lead us directly to determining what is so and therefore what can be applied successfully to practice. The next steps depend on what is being learned by practitioners from experience and from field studies, and by the interplay of those two sources of information and ideas.

In studying these change processes, I am focusing particularly on *social inventions* and on the *diffusion and adaptation of social inventions* within organizations and between organizations. I have defined (Whyte, 1982) a social invention as

- a new element in organizational structure or interorganizational relations;
- new sets of procedures for shaping human interactions and activities and the relations of humans to the natural and social environment;
- a new policy in action (that is, not just on paper); or
- a new role or a new set of roles.

I claim that social inventions are as important for understanding social change as mechanical and chemical inventions are for understanding technological change. We should not assume, however, that, once successfully applied at one point in an organization, a social invention will automatically spread to other parts of that organization. I have encountered a number of cases in which the organization lapsed into doing "business as usual" following the solution of the problem that gave rise to the social invention. Even if a social invention does spread widely within a single organization, that does not guarantee its diffusion across organizations.

For understanding both the creation and diffusion of social inventions, I am focusing on *organizational learning* (Schön, 1983b). Purists may argue that it is individuals and not organizations that do the learning; nevertheless, the organization is the major arena in which information and ideas about organizational behavior are learned, taught, and reinforced through experience. The focus on organizational learning therefore guides us through the exploration of the creation, diffusion, and adaptation of social inventions.

Applying this framework to the study of participation, I am seeking in Parts I and II to answer the following questions: How does the need for participation come to be recognized—by researchers and by practitioners? How are participatory processes initially structured? How do they become diffused through an organization? How does diffusion spread from one organization to another? What conditions are required for participation to contribute to both organizational efficiency and members' personal satisfaction? More generally, through studying organizational learning, I am seeking to discover what leads organizational members to go beyond solving particular problems toward learning new ways of organizing work processes.

In Parts III and IV, I look more generally for the theoretical and practical implications of the structures and processes examined in

Parts I and II. What can we learn from these ways of doing research and theorizing in order to advance scientific knowledge? And how can we learn to apply more effectively to practical problems what we have been learning in research?

ON THREE TYPES OF SOCIAL THEORY

As the consequences of human actions can be remote but also important, humans inevitably develop theories regarding the way the world works, at least within their immediate environment.

It is a mistake to assume that only scientists have theories. It is impossible for anyone to behave in an orderly fashion without developing some kind of theoretical framework to provide a context for guiding actions in search of particular consequences. We need to distinguish among several types of theory, along the following lines:

Local theory. Max Elden has drawn attention to the importance of recognizing the local theory in use by members of organizations (Elden, 1979). Furthermore, in any organization where there are important cleavages between different levels or segments, there may be several local theories. Thus there can be one local theory held by members of management and another local theory held by workers. Local theories are not written out or explicitly stated but a researcher can deduce their general outlines through observing consistent patterns of behavior and through interviewing and examining written communications.

Formal theory. Formal theory consists of more elaborate, systematic, general, and explicitly stated propositions. The existence of this body of theory is widely recognized. Formal theories are often developed by powerful and/or socially elite individuals who use the theory to influence and control others. Some elements of formal theory may be based on scientific research, but others are based upon unsupported assumptions. Nevertheless, formal theory gives the believer a coherent view of the way the world works—however accurate or inaccurate that view may be.

In industrial relations, until recent years the predominant formal theory followed by American management arose out of the work of Frederick W. Taylor and his followers in the scientific management movement. In agricultural research and development, no such formal theory emerged in written form, yet what conventional practitioners did and said clearly reflected a formal theory regarding the appropriate relations between professionals and farmers.

Scientifically grounded theory. This refers to a set of propositions that have their primary basis in empirical observations, measurements, and experiments. At any time, researchers may discover errors and incorrect inferences out of scientifically grounded theory, but science advances through the correction of errors and the reinterpretation of empirical data.

In this book, I hope to contribute to scientifically grounded theory. I must also deal with local theory and formal theory. Although local theory in particular and also formal theory to some extent emerge out of past patterns of behavior, they also tend to shape present behavior. We need to understand local theory in order to fit proposed innovations into the preexisting cognitive map of the members of the organization. Because local theory differs from locale to locale and from organizational segment to segment, it is impossible to generalize beyond pointing out its universal existence. Since formal theory is articulated and diffused so widely that we can trace its impact, we will focus on the relation of formal theory to behavior.

To answer the questions stated above, we need to view them in relation to these three types of theory. Only through understanding the local theory or theories that implicitly guide the actions of workers, farmers, managers, and professionals can we understand the baseline from which change processes begin. Only through understanding the formal theory guiding decision making by those in superior positions can we make sense out of the problems those superiors have in changing their own behavior. Only through systematic observation and interviewing in the field of action projects can we contribute to the building of scientifically grounded theories of participatory processes and structures. In this book I aim to contribute to the understanding of the relation between theory and practice for all three types of theory.

PART I

Participation
in Agriculture

2. Discovering What Ain't So in Agricultural Research and Development

"It is better to know nothing than to know what ain't so."

Josh Billings

The wisdom of the nineteenth-century American humorist focuses our attention on one of the basic problems of human learning. If you acknowledge that there is something important that you don't know, then you engage in an open-minded inquiry that is likely to advance your learning. If you think you know something that "ain't so," then you continue to act on this misconception, in spite of increasing failures and frustrations. As humans generally do not abandon a theory simply through the discovery of its faults but tend to persist in error until they envision at least the glimmerings of a more adequate theory, the learning process can be long and painful.

In this chapter we begin an exploration of what we call organizational learning. In the fields we have been studying, the first step in organizational learning is the discovery of "what ain't so" in conventional formal theories. The facts do not speak for themselves. They are always interpreted within some implicit or explicit theoretical framework. When that interpretation does not seem to make sense, we do not simply abandon the theoretical framework that has been guiding our thinking. We ask ourselves first whether we or others have made mistakes in determining what the facts are. If that tactic fails, we can fall back on the old saying that "the exception proves the rule." If that excuse does not appear to be sufficiently scientific, we may then begin to tinker with the theory in the hope that some minor adjustments will eliminate the clash between facts and framework. Only when the continuing discovery of discordant facts makes it too difficult to fit facts and framework together do we begin to think of abandoning a conventional framework.

We begin our exploration by reviewing the accumulating evidence for the inadequacy of the formal theories that have long prevailed in industrial and agricultural development. In the process I will describe my own learning experience and also interpret the learning experience of practitioners and researchers in these two fields. I do not mean to imply that I have shaped the thinking of practitioners and researchers. Whatever influence I may have had has been minor. In large measure I have been learning from studying ways in which practitioners and researchers acquire their organizational learning. I build primarily on my own research and that of colleagues working in these fields because that is the best way I know of telling an important story.

LEARNING FROM THE PUEBLA PROJECT

The reorientation of my own thinking on agricultural research and development stems particularly from contacts with the famed Puebla project in Mexico (CIMMYT, 1975). In an earlier publication (Whyte, 1982:5-6) I presented the following discussion of the reorientation that came out of this project.

> Located in one state of Mexico, the project's purpose was to demonstrate how small farmers could increase their yields of corn.
>
> Puebla was primarily a demonstration project rather than a research project. The designers of the project thought they already knew how to help the small farmers grow more corn, and the research was designed primarily to measure the effectiveness of this technology transfer project. The project involved not only the introduction of improved methods of growing corn but also assistance in securing credit for the farmers, who would need additional funds to buy the inputs necessary.
>
> Over a period of several years, the project enrolled increasing numbers of farmers and demonstrated approximately a 30 percent increase in corn

yields—significant but hardly impressive compared with results then being achieved with high yielding varieties of rice and wheat. Furthermore, the number of adopters of the Puebla project technology, as measured by the number of farmers receiving credit through the program, leveled off at a point where only a quarter of the corn farmers in the program were participating. This led the Mexican professionals implementing the program to wonder why adoption was not continuing to grow. Rather than falling back on the traditional explanations of peasant traditionalism and resistance to change, they went out into the field to observe and study the nonadopters.

The revelation that was key to my reformulation was put to me in this way by Mauro Gomez, Puebla Project general coordinator (1970-1973):

> In Mexico we have been mentally deformed by our professional education. Without realizing what was happening to us, in the classroom and in the laboratories we were learning that scientists knew all that had so far been learned about agriculture and that the small farmers did not know anything. Finally we had to realize that there was much we could learn from the small farmers.

To oversimplify a complex set of results, the Mexican field workers discovered that the basic reason some of these farmers were not adopting the Puebla recommendations was because they were making twice as much money following their own methods. The Puebla program was geared to the monocultural production of corn—that is, planting corn in rows. The most successful nonadopters planted beans between the rows of corn. They were making much more intensive use of their small plots of land and also making more efficient use of fertilizer, which now served two crops instead of one.

When the Mexicans made this discovery, they naturally asked themselves, "Why is it that we have been telling them they should not plant anything between rows?" Not finding any rational explanation, they recognized the force of tradition: "That is not the way they raise corn in Iowa." In other words, their recommendations had been based implicitly upon the model of farming in the midwest corn belt. The monocultural strategy made sense in Iowa where affluent farmers plant large acreage of corn and use tractors, which require space between the corn rows for most operations.

Promoters of the Puebla program realized that where land and capital were in short supply and labor was relatively cheap and abundant, tractors were not practical. However, instead of recognizing that the rationale for leaving empty space between rows of corn depended upon the use of the tractor, they simply proceeded on the implicit assumption that, since the Iowa corn farmers were highly efficient, their methods must be applied in Puebla. In this case, we must ask, who is tradition-bound, the agricultural professional or the peasant farmer?

The traditionalism of the agriculture professionals is strikingly illustrated in the basic Puebla report of CIMMYT, the International Center for Maize and Wheat Improvement, which was responsible for the project. The report has a schizophrenic character. The authors faithfully describe the slowing down of the adoption process and the discovery that farmers intercropping beans and corn were making up to twice as much money off of their crops as those who faithfully followed the Puebla recommendations. Furthermore, they describe how, three years after the project's beginning, project officials endorsed intercropping and stimulated the growth of organizations of corn and bean farmers. At the end of their report, however, they arrive at this extraordinary conclusion:

> Clearly, the job of adjusting and delivering adequate technology, as well as that of inducing farmers to use the recommended technology is very difficult and it is far from being accomplished in the Puebla area. (CIMMYT, 1975)

Of course, it is difficult to persuade small farmers to adopt a new agricultural technology when it promises to cut their crop income in half. How could a group of highly competent agricultural professionals come to a conclusion that bore no relation to the facts they themselves had documented? To answer that question, we must distinguish between accidental and systemic errors. An accidental error is one which may be committed by anyone at any time; a systemic error is caused by the conceptual scheme the researchers bring to bear upon the problem. The designers of the Puebla Project began with a conceptual scheme that visualized the development process as a problem in the transfer of technology in ways designed to overcome the resistance to change on the part of passive peasants. Their own findings were clearly incompatible with such a scheme, but, as historians and sociologists of science have noted, the discovery of discrepant facts may not be sufficient to overthrow an established theory—or, I would add, a more modest construct such as a conceptual scheme. Especially in the early stages of the development of a science, those attached to the established paradigm tend to ignore the facts that don't fit or to make patchwork adjustments in the theory. A popular theory is discarded only after it is confronted with overwhelming contrary evidence and the emergence of a new theory which fits both the old facts and the new facts that have now become available. The writers of the Puebla Project report stayed with their defective conceptual scheme because they had nothing better to put in its place. It remained for those who followed their pioneering work to move toward the new paradigm.

These reflections prompted me to abandon any thought of further studies of peasant resistance to change. I did not go to the other extreme to assume that small farmers are always eager to embrace change but simply that, in general, they are no more resistant to change than are the professionals in their own field of activity. Therefore, when small farmers decline to adopt a proposed innovation, we can generally assume that either (a) they have enough sense to know it would not work, or (b) they lack the money to buy the necessary inputs or cannot get those inputs in local markets.

DISCOVERY IN POTATO RESEARCH

Later, I began learning with potatoes the same lesson I learned with maize and beans in the Puebla Project. In 1976, I accompanied economist Douglas Horton, Head of the Social Science Unit of the International Potato Center (CIP), and agricultural economist Anibal Monares on a mission to ICA (Instituto Colombiano Agropecuario), the agricultural research organization of the government of Colombia.

Since the 1930s, the Rockefeller Foundation had provided substantial funds to support ICA, enabling very able Colombian and American plant scientists to work in various fields, including potatoes. CIP was not being asked for biological information or advice but rather for guidance in establishing a viable seed potato program.

Development of such a program depended on integrating biological knowledge with knowledge derived from economics and organizational behavior. Seed production for potatoes is a much more difficult problem than seed production for grains because potatoes are vegetatively propagated. That is, potatoes generally are grown from potatoes—from the "eyes" or sprouts that emerge from the ripe tuber. In the United States and Europe it has been customary to cut potatoes grown for seeds into pieces, with an eye embedded in each piece. In this way one good-sized potato can be used to seed six to eight potato plants. When plant scientist H. David Thurston was working with ICA in the 1950s, he was told by his Colombian colleagues that this method would not work: It was necessary to plant the whole potato. Like a good scientist, Thurston decided to test that conclusion by planting the cut pieces as he would have done in the United States. Results showed him that his informants had been right. Almost all the cut tubers rotted in the ground.

These differences in planting methods apparently related both to history and to differences in soil, climatic conditions, and plant pathogens. Potatoes were first grown in either Peru or Bolivia hundreds of years ago (both countries claim the origin of the plant). For centuries potatoes have grown along with the diseases and pests that prevail in that region. This means that any successful Andean potato farmer must devote special time and effort and money to the techniques and the chemicals required to eliminate or reduce the prevalence of disease and pests.

This naturally led researchers and program administrators to the conclusion that the production and distribution of "clean" (disease-free) seed potatoes was of fundamental importance for high-yielding healthy potatoes for the consumer market. How could this be done? Because the rate of multiplication of potatoes from seed potatoes is so low, it would not be economically rational for any government to establish its own agency to control the production of seed potatoes to be sold to all farmers who did not choose to grow their own seed potatoes. This meant that seed potatoes sold to growers would be produced by farmers, but, to ensure the quality of their output, a government agency would have to inspect and certify—or disqualify—their fields.

In the United States and Europe the bulk of seed potatoes is grown by farmers, but not by just any farmers. The farmer who wishes to grow and sell seed potatoes must apply to a government agency to be certified as an official grower. Before harvest time a government official makes an exhaustive and painstaking inspection of the plants throughout the designated field. The agency has different tolerance levels for different diseases, and these exacting standards can even result in condemnation of the entire field if the inspector discovers even a very small incidence of an especially serious disease commonly known as ring rot (*Pseudomonas solanacearum*). In this case, it is against the law for the farmer to sell his crop as certified seed potatoes. He can sell the potatoes in the consumer market, but there they will only command about half the price of certified seed potatoes. Condemnation of such a field therefore imposes a substantial financial loss on the farmer.

On the mission to Colombia I learned that this was not the first ICA effort to establish a national seed certification program. Cornell plant scientist Karl Fernow had been striving to develop such a seed certification program in the 1940s (Fernow and Garcés, 1949). There was another effort mounted in the 1950s. In fact, in that era ICA plant scientists reported that they had established a seed certification program, but it had later disintegrated. ICA was now preparing to make the third or fourth try to establish such a program.

Without knowing in detail the history of past failures, I began to wonder whether ICA was aiming for an unreachable goal. Could some adaptation of an American or European seed certification program work in a region where climate, soils, and plant pathogens were much more adverse for potato growers? Besides, one had to consider the capacities of the governments of the region to inspect and control the seed potato production process. Especially when the government is led by a dictator, we may think it is powerful, but—although the armed forces may determine who controls the government in the capital city—such a government may have little capacity to control and regulate the performance of individual farmers. Its limited ability may be further undermined if some of the farmers to be regulated and controlled are members of influential families in their area.

I wondered how farmers got along without a seed certification program. In the Andes, insofar as possible, small farmers grow their own seed potatoes. Potato yields are substantially higher at lower elevations, but virus and insect infestations are also much more severe. Therefore, whenever farmers can use land at higher elevations, they concentrate growing of their seed potatoes at those locations.

In selecting the tubers they will eventually plant for consumable potatoes, the small farmers follow a strategy opposite to that applied in American and European seed certification programs. In those programs, the strategy is to inspect for diseased plants and to condemn plots or a whole field if the infestation appears particularly serious. The Andean farmers also make a meticulous inspection but follow a different logic: They select for seeds those plants that appear to be particularly clean and healthy, using the other tubers for home consumption or sale to consumers.

It is useful to know the indigenous seed selection strategy, but that leaves unanswered a major question: Would the Andean potato farmers be better off if they could buy government-inspected, disease-free seed potatoes instead of growing their own?

To answer that question, Douglas Horton and his associates in the Social Science Program of the CIP worked with potato farmers in the Mantaro Valley of the central highlands of Peru, a major potato growing area. Farmers participating in the experiment were persuaded to purchase seed potatoes from the government potato program and plant them in one plot to compare results with another plot where they had planted their home grown seed potatoes.

This research led to the following conclusion (Horton, 1984:46):

> In on-farm experiments, the use of improved seed increased yields on average by 15-20%. Due to the high cost of the improved seeds, however, its use reduced farmers' net returns below the level obtained when using their own seed.

Horton then goes on to explain this startling conclusion (Horton, 1984:46-47):

> It is generally believed that if small-scale farmers would use certified or "improved" seed, they could substantially increase their yield and income.
>
> Surveys and on-farm experiments indicate that farmers' seed is not as bad as it is generally assumed to be and that for most farmers the use of presently available "improved" seed is uneconomical. Data recorded from farm-level experiments indicate that yield-reducing virus diseases are not as common as previously assumed. . . . There are two important reasons for this. First, farmers' native varieties are not as severely affected by yield-reducing virus diseases as are most modern varieties. Second, farmers' seed management practices tend to minimize the spreading of viruses. . . .
>
> In the Mantaro Valley project, two things become clear: first, that there was little "demonstrated technology" that could be transferred to farmers without local refinement or adaptive research; and second, that farmers are not passive recipients of recommended technologies but active researchers and developers in their own right.

As Horton and others have pointed out, the conventional wisdom regarding the transfer of technology to small farmers is based on mythology rather than on empirical research on small farmers. This is reflected in the concept of "the myth of the passive peasant" (Whyte, 1981; Whyte and Boynton, 1983). According to that myth, there exists a wide body of useful knowledge that could be transferred to small farmers if only the improved technologies and systems could be introduced to them and means could be found to "overcome resistance to change." The record demonstrates that for many years social scientists studying the diffusion of innovation in agriculture have been guiding their research on the basis of this myth. The record indicates that the top-down research and development strategy does not work.

When we place the misconceptions that guided the Puebla Project alongside the Andean potato story, the evidence suggests a broad pattern of wasted investments designed to implement top-down strategies of agricultural research and development. And those programs were promoted and guided by outstanding plant scientists.

I am not arguing that the money invested in agricultural research in general has been wasted. Clearly the plant, soil, and animal scientists have made enormous contributions to agricultural production around the world. I am arguing that, especially for small farmers, their contributions could be enormously increased if they discovered ways of integrating formal research knowledge with the experiential knowledge of small farmers.

Discovering "what ain't so" is an important first step in the organizational learning process; but if learning stops at that point, no practical results are achieved. That discovery tells you what *not* to do; it does not tell you what to do. Linking that discovery to action requires finding and testing new action options. Furthermore, for that learning to be widely shared and acted on, organizational leaders need to visualize and articulate a new cognitive map, that provides a framework for evaluating old and new action options.

RELATING THEORY TO PRACTICE—AND VICE VERSA

Here we have seen how agricultural research and development professionals were misled by their failure to understand the difference between formal theory and scientifically grounded theory. To be sure, they were basing much of their development work on scientifically grounded theory in the biological sciences as it had evolved in their laboratories and experiment stations, but that theory did not tell them how to organize the research and development process so as to work effectively with small farmers.

In their conventional application efforts, they were unconsciously misguided by a formal theory whose nature we can describe from written documents and from what the professionals tell us. As Mauro Gomez learned from the Puebla Project, their university education taught the professionals "that scientists knew all that had so far been learned about agriculture and that the small farmers did not know anything." That basic assumption led to the technology transfer strategy. Then, as the experience of the professionals indicated that small farmers were not readily following recommendations of the professional experts, they fell back on the myth of the passive peasant. That myth in turn led to a search for ways to get the small farmers to do what the experts had decided was good for them.

It was only as some of the Puebla and CIP professionals, and other unconventional professionals in other parts of the world, began to reflect on their own experience in working with small farmers and design research to test and further develop what they were learning that they were able to break the bonds of their misguided theory of agricultural research and development.

The following chapters in Part I continue our exploration from "what ain't so" to some better approximation of what is so in this field.

3. The Context for Organizational Learning in Agricultural Research and Development

In this and the following chapters, I trace the process of organizational learning through the development of participatory action research (PAR) in agricultural research and development. Here I concentrate particularly on Latin America, but much the same story could be told focusing on Asia or Africa. In fact, for decades there has been an active flow of information and ideas, along with agricultural R&D people, among the world's regions and as a result it is impossible to tell the full story of PAR in any region without some reference to developments in other regions.

This chapter provides a context and a general overview of this line of development. Chapter 4 focuses primarily on one national program, the Instituto de Ciencia y Tecnología Agrícolas (ICTA, Institute for Agricultural Sciences and Technology) in Guatemala. Chapter 5 focuses primarily on CIP, the International Potato Center.

So as to link concrete behavior, structures, and social processes with an evolving theoretical framework, I concentrate on particular cases. Why focus on ICTA and CIP? The reasons are both scientific and personal.

ICTA seems to be the first national research program designed to include a strong element of small-farmer active participation in the R&D process. This element is called on-farm client-oriented research (OFCOR) in recent publications of the International Service for National Agricultural Research (ISNAR). ICTA also involved a more highly developed program of interdisciplinary collaboration among plant scientists and social scientists than was present in any other national program at the time ICTA was created. Some of the main strategies and research methodologies developed at ICTA have since been adopted or adapted by many other national programs. For example, a method for making a quick survey of small-farmer farming practices has become so widely known that it is often referred to elsewhere as the *sondeo,* without translating that Spanish word.

At the international level, CIP represents much the same combination of strengths. So far CIP has gone farther than any other international program in integrating a broad range of the social sciences with the plant, animal, and soil sciences and agricultural engineering. The international programs were originally staffed exclusively by biological scientists. Economists were the first social scientists to be invited into the international centers, but, in the early years, they were expected to contribute primarily by doing cost-benefit analyses, comparing at the national level the cost of agricultural research with the benefits flowing from adoption of the higher-yielding plant varieties created at the centers. As some economists ventured to examine cost-benefit questions at the farmer level, this eventually opened the way for involvement of anthropologists and sociologists.

CIP was also the point of origin of the "farmer-back-to-farmer" methodology, a model for farmer participation in the R&D process, which has become widely known and practiced elsewhere. As we shall see, that model bears strong resemblances to participatory models developed in ICTA.

The personal rationale involves both my own fieldwork and past association with some of the key figures in the cases to be described. In the 1970s, I was involved in a field study of ICTA (see Gostyla and Whyte, 1980; Whyte and Boynton, 1983). In that project, I became acquainted with Astolfo Fumagalli, Peter Hildebrand, Sergio Ruano, and Robert Waugh. Hildebrand was a collaborating author in *Higher Yielding Human Systems for Agriculture* (Whyte and Boynton, 1983). Ruano guided me to one of the ICTA project sites with small farmers and later came to Cornell to get his Ph.D. in the sociology of develop-ment. I was a member of his doctoral thesis committee. Later he was coauthor of an impressive follow-up study describing and evaluating ICTA (Ruano and Fumagalli, 1988). That study, along with Ruano's criticisms of earlier drafts of my chapters, has substantially strength-ened my discussion of ICTA and related matters.

Douglas Horton, director of CIP's Social Science Unit, received his Ph.D. in economics at Cornell University during a period (1961-76) when I was heavily involved in research in Peru, where CIP is based. I served on his doctoral thesis committee, and he participated in a seminar on our Peruvian research that I conducted with Lawrence K. Williams. Cornell's involvement in social and economic research in Peru began with anthropologist Allen R. Holmberg in the 1940s, and in following decades Cornell was a major center for research and teaching in Andean studies across a broad range of disciplines. In the mid-1970s Horton got me involved in a brief field project with CIP, and he and his associates have continued to supply me with a flow of CIP's reports and publications.

SETTING THE CONTEXT

We need first to place agricultural research and development in its broad environmental and historical context. The prevailing system of land tenure and the social class structure associated with that system provide basic starting points for analysis.

Throughout Latin America and in many other developing countries, agricultural land has been unevenly distributed, with a high proportion of farm land owned by a small number of families or commercial com-panies. These more affluent families or companies have also gained control over more favorable farming areas, in terms of soil fertility and access to irrigation.

In Africa and Asia the colonial powers fostered export agriculture. In Latin America, liberated from Spain and Portugal in the early years of the nineteenth century, foreign firms and affluent families with strong ties to Europe or the United States similarly emphasized export agriculture.

The farming system practiced by large landholders involved not only specialization in single crops but also heavy expenditures for fertilizers and other chemical inputs, mechanical equipment, and hired labor. The farming systems of small farmers contrasted sharply with the pattern of the large operators. They had to farm primarily for home consumption, hoping to grow a modest surplus for sale to provide money for needs that cannot be met by their land. This has made specialization impractical. Small farmers have generally combined a variety of crops with animal husbandry.

Through the first half of the twentieth century, government planners gave little thought to the special needs of small farmers in developing countries. They tended to assume that the biological improvements arising out of agricultural research were scale neutral: Any advance in knowledge that would benefit large farmers would also benefit small farmers.

The research programs and agricultural experiment stations established by governments and private foundations were far better adapted to the interests of large farmers than to those of small farmers. Experiment stations generally reflected a monocultural emphasis: creating improved varieties of particular crops and determining the best methods of cultivation of each species. The experiment stations were generally located on fertile land with ample water available, and the scientists were concerned with discovering the best combination of fertilizers and other chemical inputs—with little regard for cost as long as the value of the crops raised experimentally seemed to justify a high level of expenditure.

The shift of emphasis toward farming systems and farmer participation was beginning to develop in the 1960s in various areas of the developing world. Richard Bradfield had been a key figure in the 1940s in launching the Rockefeller Foundation's Office of Special Studies, which led to the development of high-yielding varieties of wheat in Mexico and the creation of CIMMYT (the International Maize and Wheat Improvement Center). In the 1960s, when he became particularly concerned about the productivity of small farms under tropical conditions, Bradfield was working with the International Rice Research Institute in the Philippines. Inspired by what he had observed on small farms in Taiwan, Bradfield devised a system extraordinarily intensive in use of land through intercropping, relay planting, and sequencing of planting so as to get three or four full growing seasons within a year.

The Bradfield system was not a practical model for small farmers since it depended on an extraordinarily high level of farm management skills, very large expenditures for inputs and use of machines, as well as abundant irrigation water. Nevertheless, the enormous yields achieved by Bradfield impressed many scientists with the potential for improving the income of small farmers through intensive use of their land.

Small farmers were absent entirely from the Bradfield project, but others following him not only focused their attention upon farming systems but also began developing participatory experiments with small farmers (Harwood, 1979). In Africa, M. P. Collinson (1972) and David Norman (1973, 1980) took the lead in investigating farming systems under indigenous conditions.

Studies of indigenous farming methods led researchers to question the value of plowing tropical soils, as traditionally done in temperate climates. Tropical soils often give better results if not disturbed by plowing. This discovery has led to a growing number of experiments in "minimum tillage"—a fancy new name for a very old principle. Ironically, scientists were finding that, in some conditions, the "primitive" digging stick is a more useful tool than anything provided by modern technology. (Now many farmers even in temperate zones are experimenting with minimum tillage.)

Freeing themselves from the technology transfer interpretation that had misled the Puebla planners, several Mexican agricultural scientists who had worked on the Puebla project led a strong move into farming systems research and participatory research on farmers fields. CIMMYT had carried out the Puebla Project in association with the Colegio de Postgraduados, the Mexican Graduate Agricultural University at nearby Chapingo. By all accounts, the man most influential in gaining acceptance of this reinterpretation was Leobardo Jimenez, who had been the first field director of Puebla and later became dean of the Colegio de Postgraduados and subsequently deputy director of the National Agricultural Extension Service in Mexico. Also a veteran of the Puebla Project, Antonio Turrent (1978) continued carrying out systematic studies of interplanting. His project reinforced the conclusion gained in Puebla that small farmers would do much better interplanting maize and beans rather than planting either crop alone. In his experiments with interplanting corn and castor beans, he found that this combination yielded 2 to 6.7 times as much income, depending on the market price of castor beans.

By 1979, official reports of the Instituto Nacional de Investigaciones Agrarias (INIA, the Mexican National Agricultural Research Institute) showed that 56 percent of all experiments were carried out on the fields of small farmers. By this time scientists were ready to draw general conclusions regarding the advantages of intercropping. As Turrent wrote,

> The patterns of cultivation that formed parts of the system of peasant agriculture are rational, and where there exists an ample opportunity to improve them, as a general rule the productivity of the land under these patterns of cultivation is potentially greater than that which is achieved with monocultural systems. (Turrent, 1978)

FROM ORGANIZATIONAL LEARNING TO ACTION

That statement provides a suitable conclusion for this chapter, as it states clearly the problem of concern to us: How do you integrate the information and ideas gained by small farmers with the information and ideas generated by professional researchers?

That question has to be answered at several levels:

At the farm level, through establishing a pilot model that works on a small scale;

At regional and national levels, where researchers and administrators strive to develop organizations capable of adapting learning at the micro-level to practice in national programs; and

At the international level, where various international centers are striving to discover means of helping national programs meet the needs of small farmers.

The question needs to be answered also in interorganizational terms: Within the research organization itself, how do you integrate the new activities of the units carrying out participatory action research involving small farmers with the previously well-established agricultural experiment station programs? As the International Service to National Agricultural Research phrases the question: How do you integrate on-farm client-oriented research (OFCOR) with on-station research (OSR)?

Looking outward from the research institute or agency, how do you integrate its activities with those of other organizations involved in the agricultural and rural development field? That question requires us to examine the relations between the agricultural research institute and the agricultural extension agency, the agricultural bank, and (in some cases) the land reform agency and the agency established to promote and regulate cooperatives.

In other words, development of a methodology for small-farmer participation in the research and development process is a necessary step toward building an effective national program but is only a first step. A series of complex social, economic, and technical problems must be solved before what has been learned at the micro-level can be applied effectively at macro-levels and also across the various organizations involved in the agricultural R&D process.

4. Developing the Guatemalan ICTA Model

The Instituto de Ciencia y Tecnología Agrícolas (ICTA, Institute for Agricultural Sciences and Technology) arose under national conditions similar to those facing many third world countries but with a concentration of wealth more extreme than in many nations. As reported in the 1970 National Development Plan (Ruano and Fumagalli, 1988:9).

> One percent of the population owned about 80% of the land; 5% of the population received 34.5% of the national income; 20% of the labor force was unemployed and 52% underemployed.

Development of national agricultural research had begun in 1930 with the creation of the Instituto Químico Agrícola Nacional (IQAN, National Chemical-Agricultural Institute). In 1944 the IQAN became the Instituto Agropecuario Nacional (IAN, the National Agricultural and Animal Husbandry Institute). During the World War II period, Guatemalan research was supported by grants from the U.S. Department of Agriculture, which was particularly interested in quinine for troops in the tropics.

> The organization of all these entities was always carried out under the same operational and administrative design; modeled after the style of North

American research units, but without the support of the university, which occurs in that country. (Ruano and Fumagalli, 1988:15)

Planning for the establishment of ICTA began in 1970. The leading Guatemalan in this planning was Astolfo Fumagalli, who had been involved earlier with the projects supported by Rockefeller Foundation's Office of Special Services in Northwest Mexico, which achieved the green revolution breakthroughs in high-yielding varieties of wheat. According to Sergio Ruano,

> The Office of Special Studies [OSS] . . . is the first or one of the first examples in the world of real research on farmers' fields. Contrary to what others claim, it was not traditional "farm management." I believe the OSS was really the principle source of FSR [farming systems research] because it began to develop methodologies of "on-farm" [research] and the concept of the "farmer's managed trial." (personal communication)

Fumagalli and his associates also studied the experience of other projects. According to Ramiro Ortiz (personal communication), they picked up valuable information and ideas especially from Colombia through projects carried out in Rio Piedras and Caqueza (for an account of the Caqueza project, see Zandstra, Swanberg, Zulberti, and Nestel, 1979).

Although Fumagalli's experience with the Mexican program may have convinced him of the value of linking experiment station research with on-farm research, ICTA was created to cope with problems different from those faced by the Mexican program in two important respects.

First, the OSS program was monocultural, focused upon a single crop. ICTA was created to focus on farming systems research, involving the integration of a variety of crops with animal husbandry.

Second, the OSS program worked primarily with farmers owning large tracts of land, having access to irrigation through heavily financed government development projects. These relatively affluent farmers were much closer in levels of education and social status to the national and international scientists working with OSS than were the small farmers in Guatemala. Furthermore, without disregarding the importance of irrigation, ICTA was designed to find ways of assisting small farmers who had to depend on rainfall.

In other words, this early Mexican program may have planted important seeds, but Guatemala had to find new pathways to help small farmers with on-farm research relevant to particular local farming systems.

In the planning process leading to the creation of ICTA, the Guatemalan government drew on the guidance and support of the Rockefeller Foundation, two international research centers (CIMMYT and CIAT, the International Center for Tropical Agriculture), and the U.S. Agency for International Development (AID). ICTA was created in 1973 with Astolfo Fumagalli as its director general and Robert K. Waugh, an American supported by the Rockefeller Foundation, as associate director.

Initially it was not clear what relationships ICTA would have within the governmental agricultural bureaucracy, but it was understood that ICTA should have substantial autonomy in building the new research program. At this time ICTA reported to higher levels in the Ministry of Agriculture through Mario Martinez, who was just as dedicated as Fumagalli to finding new ways to assist small farmers.

ICTA planned from the outset to establish mutually supporting relations between on-station research and on-farm research, but how this was to be done was not laid out in the planning documents. In 1975 ICTA established Technology Testing Teams to assume the main responsibilities for carrying out on-farm research. Those teams then began working out their own methodology for such projects.

In October 1975, ICTA brought in American agricultural economist Peter Hildebrand with Rockefeller Foundation support. Hildebrand's assignment was to create a socioeconomic research unit to develop further the methodology of on-farm research with small farmers.

At the time the guiding rhetoric for ICTA was phrased in terms of "transfer of technology," but Hildebrand interpreted the phrase in an unconventional way. In previous experience with small-farmer programs in El Salvador, Hildebrand had become convinced that any such program must be built on intimate knowledge of the farming systems being practiced locally in areas where ICTA carried out on-farm research.

As Hildebrand surveyed the scene in Guatemala, he was impressed with the enormous gap between conditions on experiment stations and those on the peasant farms. For example, in Jutiapa, not far from the experiment station, the small farmers were struggling to eke out an existence on hillsides, on rocky terrain of low fertility; they were using bullocks for plowing and were able to afford far fewer inputs than recommended by plant scientists.

Hildebrand sought to persuade one experiment station director to move most of his experimental program off the station and onto a hillside typical of peasant farming. The proposal provoked an indignant rejection. In fact, in the early months, members of the socioeconomic unit were seen by the station plant scientists as cranks, and the unit was unable to get any cooperation from the established experimental program. Finding itself blocked in fitting its program into the established structures, the unit won top-level approval to develop its own methods of on-farm research.

The social scientists began with a study to delimit an area where the farming system practiced by small farmers was relatively homogeneous. The purpose was to make sure that successful experiments would provide conclusions applicable throughout the area. At the same time, to get systematic information on indigenous farming systems, the unit developed a program of *registros,* simple farm management records to be filled out daily by the farmer or a family member recording the amount and type of labor, the tools and power sources used, amounts of fertilizer, pesticides, or other inputs applied, and so on. Members of the unit worked with the farmers to develop a balance between the researcher's desire for a highly detailed record of farming practices and expenditures and the small farmers' need for a system that was simple enough for them to understand and more helpful than burdensome.

Not having access to land on experiment stations, the socioeconomic unit rented small plots from local farmers and paid the farmer whose land it rented for his labor in the experimental process. The aim was not to use the small farmer as a hired hand but to involve him as a consultant *(asesor)* and participant in the research-planning process. The unit proposed to try only those innovations that its farmer-consultants considered reasonable and promising. The rationale was that any innovation that seemed impractical to local farmers was not likely to gain acceptance.

The strategy was to start with minor changes, and especially those that required little or no additional expenditure for inputs compared to the farmers' traditional practices. If a modest experiment yielded concrete benefits, the participating farmer would be encouraged to undertake further and more far-reaching changes.

The first on-farm experiments were carried out under the direction and control of professionals. Any innovation that did not work out was referred back to the plant scientists on experiment stations for advice and further study. Innovations that yielded good results moved into the second stage of farmer field trials. At this stage the socioeconomic unit gave up control and shifted into the role of consultant and observer. Farmers now tried out on their own fields, with their own money and labor, the innovation they had tested earlier. Innovations that did not work at this stage were referred back to the professionals for advice and further study. Those that did work were assumed to be ready for diffusion and general adoption throughout the farming area. In this stage, the socioeconomic unit had become involved in the diffusion process, which is normally thought to be the jurisdiction of the extension service.

While refining its methodology for on-farm experiments and field trials, the socioeconomic unit was also improving and speeding up its system for making baseline studies of farming systems. The traditional style of social science research has impeded its integration within agricultural R&D programs. Such research takes so much time that conclusions are reached after planners wish to act. Furthermore, the action implications of such research are often difficult for the administrator to discern.

The socioeconomic unit changed this pattern. At first, it conducted exploratory research to determine the major agronomic and socioeconomic features of the area; results were made available immediately to other programs for planning purposes. The unit then proceeded to study the area more in depth, with final recommendations ready for publication a year later. Eventually, ICTA leaders decided that the longer-range study was too costly and not necessary for planning. The unit then concentrated on improving its capacity to carry out exploratory research that could be quickly applied by agronomists, doing a reconnaissance of an area in one or two weeks. The unit had become more familiar with the general characteristics of systems used by farmers; this knowledge facilitated the survey process by directing interviewers' attention toward key aspects of the farmers' practices.

At this time, ICTA operated in somewhat decentralized fashion in six regions, with the experiment station of each region being the major center of research activity. In order to involve agronomists in the on-farm research, the socioeconomic unit invited their participation in the field surveys wherever a new field project was being developed. Researchers were organized in pairs consisting of one natural scientist and one social scientist; members were rotated daily within pairs to control against interviewing bias. At the end of each day, the members met to discuss their work. They tried to identify common patterns in their findings and fill in weak spots by following up on particular themes the next day. This activity provided valuable cross-fertilization of information between disciplines.

The reports that the unit produced were available almost immediately upon completion of the fieldwork, written in clear and precise form that natural scientists can understand. The participation of agronomists in the surveys helped the unit direct its research to areas of technical concern to the rest of the institute, and at the same time it put technical people more in touch with farmers' problems. These reports were becoming increasingly useful in regional planning processes.

In the early stages, ICTA's budget provided substantial support for education and training of its professional staff. ICTA followed a conventional strategy in supporting some staff members in graduate degree programs outside of Guatemala, but it was not at all clear what sort of training ICTA should provide inside Guatemala. Looking around the world and finding no programs like the one ICTA was developing and therefore no established models for training, ICTA's planners had to devise their own training model.

Serious commitment to this objective is indicated by the ten-month training program for all professional-level recruits before they were assigned to particular projects. The most novel feature of this program was the training plot *(lote de entrenamiento)*. Each trainee was required to farm a small plot he rented, paying for all the inputs used and gaining the profits or suffering the losses of success or failure. This was a powerful learning experience.

> In the first years, the tendency was for many graduates to use the technology that they brought from the university and the (officially) established recommendations. The majority failed. Following these experiences, new graduates have learned to consult others and particularly the local farmers themselves. These [graduates] have had greater success. (Ruano and Fumagalli, 1988:50)

So far I have described the evolution of the socioeconomic unit methodology and given some indications of its contribution to ICTA, but I have not focused on the problems of integrating it into a research organization dominated by plant scientists and organized according to two structural principles: crop specialization and regional decentralization. Directors of crop improvement programs (maize, beans, sorghum, and so on) worked in the central office, guiding experimentation in their particular crops in the six regions. The headquarters of each region was located on an experiment station, now renamed production center. It was the responsibility of the regional director to coordinate the activities of various specialists who were developing research on cropping systems and conducting experiments on farms as well as at the production center. Ways to coordinate these new lines of research had to be discovered in practice.

At first the Technology Testing Teams were reluctant to use the methods developed by the socioeconomic unit. They had established their own system before these newcomers had arrived on the scene, and the agronomists were not accustomed to responding to initiatives from social scientists. Team members particularly resisted responsibility for carrying out *registros* as they had had no experience with or training for this time-consuming task.

When Ramiro Ortiz, a plant scientist, had been technical director of one of the ICTA regions, he had worked closely with Hildebrand and became convinced "that Hildebrand's contribution should be better exploited" (personal communication from Ortiz).

When Ortiz became technical director of the national program in early 1979, he strongly supported the *registro* and made developing farm management records an integral part of the responsibilities of Technology Testing Teams.

While noting that Hildebrand did not start on-farm research (OFR) in ICTA, Ortiz offers this evaluation:

> Socioeconomic's or Hildebrand's contribution to the OFR approach used within ICTA was in raising the issue that we should try to learn more from the traditional systems (in order to plan relevant OFR activities) and in letting farmers get more involved in the on-farm activities conducted by ICTA. (personal communication)

Also in 1977 the ICTA administration decided that a member of the socioeconomic unit should be assigned to each regional production center. Although this appeared to be an important step toward integration of OSR and OFCOR, it did pose problems for the socioeconomic unit. At that time the unit did not have enough staff to place university graduates in each regional center and therefore had to send out *peritos* (agricultural high school graduates), whose lower status placed them at a disadvantage in dealing with the university graduate *ingenieros agrónomos*. Being especially qualified through experience working closely with farmers, the *peritos* were expected to guide the professionals in developing farmer records and in carrying out on-farm intercropping experiments according to the socioeconomic unit's methodology, but university graduates did not respond readily to the guidance of high school graduates.

In this case, more than a status problem was involved. In general, the crop improvement program heads in the central office and the regional directors had not made adjustments in work loads to allow for collecting farmers' records and for expansion of the on-farm research within work already in progress. The professionals naturally tended to do their accustomed work first and delay the new tasks brought to them by the *peritos*.

In the course of a year, ICTA leaders noted a marked improvement in regional response to these new responsibilities initiated by the socioeconomic unit, as professionals from its central office were able to spend more time in the field with regional directors and their staffs. These professionals were able to help regional *peritos* to fit their work into the established program and to demonstrate how socioeconomic unit projects could strengthen these programs. The new methodology for field surveys was a major influence in strengthening the unit's relations with plant and soil scientists in the regions. As the surveys were carried out by pairs consisting of a social scientist and an agronomist from the regional organization, the success of this program helped representatives of the two units to appreciate the value of each unit's participation in the joint effort. By 1979, regional directors were generally reporting that farmer records and area agro-socioeconomic surveys had become basic elements in their programs.

In an earlier period, ICTA had been in the same division of the Agriculture Ministry with the much larger national extension agency, The Dirección Nacional de Servcios Agrícolas (DIGESA), and the Banco Nacional de Desarrollo Agrícola (BANDESA), the Agricultural Development Bank. With the encouragement of consultants from the Rockefeller Foundation, ICTA was separated from DIGESA and BANDESA and established as a semiautonomous unit. This organizational divorce may well have been necessary to enable ICTA to develop its innovative program, but the new strategy of ICTA did not mesh with the policies and practices of the larger agricultural extension and credit organizations.

The problem was not simply the natural rivalries among bureaucratic organizations but rather the incompatibility of assumptions regarding the nature of small farmers. ICTA assumed that the farmer was a thoughtful individual who adapted more or less successfully to difficult conditions, and that, in developing technology appropriate to these conditions, professionals had much to learn from the farmers' experience and ideas. Research and development should therefore be a process in which farmers participated.

DIGESA was operating according to more traditional assumptions. The farmer was seen as an irrational individual, who could not be trusted to further his own best interests. He therefore needed direction and close supervision by technicians who designed farming practices to benefit him. DIGESA's orientation was illustrated by its role in the supervision of BANDESA's credit program. For a farmer to qualify for credit, he had to sign a contract to follow a plan worked out for him by a DIGESA agent. The DIGESA agent helped the farmer deal with BANDESA and then supervised him to make sure that he stuck to the plan.

DIGESA was doing most of its extension work with farmers on a one-to-one basis. This necessarily limited the number of farmers reached with technical assistance. In administering and supervising BANDESA's loan program, a DIGESA agent could serve only forty-five or fifty farmers a year. With approximately 500 agents, DIGESA could serve only 25,000 farm families in one year. To reach even half the number of farm families in Guatemala, that model would have required 5,000 agents—obviously beyond the nation's financial and managerial capacity. Furthermore, we heard complaints that DIGESA agents gave so much attention to credit that they had little time to attend to farmers' other needs.

Recognizing the need for a new extension model to link up with its new research model, ICTA began its own small-scale research extension projects. Here ICTA worked out a collaborative relationship with a nongovernmental organization, World Neighbors, based in Oklahoma and sponsored by the Lutheran Church. World Neighbors began work in the Chimaltenango area in 1962, setting up a small health clinic (Miller, 1989). In 1963 Carroll Behrhorst, a physician who directed the health program, teamed up with Wayne Hagen, a Peace Corps volunteer, to start an agricultural development program. Over a period of some months, supported by a $25,000 grant from World Neighbors, Hagen trained fifty local volunteer farmers in improved farming methods adapted to their own conditions.

In 1968 Oxfam joined World Neighbors in supporting intensified agricultural projects, and the apparent success of work along these lines later attracted other donors. In 1970 the two main sponsoring organizations decided to develop a more concentrated project in the village of San Martín Jilotepeque, which appeared to offer a strong leadership base in the local church (Gow et al., 1979). The formal involvement of World Neighbors had ended in 1972, but the momentum of the project continued and spread its influence to neighboring villages and even other nations.

By the time ICTA came in contact with the project, farmers were already working in organized groups and experimenting with agricultural innovations. They had begun to increase yields through the use of soil and water management practices that the project had introduced.

In 1974 ICTA worked out a project to involve the local farm leader volunteers in testing some of ICTA's technology. Organizational arrangements for implementing the research were not clear at first, but they were gradually solidified and formalized. Three informal farm leaders were put on ICTA's payroll, to collaborate with an ICTA technician assigned to the project in managing agronomic trials throughout the community.

This arrangement overcame the limitation of extending technology to farmers on a one-to-one basis. Professionals dealt with farm leaders, and the farm leaders took responsibility for communicating information and managing experiments with organized groups and communities. Farm leaders in the San Martín project were able to manage approximately sixty field trials per year, compared with the average of twenty-five for the professional agronomists in the ICTA program. Of course, these trials were not as neat and scientific as ICTA's more controlled experimental work, but they provided data to the research program and were of high credibility to the participating farmers. The farmer paraprofessionals working with ICTA extended their work into eleven villages, providing one-to-one technical assistance and holding regular instruction and discussion meetings with the villagers. By 1979 the paraprofessionals were working actively with two large farmer cooperatives, thus further extending their outreach through linking up with indigenous organizations.

Stimulated by the success of the San Martín project, two ICTA *peritos* in the Quetzaltenango region recruited and trained local farmers in the planning and implementation of on-farm experiments. Working with six paraprofessionals in an adult education program financed by the

Ministry of Education, one *perito* directed a program of 141 on-farm experiments in a single year. Working with six unpaid leaders of a co-operative, the other *perito* managed a program of 119 such experiments.

This sudden expansion grew beyond the capacity of ICTA to make systematic observations and measurements of yields in all cases. ICTA leaders were enthusiastic over the value of the data acquired, however, and regarded the experience as a challenge to ICTA to develop methods of observation and measurement to cope with the expanded volume of experiments, which promised to shape the pattern of field activities.

With such programs ICTA was in effect bypassing DIGESA and justifying its activities as fulfilling its legal mandate to promote the use of the new technologies it developed. Whatever the justification, this apparent duplication of extension activities raised basic policy questions regarding the responsibilities of the two organizations.

1980 marked the beginning of a new stage in ICTA's development. This coincided with the appointment of a new director general for ICTA and also the onset of serious financial problems in the face of government imposed austerity programs in response to a downturn in the Guatemalan economy.

The director general did not have the same commitment to ICTA's innovative program as the founding director general and also had to cope with a more difficult financial situation. He did not eliminate the socioeconomic unit, but neither did he support it in its original form. The planners had assumed that Peter Hildebrand would continue to lead the unit until some of those sent abroad for graduate degrees had completed their educational program and had returned to assume leadership positions in ICTA. The director general decided that it was not necessary to wait so long and terminated Hildebrand's contract in 1980. In the following months, Guatemalan social scientists dropped out of the program so that, until 1986 when ICTA again began hiring social scientists, the socioeconomic unit was staffed by two social scientists and thirteen technical high school graduates in agronomy.

EVALUATING ICTA PROGRESS, 1973-1986

The ISNAR study of ICTA was carried out by Sergio Ruano and Astolfo Fumagalli, both of whom had been very involved in the early development of ICTA—Fumagalli as its director and Ruano as a member of the socioeconomic unit. At the time of undertaking this study, they were no longer employed by ICTA. To build on their intimate knowledge of the first years, they returned to gather documentary data and to interview fifty-four people, including "administrators of research programs, scientists in programs and various disciplines, scientists and technicians in OFCOR, and farmers participating in OFCOR" (Ruano and Fumagalli, 1988).

They report impressive indications of progress along the following lines (Ruano and Fumagalli, 1988, p. 87):

- ICTA has institutionalized the process of diagnostic agro-socioeconomic studies in all areas of the country (p. 95). This means that wherever ICTA plans to develop OFCOR projects, the process of doing the baseline studies is well understood and ready for use.
- One hundred percent of the technology generated or adapted by ICTA has been (or is being) tested on farms (pp. 97-98).
- Small farmers have been participating actively in managing their own on-farm testing. The authors found no cases where this on-farm testing was being managed by ICTA professionals (pp. 98-99).
- With active small farmer participation, the technologies developed by ICTA have been diffusing widely.

This has been achieved in spite of hardly being able to count on the participation of extension, because the technology has been diffused very largely by the farmers. (p. 98)

To date studies have proved that the most successful technology generated by ICTA has largely been diffused by the farmers themselves. This is the case with wheat, rice, maize, beans, potato, sorghum, and cattle, etc. (p. 99)

- In several cases, ICTA has involved small farmers in evaluating and selecting among alternative materials before the on-farm testing begins. Furthermore, the professionals are encouraging farmers to include their own materials in the testing program.

Various programs are using genetic sources of the producers in their variety improvement projects. (p. 100)

- In interviews at all levels, informants found the Technology Testing Teams and socioeconomics unit the most important for carrying out ICTA policies and programs. These particular social inventions are the most distinctive features of ICTA, as nothing resembling them existed previously in the agricultural research system of developing countries.

DEFICIENCIES AND LIMITATIONS

Ruano and Fumagalli (1988) also noted some deficiencies and limitations that have retarded progress. The most obvious problem has been financial. Beginning in 1980, Guatemala entered an economic crisis, leading government to impose budget cuts on ICTA. The effects of these cuts are illustrated in the inventory of ICTA motor vehicles, as OFCOR requires extensive automotive travel—and on roads that punish the vehicles much more than use on major highways does. This inventory for 1986 shows ICTA owning 169 vehicles. Of that total, 91 percent were purchased from 1973 through 1981.

The austerity program also severely restricted travel expenses, on which OFCOR personnel depended much more heavily than did those professionals assigned to on-station research. However, the authors note one beneficial effect of the austerity program: It required ICTA to depend even more on farmer participation. Assuming that the results are satisfactory, the economic advantages of this strategy are clear. At the time of my field studies, ICTA was paying its *peritos* about half of the salary of university graduate professionals—and the *peritos* were implementing major parts of the OFCOR program. The local farmer paraprofessionals employed in the San Martín Jilotepeque project were receiving about a quarter of the pay of the university graduate scientists; and the paraprofessionals needed little travel support money because they were working around where they lived, which also enabled them to organize and observe far more projects than could be handled by the professionals. Besides, in some countries, administrators of agricultural R&D programs have found it necessary to offer hardship pay to persuade their professionals to go out and work in the "boondocks," far away from major cultural and commercial centers. The paraprofessionals require no such inducements because they are already living where they want to work.

In spite of the general opinion that technology testing and socioeconomics are the most important units in carrying out the ICTA mission, Ruano and Fumagalli (1988) found members of those units at a status disadvantage in relation to the professionals in the commodity programs involved in on-station research (OSR). The experiment station still seems to be the mainstream for career advancement. "In general, the technologists considered most capable have been recruited into the commodity programs" (1988:93).

The authors also note a decline in interunit and interdisciplinary collaboration. In the 1980s leaders of OFCOR were less successful than in earlier years in involving on-station researchers with them in on-farm research. To some extent budgetary limitations may have been a factor in this decline because the OSR personnel had little travel money to devote to this purpose. But that could not have been a factor in the observed decline in integration observed in the annual reporting and planning meetings. Ruano and Fumagalli note that, after they had given their reports, some of the OSR people left the meetings before the technology testing and socioeconomic reports were given and discussed.

Perhaps the most serious deficiency noted by the authors is one that we have already emphasized, the absence of research extension collaboration. "Up to 1985 this was the only function for which there existed no mechanisms for institutionalization (Ruano and Fumagalli, 1988:102).

In 1976 the directors of ICTA and DIGESA had agreed that their two organizations should collaborate in some activities, but this top-level agreement was never implemented in practice.

> Unfortunately, this technological linkage did not yield the hoped for results, due to the fact that the extension agents who participated were required also to complete their normal work load traditionally assigned to them in DIGESA. In all cases, the principal problem was the same because in the extension organization it is middle management, for example, the regional directors, who define the operational plans, independently of top management. (1988:102)

ORGANIZATIONAL REVITALIZATION?

Through their own experience some of the leaders of Guatemalan R&D programs had become concerned about the absence of ICTA-DIGESA collaboration. Their efforts to resolve this problem may be ushering in a revitalization of the Guatemalan program.

After many months of discussion and planning—and with financial
support of the Inter-American Development Bank—the Fondo Inter-
nacional de Desarrollo Agrícola (FIDA) and the 1986 Guatemalan
government gave birth to a new organization: El Proyecto de Genera-
ción y Transferencia de Tecnología Agropecuaria y Producción de
Semillas (PROGETTAPS, Project for the Generation and Transfer of
Technology in Agriculture and Animal Husbandry and for the Production of Seeds).

Internally, PROGETTAPS has been sponsored particularly by ICTA
and DIGESA, with the participation of other governmental agencies in
the agricultural and animal husbandry sectors. The new project has
brought together joint teams of researchers and extension agents, supported by new job descriptions and a budget specifically designed to
support such collaboration.

After playing a key role in ICTA and in the planning for creation of
PROGETTAPS, Ramiro Ortiz became a consultant to that organization.
As he has reported (Ortiz, 1990), PROGETTAPS has been operating in
five of Guatemala's six agricultural regions. In each region its activities
are jointly coordinated by ICTA's regional director of technology testing and, for DIGESA, by a university graduate with extension experience. They are jointly responsible for what is known as a Modular
System for Technology Transfer (MSTT). At its creation in 1986, in
each region that unit was staffed by four agronomists engaged in
on-farm research and each one was assigned from three to seven extension agents (technical high school graduates), the number depending
upon the number of extension offices in an area covered by the researcher. As the program involves more and more farmers, the numbers
of researchers and extension agents has been increasing.

PROGETAPPS has been built on a base of active farmer participation
in program planning and field operations. In the field, each extension
agent works with from ten to fifteen rural leaders who have been
recruited and hired by the Ministry of Agriculture as *Represantes
Agrícolas* (RAs) on recommendations from their communities. According to Ortiz (1990, p. 183), the RAs

> have been a key element in the transfer process conducting some transfer
> plots, farm records, and transfer activities with groups of farmers that they
> have formed. They have also brought information to better guide the
> research programs in identification of new technologies for transfer, and
> helped in establishing a seed distribution system.

In each area, PROGETTAPS has also established consultative groups of farmers who meet with program coordinators and staff to evaluate and discuss the research extension work plan for the coming year. In addition, many of these farmers are involved in testing and adapting new technologies in their own fields.

In this program, extension agents do not simply try to deliver to farmers technologies given them by researchers. They gain some experience in on-farm research to enhance the research extension relationship, and they play important roles in facilitating the feedback process from farmers. Jointly with researchers, they participate in the training supporting the new research extension model.

Although it is still early to evaluate PROGETTAPS, Ortiz has reported some impressive indications of progress. In just three years, PROGETTAPS has involved as active participants in its program 200 percent of the farmers anticipated in the 1986 plans. By 1989 early projections of the harvest in the program areas showed an increase of 16,200 metric tons of food over the 1986 base line level—"enough to satisfy the annual food requirements of a little over 26,000 additional typical rural families."(p. 185)

5. Potatoes, Peasants, and Professionals

Characteristic of Central America, in the farming systems of small producers in Guatemala, maize and beans are the principal crops and therefore were the initial focus of much of ICTA's research. In the farming systems of small producers in the Andes, potatoes are the principal crop, a situation that led to the establishment of CIP, the International Potato Center, based in Peru.

Why devote such attention to potatoes and to CIP? Shifting our focus now to potatoes gives us an opportunity to view another farming system while at the same time examining the impact of an international research agency on small farmers and their farming systems. Founded in 1971, CIP had the opportunity to learn from previously established centers, as a basis for its own innovative thrusts. Besides, the potato is important nutritionally and economically.

> Increases in potato production have made this vegetable the most rapidly expanding major food crop in the third world—and its fourth most valuable crop in monetary terms. Potato consumption is doubling every ten to fifteen years. (CIP, 1984:vii)

The potato is also interesting because it involves an especially wide range of biological, economic, and social problems. The potato has been a relatively high-cost product for farmers but offers a high potential for farmer income—if farmers can pay the cost. For all of its problems in cultivation, potatoes can yield far more per hectare in tonnage and monetary value than can wheat, maize, or rice.

The 1980-1982 yield figures (CIP, 1984:17) indicate that North America had the highest yield, 29.1 tons per hectare, with countries of western Europe and other developed nations all exceeding 20 tons per hectare. In that period the average for Africa was 7.1 tons compared to 10.5 tons per hectare for Latin America. On individual farms, yields of well over 40 tons per hectare have been reported.

Enormous improvements in the economics of potato growing are possible as agricultural research and development programs work with farmers to reduce the costs of potato production, storage, and distribution. This can be achieved through reducing the expense of producing seed for potato, reducing the loss of the crop through disease and insects, and also reducing the post-harvest losses. Those losses are a particular problem for the potato since it is generally more profitable to farmers not to have to sell the total production at the time of harvest, when prices are likely to be low, but the storage of potatoes is much more difficult than for the grains.

In Chapter 2 we pointed out the enormous waste in time and money in potato research over many years as the professionals misdiagnosed the problems of using "clean" potato seeds on the farms of the small producers. The diagnosis was not based upon any intensive studies of the experience of small farmers in growing seed potatoes. In effect, the biological scientists began with their own on-station research (OSR) and then sought to build on this base a development program to provide farmers with certified seeds. It was only after decades of making their way down this blind alley that the agricultural professionals discovered, through the research of CIP's social scientists, that the yield advantage of farmer use of certified seed potatoes was not great enough to cover the farmers' additional costs, at least in the Peruvian highlands.

We cannot assume that this same conclusion would hold true for small farmers in all other third world countries. On the other hand, the findings of this CIP project were so at odds with the conventional wisdom of the agricultural professionals as to suggest a more skeptical stance toward the development of national seed potato programs. Before embarking on such a difficult and costly program, agricultural professionals need to tap the experience and ideas of small potato farmers and invite them to participate in small-scale experiments to compare the costs and benefits of using government-approved clean seed potatoes with the costs and benefits of using their own seed potatoes.

In this chapter, we move on from "discovering what ain't so" to examine three cases of small-farmer participation in potato research: post-harvest storage research, production and distribution of "true" potato seeds, and digging for ancestral knowledge.

CIP DEVELOPS AN ON-FARM
PARTICIPATORY RESEARCH PROGRAM

Among international agricultural research centers, CIP appears to have been out in front with on-farm participatory research and in the involvement of a broad range of social scientists. Those breakthroughs were initially opposed by traditionally minded plant scientists. Douglas Horton (1990, p. 218) gives this account of an early experience of Michael Twomey, who, in late 1973, became the first economist to join CIP. In order to learn about indigenous methods of potato cultivation, he requested travel expenses to go to the highlands and plant a potato trial on the farm of a peasant family.

> CIP's Director of Research, a mycologist by training, denied the request for three reasons: First, economists should concentrate on economics and leave experiments to biologists, who have the required training and experience. Second, research should be done on the experiment station, where non-experimental variables can be controlled, not on farms. Third, extension-type on-farm work was beyond CIP's mandate, and should be left to Peru's National Potato Program. Undaunted by the veto, CIP's young economist arranged for his own transportation to the highlands and planted the trial anyway. (Horton, 1990:218)

Douglas Horton, Twomey's successor as CIP's chief economist, managed to gain legitimacy for on-farm research and also was able to broaden CIP's social science base by bringing in anthropologists and sociologists. The earliest example of this broadened base of interdisciplinary collaboration involved a post-harvest storage research project carried out by a team of social anthropologists and plant scientists.

At first the team members were divided by their disciplines in their diagnoses of the storage problems. The plant scientists assumed that all tubers not of quality for commercial sale were a total loss to the small farmers, whereas the anthropologists had learned that

> *all* potatoes were utilized by farm families in some form. Potatoes that could not be sold, used for "seed" or immediate home consumption were fed to animals, mainly pigs, or processed into dehydrated potatoes . . . storable for as long as 2 to 3 years. In addition, some wives informed him that in culinary quality the shrivelled partially spoiled potatoes were sometimes preferred. (Rhoades and Booth, 1982:129)

Further research by interdisciplinary teams indicated that the small farmers were concerned about the post-harvest losses and interested in finding better means of preserving their potatoes. As the anthropologists and the biological scientists worked together, they were able to sharpen their questions regarding particular post-harvest concerns. They found that the farmers stored their seed potatoes in the dark, which resulted in the potatoes growing long sprouts that were generally removed before planting. The farmers were concerned about the time and labor required for desprouting.

> Thus, farmer losses were not merely physiological but social and economic ones as well. The team now appeared on a common ground with the farmer. From drawing knowledge from farmers in both disciplines, a common agreed upon problem was defined: *"seed" potato storage* with specific emphasis on reducing sprout length and improving seed tuber quality. (Rhoades and Booth, 1982:130)

Any model for seed storage acceptable to small farmers would have to be usable on their own property at minimal expense. The research team now worked to integrate this economic requirement with what had been learned by plant scientists regarding storage of seed potatoes. Research had demonstrated that seed potatoes were best preserved on the farm when they were exposed only to diffused light, protected from direct sunlight, but also not left in dark storage areas. Furthermore, this storage model could not be used for the potatoes destined for consumption in the home.

It did not seem possible to introduce diffused light into dark traditional multipurpose stores. Diffused light produces 'greening' in potato tubers which renders them inedible and unmarketable. Only potatoes destined for 'seed' could be stored in indirect light. Also, due to security and convenience needs, any physical storage changes have to blend into the existing farm compound. (Rhoades and Booth, 1982:130)

The next step was for the professionals at the research station to develop and test seed trays that might be utilized by small farmers. The professionals then got some of the small farmers to try out the new technology.

Farmers expressed interest in the new storage technology, but concern over unavailability and the cost of seed trays. Responding to this feedback, the technologists designed simple collapsible shelves constructed from locally available, rough-hewn lumber, which were used in the second series of on-farm trials.

Now the farmers were able to build the new storage models from readily available local materials. In 1979 the post-harvest team conducted a survey revealing that at least forty farmers in the area had adopted the new technology. By the next year the number of adopters increased to over 120, so the innovation appeared to be spreading rapidly.

The researchers reported that this was not simply a case of farmers adopting technology presented to them by CIP.

Farmers rarely copied exactly the prototype store designs. They blended the new ideas with local architecture and, if a new store was constructed, made changes to suit their own concepts of space and design. Farmers were proud of these changes and the CIP post-harvest team is convinced farmers will be more likely to accept changes if they actively participate in this final research process. (Rhoades and Booth, 1982:132)

A report on this post-harvest applied research project would not be worth the space we have devoted to it if it had not also led to a significant rethinking of the research and development process. The CIP researchers utilized their experience on this project to create the farmer-back-to-farmer model, which is well adapted to the study of many problems beyond post-harvest storage. In this model, research in the field begins with a study of problems faced by farmers, against a background of basic disciplinary research and linked to applied disciplinary research about farm problems. As the interdisciplinary team begins a study of the farmers' problems, the first stage is called constructive conflict. That is, professionals from different disciplines begin with different preliminary diagnoses and then attempt to arrive at a common problem definition. There follows interdisciplinary team research, leading to a proposal for potential solutions. Both on the farm and on the research station, the third stage involves testing and adaptation of the new model. This leads to a solution better adapted to the farmers' problems. To determine whether this has been successful, the fourth and final stage involves farmer evaluation of the new technology. If that technology is accepted and utilized with good results, the problem has been solved. If the new technology is not accepted by the farmer or is initially accepted and later abandoned, professional researchers recycle the research processes, starting with a diagnosis of the problems leading to lack of acceptance. The CIP team visualizes the farmer-back-to-farmer model as shown in Figure 5.1.

Note that this model is similar to the ICTA model developed in Guatemala by Peter Hildebrand. In Figure 5.2, the ICTA model is contrasted with the conventional agricultural research and extension model. The ICTA model depicts the flow of information and action in a straight line rather than in a circle, but ICTA provides for feedback loops, which are depicted in circular form in the farmer-back-to-farmer model.

In comparing the two figures, we note that only the diagram for the conventional research extension model shows a place for extension in depicting the flow of information and action. The Honduran case (described in Chapter 6) indicates how extension can be integrated more effectively into the R&D process through the participation of extension agents in the field surveys, which provides the informational base guiding future experiments and action projects.

PRODUCTION AND DISTRIBUTION OF "TRUE" POTATO SEEDS

The cases described up to this point represent two stages in the evolution of thinking regarding farmer participation in agricultural research and development. The first stage involved the discovery of major problems when the research of plant scientists was not linked directly with the information and ideas possessed by the farmer. We

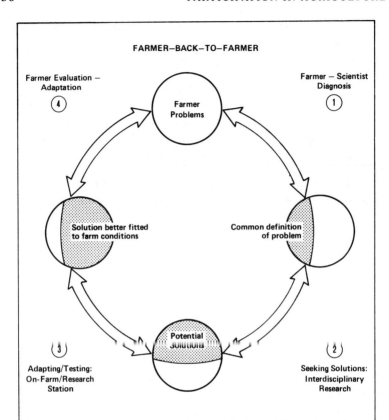

The farmer-back-to-farmer model <u>begins</u> and <u>ends</u> with the farmer. It involves <u>four</u> major activities each with a goal. The hatched areas in the circles indicate an increasing understanding of the technological problem area as research progresses. Note that research may constantly recycle.

	Activities	Goals
1	Diagnosis	Common definition of problem by farmers and scientists
2	Interdisciplinary team research	Identify and develop a potential solution to the problem
3	On-farm testing and adaptation	Better adapt the proposed solution to farmer's conditions
4	Farmer evaluation/adaptation	Modify technology to fit local conditions; understand farmer response

Figure 5.1. Farmer-Back-to-Farmer. (CIP, 1984:111)

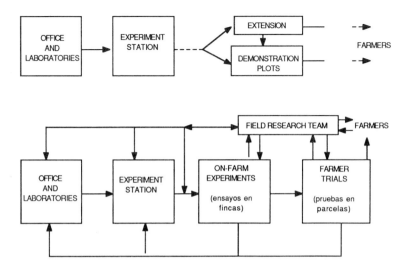

Figure 5.2. Conventional Model (above) contrasted with ICTA Model (below).
(Whyte and Boynton, 1983:200)

noted the enormous waste of money and high-level scientific talent
through misdiagnosis of the problems of maize growers in Puebla. We
have noted a similar enormous waste through years of misdiagnosis of
the problems of potato growers.

While it is important to stop wasting talent and money on unproductive research, the conclusion that any particular line of research is
unproductive does not automatically tell the researchers what needs to
be changed and how to make the changes.

The second stage in this learning process involved the introduction
of farmer participation into the research and development model. We
have followed this stage in Guatemala and Honduras, with brief com-
ments on similar developments in Asia and Africa, and finally with the
presentation of the case of post-harvest storage research by CIP.

Although these participatory models represent both scientific and
practical advances, we should not assume that the only research that
will be useful to farmers is that which begins and ends on their own
fields. The high-yielding varieties of wheat and rice developed in
international and national research programs could not have been created by farmers by themselves, and some of these varieties have been
utilized with favorable results by small farmers.

Researchers have long recognized the enormous potential gains that could be possible through research on nitrogen fixation. Certain legume plants (beans, for example) take in nitrogen from the air and thus enrich the soil. If a nitrogen-fixing variety of maize could be created, it would have great advantages for small farmers who are hard pressed to pay for chemical fertilizers. Obviously, the creation of nitrogen-fixing varieties of grains is not an assignment that can be carried out by farmers.

The growing of "true" potato seeds was another scientific problem that could only be solved by research scientists. If true potato seeds can be grown in test tubes and multiplied through planting those seeds and then producing sprouts in trays of sand or soil, this methodology has important potential advantages for farmers. The test-tube and seed sprouting process relieves the farmer of the need to devote a substantial portion of the farm to the growing of seed potatoes. Also, with this method the seeds can be produced with greater assurance that they are entirely disease free.

On the basis of previous research in certain national programs and in CIP, scientists had learned how to produce large numbers of clean potato seeds and multiply them into an enormous number of sprouts under laboratory conditions. Would this methodology be beneficial to small farmers, considering the expense of buying the true seeds or seed sprouts from commercial producers or from an agricultural research station? Would it even be possible for the small farmers themselves to adapt the methodology so that they produced their own seeds and sprouts?

Those questions have now been answered in a CIP report on researchers and farmers in the Delat area of Vietnam.

> This is the first known case where farmers are applying tissue culture techniques on a commercial basis to generate planting material for seed and table potato crops.
>
> Tissue culture methods are being successfully used by farmers with a minimum of facilities and training. Previously a laboratory operating under sophisticated conditions was thought to be necessary. (CIP, 1984:115)

The story begins in 1973 when a high Vietnamese official visited a laboratory at Orsay University in France. There he learned about methods to produce true seeds and to carry on the multiplication process in the laboratory. By late 1977, following the return of a Vietnamese scientist who had learned the techniques in France, the research station in Delat was producing and multiplying the true seeds. The plant scientists at Delat found that there were enormous possibilities of multiplication by this method. Starting with a single plantlet that could produce four cuttings in less than a month, subsequent in vitro (test-tube) multiplications could theoretically produce 12-16 million plantlets in a single year. Each plantlet transplanted into the field would produce several tubers.

In Vietnam, potatoes can be grown all year around, but the hot and humid climate has presented serious problems in producing disease-free seed potatoes. The research station had mastered the method of producing such disease-free stock, but it remained to be seen to what extent this process would be economically viable for farmers.

For the methodology to be used by farmers themselves, "it was necessary to find substitutes for large numbers of expensive and often unavailable testtubes" (CIP, 1984:117-18). The researchers also found that it was not practical in Vietnam for small farmers to grow plants in test-tubes because the plant material would deteriorate rapidly in the hot climate, and farmers could not afford refrigeration.

> Instead of large numbers of testtubes, use of cuttings derived from plantlets in testtubes was explored. Through trial-and-error including the use of washed sand in beds it was discovered in vitro cuttings could be multiplied in non-sterile conditions in subsoil mixed with manure . . . and the multiplication rate was the same as for sterile conditions. (1984:118)

In 1979, the leader of the Delat program participated in a CIP course in the Philippines to learn about rapid multiplication techniques and how to obtain improved germ plasm from CIP. The CIP plant materials were introduced into Delat in 1979-80. By 1981, farmers were buying the seed material from the Delat station and beginning to undertake their own multiplication, adapting the recommendations of scientists to their own local conditions.

> Finally, several farmers took a more sophisticated step and began to multiply plantlets in vitro. After several attempts, the most successful farmers developed family sized laboratories in their homes as well as rooting areas for rapid multiplication adjacent to the house. Equipment and instruments, mostly home made, were kept inside. These farmers recovered their total investments within a few months. (CIP, 1984:119)

In 1983 twelve of these farmers produced and sold nearly three million rooted plantlets to cooperatives for transplanting directly to the field. There the field experience showed average yields of 18 tons per hectare, double the amount that had previously been achieved with native varieties grown from seed potatoes.

The Vietnam true seed story is a striking case of collaboration between researchers and farmers. The researchers necessarily had to develop the methodology to produce and multiply the seeds and to test the methods to determine that the potential advantages in increased yields and reduction of losses from disease were indeed enormous. At this point there was no farmer experience on which to build. If professionals did all the growing and multiplying, the cost of their products would have severely limited the utilization of the plant material by the small farmers. In Vietnam the farmers themselves went into the business of multiplying the sprouts from true seeds, thus not only contributing to the economy of their area but also establishing themselves as successful business people.

DIGGING FOR ANCESTRAL KNOWLEDGE

When I first heard the words "applied archaeology" they seemed to represent an impossible concept. I recognized the scientific basis of archaeology and the humanistic and artistic values served by archaeology, but how could such research yield practical gains in today's agriculture or in other fields?

Of course, I recognized that in some countries the remains of ancient terraces and irrigation systems indicated that remote ancestors might well have developed farming systems superior to those practiced by small farmers today, but I did not see how that idea could be tested in archaeological research—until I encountered the raised field agricultural research project in the Lake Titicaca region of Peru.

The Lake Titicaca region is in the *altiplano* (high plains) of Peru and Bolivia. This has been known as a very poor farming area, with infertile soil and extremely adverse climatic conditions. The *altiplano* is approximately 12,500 feet above sea level, an altitude at which farming is precarious, with the ever-present threat of drought, severe frosts, or hailstorms that can wipe out or severely damage crops. The region has only one ecological asset for farming: Farmers with land bordering the lake can readily build their own irrigation canals to tap one of the world's largest (and purest) bodies of inland water.

Beginning in 1981, Clark L. Erickson led an international and multidisciplinary team combining archaeology, agronomy, and agricultural communications working with indigenous farmers in the raised fields research and development project.

> Raised fields are constructed by excavating parallel canals and piling the earth between them to form long, low mounds with flat or cambered surfaces. These raised platforms increase soil fertility, improve drainage in low-lying areas, and improve local micro-environments, primarily by decreasing frost risk. The canals between raised fields provide vital moisture during periods of short- and long-term drought. Water in the deep canals might have been used to cultivate aquatic plants and fish, as well as attract lake birds that were an integral part of the prehistoric diet. The raised fields of the Lake Titicaca region are diverse in form and in size, but generally range from 4-10 m wide, 10 to 100 m long, and are 1 m tall.

> The prehistoric raised fields, covering some 82,000 hectares of low-lying land around Lake Titicaca in both Bolivia and Peru, have been badly eroded by a combination of wind, rain, flooding, and modern urbanization, but their remains can be seen clearly on the ground and in aerial photographs. (Erickson, 1988:9)

Since raised field farming had been abandoned before the Spanish conquest (for reasons as yet unknown), the chronicles of the conquerors and early explorers provide no information on this ancient farming system. The applied archaeology project had three interrelated aims:

(1) reconstruct some approximation of the ancient raised field system;
(2) study the farming system required for efficient utilization of the raised fields and the results achievable under such conditions; and
(3) compare the results achieved on raised fields to those achieved by conventional research and development strategies in order to determine whether the raised field system offers a promising research and development strategy that would be suitable for wide application.

One of the most significant aspects of the project was that the farmers themselves collaborated in developing and adapting this ancient technology for their present-day use. While the archaeologist suggested guidelines based on his research, it was the farmers themselves, who, from experience and experimentation on their own, refined the construction techniques and developed new approaches. This process generated an active interest in the raised field experiments, while at the same time, it produced a technology especially suited to the present local, social, and economic environments. (Erickson and Candler, 1989:242)

The project generated vital information on soil fertility, protection against frosts and floods, labor and capital utilization, crop yields, and diffusing of the raised field system.

In this region where land had long suffered from soil erosion, the canals provided a means of greatly enhancing soil fertility. Maintenance of the system requires an annual cleaning of the canals, in which the material removed from the water is placed on the raised platform.

> The construction of raised fields doubles topsoil thickness on the planting surface, while the canals produce "green manure" in the form of rapidly growing aquatic plants, and organic matter and other nutrients produced by the decomposition of animals. The canals also act as sediment traps for the recapture of topsoil from the platforms and also from the nearby hilltops. (Erickson and Chandler, 1988)

> The value of raised fields in the cold Lake Titicaca basin was dramatically demonstrated during a severe local frost in 1982. Crops in nearby fields were severely damaged, while potatoes cultivated on our experimental raised fields suffered only minimal damage and quickly recovered. . . . The study indicated that during a night of light frost during the growing season, soil and air temperatures on the raised fields were a couple of degrees Celsius higher, and the frost was of several hours shorter duration than on nearby fields. The water temperatures in the canals between the raised fields were even warmer than that of the soil and air, indicating that the water acts as a heat sink for storage of solar energy. (Erickson and Candler, 1988:14)

Regarding protection against floods, Erickson and Chandler report a 1986 comparison with a government experiment.

> Hundreds of hectares of mechanically prepared fields of winter wheat, improved seed potatoes, and other experimental crops were destroyed by floods, while the 2 hectares of experimental raised fields adjacent to them remained unaffected and produced a bumper crop. (1989:244)

The system offers impressive economies in the use of resources. Capital is exceedingly scarce in this depressed region, and the raised field system has practically zero capital requirements. Construction of the platforms and cleaning of the canals is most efficiently done with indigenous tools such as the digging stick. The system does have extensive labor requirements, but this is a region with surplus labor—large numbers of people leave the land because they cannot make a living there. Furthermore, the existing cultural systems of mobilizing communal labor provide efficient means of getting the work done.

In yields, the raised fields proved advantageous for several important locally grown crops. Here we concentrate on potatoes.

> Potato production during 5 years of experimentation was between 8 and 16 metric tons per hectare with an average of 10 tons. This figure is much larger than today's average potato production figures of between 1 to 4 metric tons per hectare for the Department of Puno. These larger yields are especially significant because we used local and improved potato varieties without fertilizers in the experiments, while most of the potato fields upon which current regional estimates for Puno are based were fertilized. We have also demonstrated that high yields can be sustained for several years of continuous cropping. (Erickson, 1988)

Success of the experimental plots has stirred wide interest among local farmers and also among officials in agricultural research and development. A Peruvian agronomist who conducted many of the experiments went on to direct a government sponsored project that had involved thirty communities by 1987 (Erickson and Candler, 1989:235). While governmental and nongovernmental development agencies can certainly accelerate the diffusion process, the particular strength of the raised field model is that it can be—and is being—diffused steadily even when no outside agencies are involved. As ICTA has found in Guatemala, a technology that yields clear gains on the fields of experimenting farmers is greeted by great interest from neighboring farmers, who soon begin to adopt and adapt the technology for their own use. Clearly diffusion is not a one-way process, from professionals to farmers. An innovation with really important potential will spread much more rapidly through farmer-to-farmer channels.

How widely applicable is the raised field model? Working with Bolivian archaeologist Oswaldo Rivera, American archaeologist Alan Kolata has extended earlier Peruvian projects to the Bolivian side of Lake Titicaca (Obermiller, 1990). The Bolivian program began in 1987.

Three seasons later, some 1,200 Aymaras in eight communities around
the lake are using the Tiwanaku methods to grow crops on approximately
250 acres of raised fields, while the Bolivian government has expressed
an interest in funding an expansion of the project across the Altiplano.
(Obermiller, 1990:29-30)

Erickson notes that the ancient system was once utilized on 82,000
hectares (about 316.6 square miles) in Peru and Bolivia along the shores
of Lake Titicaca. Presumably the system could be used again to provide
economically and ecologically sound agriculture on such a large land
area that is otherwise unsuitable for agriculture and even has a very low
carrying capacity for grazing animals. It remains to be seen whether
the system can be applied efficiently in other regions of the world and
under other climatic conditions. In other words, the raised agriculture
project is clearly a breakthrough, but further research and development
projects will be required to determine the full potential of this important
beginning.

THE RANGE AND SCOPE OF PARTICIPATION

We have followed the spread of participatory relationships in agriculture through several case examples. We have seen the importance of
the international network of agricultural research centers. This network
is involved in the production of information and ideas, the spread of
such information and ideas through national programs, and then also in
the use of research in national programs to enrich the international
centers. We have seen some of the national programs, assisted by
international centers, developing participatory relations with farmers.
We have also seen a flowering of interdisciplinary collaboration among
plant and social scientists that would not have been possible if all of the
research activity had been confined to the universities and experiment
stations, where researchers in various disciplines may remain more or
less isolated from each other. We have even seen how professional
social and plant scientists working with indigenous farmers can redis-
cover and adapt ancestral technologies, even under adverse conditions,
so as to master farming problems that have so far resisted the strategies
promoted by the research and development establishment.

In all of these cases, in one form or another, active farmer participation was important. Reviewing the experience of the International Potato Center, Douglas Horton (1988:244) reported, "In none of the cases examined was foreign technology applied directly by researchers or farmers. Local adaptations were needed."

This conclusion has important implications for agricultural development policies. In the past, one of the most common strategies used was to present farmers with a package of recommended practices and inputs, which were designed to benefit farmers under a wide variety of local soil and economic conditions. In some cases (BANDESA in Guatemala, for example) the agricultural bank would not grant a loan unless the farmer agreed to apply every element in the package. This requirement conflicts with the widely reported results of research and experience around the world: In many cases farmers would benefit more if they applied some elements of the package and omitted others while fitting the new elements into their own farming systems. In other words, the package strategy assumes that the professional experts have all the answers the farmers need and that what farmers have learned from experience and their own experiments is of no practical value.

6. International Diffusion in Agricultural Participation

We have been following the diffusion of ideas and information regarding participation in agriculture within Guatemala and, to some extent, within CIP, the International Potato Center. Now let us focus on international diffusion. We begin by examining the case of Honduras and then go on to consider the broader structures and processes of worldwide diffusion.

DIFFUSION INTO HONDURAS

As the first national agricultural research program designed to emphasize on-farm client-oriented research (OFCOR) particularly among small farmers, ICTA (the Instituto de Ciencia y Tecnología Agrícolas) has attracted interest among agricultural professionals and administrators around the world. Interest has been particularly strong in Guatemala's neighboring countries, where formal reports have been reinforced by personal contacts. Here I concentrate upon Honduras, where I had the opportunity to study the adoption and adaptation process in the field.

It is important to note that the leaders of the Honduran program did not simply imitate the Guatemalan model; they adopted and adapted parts of that program but at the same time recognized Guatemala's organizational deficiencies, particularly the lack of integration between research and extension.

The new program in Honduras was based upon three main principles:

(1) Agricultural research should be emphasized particularly on the farmer fields and with participation of small farmers. This meant, of course, a strategy to work with farming systems rather than single crop specialization.

(2) The research and extension organizations must collaborate in developing the new program.

(3) The research and extension organizations should work collaboratively with cooperatives and peasant movements so as to extend farmer involvement far beyond the one-to-one relationships of traditional agricultural extension contacts with small farmers.

In the 1970s, Honduras distinguished itself from other Central American countries by having several strongly organized peasant movements that were undertaking to develop agriculture in rural communities on a cooperative basis.

The new program in Honduras began on an interdisciplinary basis, made possible by previous initiatives from an international agricultural research center and an American university. Ernest Sprague, director of CIMMYT's maize program, had become convinced that conventional agricultural education failed to equip professionals with the ability to work together across disciplinary lines. Considering this ability essential to the success of national and international research, he persuaded the Rockefeller Foundation to support an experimental doctoral thesis research program for half a dozen students, ranging across various specialties. Sprague undertook to interest several U.S. universities in this program, at first without success. Professors generally refused to believe they could provide solid education in their specialty if the student was also strongly involved with other specialists. Sprague found this negative reaction initially at Cornell University, but there was sufficient support to overcome resistance and a CIMMYT-Cornell program was set up.

The six fellowship recipients ranged across disciplines including entomology, plant pathology, biometry, agronomy, and agricultural economics. Students spent eighteen months in fieldwork at CIMMYT, concentrating on research in their particular specialties but meeting regularly with other members of the group to discuss their work. In this way they gained an understanding of how the various disciplines related to each other. The plan also brought each student's major professor to CIMMYT for joint discussions with CIMMYT staff members and students regarding the group thesis research project on various aspects of maize. (This aspect of the program appears to have had an impact on the Cornell campus. Some of the professors reported that they had to travel to Mexico to understand and appreciate the work of colleagues in other disciplines.)

Following the completion of their thesis research, the six students traveled through several Central American countries. When they visited Honduras, the Minister of Natural Resources offered positions to all the team members. Three of them accepted, including Mario Contreras, who returned to his native Honduras to become director of the Programa Nacional de Investigación Agropecuaria (PNIA, National Agricultural and Animal Husbandry Research Program).

To facilitate collaboration between research and extension, Contreras saw to it that the director of the agricultural extension program had an office right next to his own. A major feature of the Honduras program involved agricultural extension agents in local area surveys. Contreras told us that at first some of the extension agents had trouble adjusting to the new style of work. Previously they had been playing the role of professional experts, telling small farmers what to do. It was not easy for them to turn around and learn from small farmers, but most learned to accept this role change.

The Honduran model did not develop farmer production information as detailed as was developed by the Guatemalan model but, rather, concentrated on securing from farmers information on their major problems. The scope of problems in the survey extended beyond cultivation practices and experiences into credit and marketing problems and community organization. While extension agents gathered the data, the implications were discussed in joint meetings of research and extension officials.

In the 1970s, Honduras was moving rapidly, linking farmer organizations with government agencies in agricultural development. The initiative was taken by Rolando Vellani, assigned to Honduras by the United Nations Food and Agricultural Organization (FAO), working with a small group of Hondurans. Starting in 1975 they visited more than forty production cooperatives based on peasant organizations to determine the factors associated with their success or failure. Although the cooperatives varied greatly in ecological conditions, Vellani became convinced that these differences were not what distinguished successful from unsuccessful organizations. Organizational leadership and the effectiveness of contacts between the base organizations and government agencies were the major factors. For example, Vellani found that farmers had great difficulty in getting credit in time to make optimal use of the inputs they purchased—a problem that seemed well nigh universal in Latin America.

Over a period of two years, the Vellani group worked closely with seven cooperatives in one area. Leaders of the seven cooperatives began to meet monthly to discuss credit, production, and management problems. In February 1979 these cooperative leaders invited Vellani and his associates to help them plan production for a newly formed regional agricultural and cattle cooperative made up of eighteen to twenty local organizations. Vellani accepted the invitation for his group and also arranged for regular Monday morning meetings of the cooperative leaders with the regional heads of agriculture-related agencies: the Ministry of Natural Resources, the agricultural bank, the land reform agency, and the government agency charged with assisting cooperative development.

On the basis of information locally available from agricultural researchers and the Ministry of Natural Resources, Vellani and the regional leaders worked out a production plan. Since the farmer organizations covered large numbers of families and large expanses of land, it was now feasible to present to the bank a plan including the costs of farm machinery as well as improved seeds, herbicides, fertilizer, and fungicides. The cooperative organization then established its own pool of machines, hired its own mechanics, and trained tractor drivers. Each cooperative was then contracting with the regional cooperative for tractor and driver.

Linking up locally based organizations with government agencies made possible economies of scale far beyond previous practice. For the first year of the program with the regional cooperative, the agricultural bank granted two loans totalling $500,000. Being able to serve so many people in such a large expanse of territory with a single loan enormously reduced the transaction costs for the bank, compared to what would have been involved if each family or even each individual cooperative had had to deal with the bank separately. Furthermore, this system made it possible for the loan money to be delivered at the optimal time for the farmers. The regional head of the agricultural bank had been meeting regularly with the Vellani group and leaders of the regional cooperative as they worked out their production and financing plans. As soon as the plans were completed, they had his informal approval, and the necessary paper work followed shortly thereafter.

The administrative costs at the beginning of this new system were a trifling amount. One or two percent of the amount requested from the bank for inputs and equipment was added to the loan to cover costs of administration. In the regional cooperative, administrative costs were kept to a minimum, with most services performed by unpaid officers, but there is, of course, a need to compensate the regional leaders for travel and living expenses for their cooperative meetings and for their consultations with government officials.

When we last visited Honduras, the Vellani group had not yet finished the analysis of the results for the regional cooperative of the 1980 crop year, but preliminary indications pointed to a yield of maize more than double that of 1979. Vellani stated that weather conditions, particularly the amount of rainfall, had been practically identical for the two years.

The success of this first regional cooperative attracted widespread attention as news spread rapidly through ANACH, the largest peasant organization in Honduras. By early 1980, six other regional cooperatives had been formed, and Vellani noted growing interest around the country in moving beyond the local cooperative base toward regional organizations.

February 1980 marked another major organizational step as ANACH and the government began regular monthly meetings in the capital city between the operating heads of all agriculture-related agencies and the leaders of the regional cooperatives from various parts of the country. This was the culmination of a process of building up farmer organizations from the grass roots to regional levels and linking them with government agencies from the regional level to the capital, Tegucigalpa.

In our experience in Peru and Central America, we have found a common misconception regarding the education and training needs of small farmers. Recognizing the potential economies of scale that can be achieved through farmers getting together to form cooperatives, professionals often decide that their first task is to provide ideological education on the values of the cooperative movement. Vellani told us that the farmer leaders had made clear to his group that their members had long recognized the advantages of cooperation and did not need any further instruction on its ideology. They had also recognized that potential economies of scale were not achievable without the ability to manage a cooperative effectively. They were calling upon the Vellani group for help and training in accounting and record keeping, production planning, and other technical subjects.

The Honduras case reflects the flow of the diffusion process from Guatamala, Mexico, and the United States, involving a national research program (ICTA), an international research center (CIMMYT), and a university (Cornell). We see that the Hondurans picked up some basic ideas abroad but did not simply imitate the structures and processes that had seemed useful elsewhere. For example, the Hondurans were well aware of the ineffective coordination between ICTA and DIGESA and took steps to develop joint activities.

At the time of our fieldwork in the 1970s, Honduras had gone further than Guatemala in working with and through local and regional cooperatives, but that may have involved exploiting opportunities in Honduras that were not available in Guatemala.

Since 1954, when the United States supported a military coup to overthrow a democratically elected government, Guatemala has been ruled by military dictators or by civilian presidents powerless to control the armed forces. The military leaders have viewed well-organized groups of peasants or small farmers as subversive, thus justifying a thinly disguised campaign of killing peasant leaders. In such a situation, even working with a locally based organization developed with the support of World Neighbors and Oxfam might have been considered a precarious enterprise, and trying to help small farmers organize themselves on a large scale would have been out of the question. The situation in Honduras in 1980 was much more favorable for working with and through strong peasant organizations. That situation may have changed, as American use of Honduras as a base for the Contra counterrevolution in Nicaragua has markedly increased the political and economic power of Honduran military leaders.

NETWORKING INTERNATIONALLY

In following developments in Guatemala, Mexico, and Peru, we have already looked at the role played by international agricultural research centers. Now we view these organizations in a broader context for the role they have been playing worldwide for the diffusion of ideas and information regarding agricultural research and development.

In the first place, it is important to recognize that the establishment of the first such center (CIMMYT) was an important social invention, which, over the years, led to the creation of twelve more international agricultural research centers around the world. Exhibit 6.1 (provided by CIP) is a brief statement on those thirteen centers and indicates how they are linked together through the Consultative Group on International Agricultural Research (CGIAR).

It is also important to recognize CGIAR as an important social invention. It is not a bureaucratic organization led by a chief executive officer or operating with a large staff to implement its program. It is a small but influential organization at the central point of a worldwide network of agricultural scientists and professionals and national and international development organizations. CGIAR does not have the power to decide policy or program for any international center, but the consultative process influences both policies and programs. However, the influence does not go just in one direction, from CGIAR to the international centers and to national programs. There have been cases in which national or international centers have initiated programs that have gained favor within CGIAR.

We have seen how CIMMYT, working with Cornell University, stimulated the diffusion process through Central America and how CIP, through developing its influential farmer-back-to-farmer model, further accelerated this diffusion internationally.

In terms of our focus, the most interesting of these centers is the one most recently established (in 1980), International Service for National Agricultural Research (ISNAR). From the early days of the Rockefeller Foundation's Office of Special Services in Mexico, leading to the later establishment of CIMMYT, down to the founding of ISNAR, we see the recognition of new needs and opportunities generating the creation of new international centers.

This evolution responded to changes in the cognitive maps of international agricultural planners. The initial conception reflected the notion of a technological fix. The international centers would develop

Exhibit 6.1

The CGIAR:
A Global Agricultural
Research System

The Consultative Group on International Agricultural Research (CGIAR) was established in 1971 to bring together countries, public and private institutions, international and regional organizations, and representatives from developing countries in support of a network of international agricultural research centers. The basic objective of this effort is to increase the quantity and improve the quality of food production in developing countries. The research supported by the CGIAR concentrates on the critical aspects of food production in developing countries, of global importance, that are not covered adequately by other institutions. Currently, the CGIAR network is involved in research on all of the major food crops and farming systems in the major ecological zones of the developing world.

The CGIAR consists of over 40 donor organizations. They meet twice a year to consider program and budget proposals as well as policy issues of the 13 international agricultural research institutes supported by the group. The world Bank provides the CGIAR with its chairman and secretariat, while the Food and Agriculture Organization (FAO) of the United Nations provides a separate secretariat for the group's Technical Advisory Committee (TAC). The TAC regularly reviews the scientific and Technical aspects of all center programs and advises the CGIAR on needs, priorities,and opportunities for research.

Of the thirteen centers, ten have commodity-oriented programs covering a range of crops and livestock, and farming systems that provide three-fourths of the developing world's total food supply. The remaining three centers are concerned with problems of food policy, national agricultural research, and plant genetic resources.

CIAT
International Center for Tropical Agriculture
CALI, Colombia

CIMMYT
International Maize and Wheat Improvement Center
Mexico City, Mexico

CIP
International Potato Center
Lima, Peru

ICARDA
International Center for Agriculture Research in the Dry Areas
Allepo, Syria

ICRISAT
International Crops Research Institute for the Semi-Arid Tropics
Hyderabad, India

IITA
International Institute of Tropical Agriculture
Ibadan, Nigeria

ILCA
International Livestock Center for Africa
Addis Ababa, Ethiopia

ILRAD
International Laboratory for Research on Animal Diseases
Nairobi, Kenya

IRRI
International Rice Research Institute
Manila, Philippines

WARDA
West Africa Rice Development Association
Bouake, Ivory Coast

IBPGR
International Board for Plant Genetic Resources
Rome, Italy

IFPRI
International Food Policy Research Institute
Washington, D.C., U.S.A.

ISNAR
International Service for National Agricultural Research
The Hague, Netherlands

SOURCE: CGIAR Annual Report, 1990. Used by permission.

new higher-yielding varieties of major food crops, beginning with the grains. The centers would then make the seeds of these varieties available to national programs and teach national personnel the methods required to get maximum yields out of these new resources.

This technological fix early yielded spectacular gains in world production of wheat and rice that became known popularly as the green revolution. This naturally encouraged the development of centers specializing in other important food crops and also one for livestock. Recognizing that difficult soil and climate conditions in some parts of the world prevented farmers from making the yield gains achieved in more favored regions, planners enlarged their focus to create new centers focusing their research on these limiting factors, and the preexisting centers began to focus more attention on problems and potentials for farming under less than optimal conditions.

By the 1970s, planners were coming to recognize three important needs not yet met:

Aid to small farmers in rain-fed agriculture. It had earlier been assumed that the green revolution technologies were scale neutral, benefitting small farmers as well as large operators. By now research was indicating that, in general, small farmers benefitted only where they had access to ample irrigation water. Furthermore, while planners had previously known that few small farmers specialized in a single crop, now they began to recognize the limitations of the traditional crop specialization research that had yielded the higher-yielding varieties. This led to a shift in interest toward farming systems research and research on farmers' fields.

More effective help to national programs. It had been assumed that, with new plant varieties and training from the international centers, national programs could handle their own research and development problems. Now planners began to realize that the national programs were no better prepared than the international centers to deal with these newly recognized problems. The problems involved not only the need to learn more about the biology and ecology of farming systems but also the need to devise better organizational structures and social systems to serve small farmers.

Broadening the disciplinary research base. The technological fix model indicated that researcher needs would be limited to plant, soil, and animal scientists and agricultural engineers. Recognition of these new needs and problems opened the way to the introduction of social scientists—economists first and later, less extensively, anthropologists and sociologists.

We should not assume that these changes in the thinking of planners came about easily or without resistance. When we first visited CIMMYT in the spring of 1975, I came upon planning documents reporting an exchange of communications between CGIAR and CIMMYT. Noting that the enormous price increases for petroleum imposed by OPEC in 1973 and again in 1975 were dramatically raising the price of fertilizer, CGIAR asked each of the centers to report how this was going to affect their own research planning. CIMMYT's responded that there would be *no effect at all*. The argument was that the higher-yielding varieties would require the same amount of fertilizer as before and would still pay off for farmers. I have noted resistance to change also within CIP, as Douglas Horton reported the research director's veto of CIP's first economist's plan to go into the field to study how Peruvian small farmers were growing potatoes. Nevertheless, the external forces toward change were strong enough and there were enough international center people recognizing the needs and opportunities for change to move the international system in the directions noted above.

ISNAR plays a central role in networking for guiding interdisciplinary research and participatory processes in on-farm research (which ISNAR calls OFCOR). Furthermore, ISNAR has taken its mandate beyond what appears in its title to devote major attention to extension and to the relations between research and extension. Through its worldwide network, ISNAR circulates a rapidly growing stream of publications focused on what has been learned through case studies of national programs and also through the comparative studies of key problems across various national programs. The reports are written in nontechnical language so that professionals in any agriculture-related discipline should find them easy to understand. I have drawn heavily on the ISNAR report on the Guatemala program (Ruano and Fumagalli, 1989) to go beyond my earlier fieldwork in that country.

In its technical assistance to national programs, ISNAR has gone far beyond technical biological initiatives to help national professionals to organize research and extension more effectively. The scope of such assistance can be illustrated from a statement made by an experiment station director to ISNAR officials during their recent visit to Costa

Rica (ISNAR, 1990). He credited ISNAR recommendations with the following organizational changes:

- administrative decentralization, with regional centers deciding on their own programs;
- budgetary responsibility for experiment station operations shifted from the central office to experiment stations;
- establishment of a Director's Advisory Committee with representatives of research programs, farmer leaders, and private enterprise;
- increased participation of station technicians in research planning;
- a redesigned accounting system better adapted to research operations; and
- improved systems of communication between research, extension, and small farmers.

Probably Costa Rican research professionals had had some of these changes in mind before ISNAR study visits but had not been able to initiate action for top-level decision makers. The involvement of high prestige international officials probably introduced valuable new ideas into Costa Rica's national programs and also provided the necessary impulse to transform good ideas, both old and new, into action.

These international networks sponsor conferences and publications that make it possible for the professional almost anywhere to get information and ideas regarding what has been done elsewhere on a problem that a professional is grappling with in his or her own organization. Such networks are powerful engines for the diffusion of information and ideas in agricultural research and development.

Also important in the diffusion of information and ideas is the Overseas Development Institute (ODI) in London. ODI has recently concentrated particularly on tracking R&D projects containing participatory elements. In 1989 its Agricultural Administration (Research and Extension) Network published *340 Abstracts on Farmer Participatory Research*. By my count, only 13 of the case reports appeared before 1980, and 7 of those bear the date 1979. This indicates an explosive growth of participatory projects and provides anyone anywhere with a wealth of case materials for stimulation and guidance.

PART II

Participation in Industry

7. Discovering What Ain't So in Industrial Relations

I got my introduction to "what ain't so" in industrial relations in 1942 and 1943 in my first study in industry. The field site was a set of plants of Phillips Petroleum Company in Oklahoma City. I focused particularly on the plants involved in transforming natural gas into high-octane gasoline.

The operations I observed were carried on in three interrelated installations, supervised by a foreman. At the heart of the process was the control room, manned for each shift by three workers: the polymerization (poly) operator as the lead man, followed by the hydro-stillman and the fractionator operator. The engine room was manned by a single engine operator. Producing some of the material used in the process, the catalyst plant was staffed by a lead operator and about ten other workers.

When it had been built a few years earlier, these installations were in the forefront of applied chemical engineering. Workers in the control room did not have college degrees, but several of them had passed correspondence school courses in chemical engineering, and many appeared to have considerable technical knowledge along with what they had picked up from experience.

At the time, foreman positions in such plants were held by chemical engineers. Tom Lloyd, the current foreman, respected the knowledge and skill of the workers and got along with them very well, but they regaled me with tales of their problems with Bill Jones and Tom Fitch, two previous foremen. Those supervisors had always given their operating instructions in great detail and had been highly critical of the men when operating results did not meet what the foremen predicted would ensue from their instructions. Through their experience, the men had learned that following instructions would not produce the results the foremen demanded, but the foremen refused to acknowledge that the workers might know more about some aspects of operations than did a chemical engineer. In order to escape the foremen's criticisms, the workers took to "boiler housing" their record of operations on the daily operating data sheet. In full detail, they wrote down the operating steps the foremen had ordered but then went ahead to operate the plant so as to produce the results the foremen had required. The foremen then proceeded to make elaborate analyses of the data produced by "boiler housing" the records in order to determine *scientifically* what operating methods would produce the best results. Working with such a combination of fact and fiction, the best laboratory-trained chemical engineer had no chance of drawing sound conclusions regarding the relation between operational steps and operating results.

By the time I began my fieldwork, boiler housing had been abandoned because the workers did not need to record fictitious data to protect themselves from Tom Lloyd. Because he was willing to learn from the workers, he gained a far better understanding of operations than had his predecessors.

In the earlier period, the conflict between workers and supervisors was based primarily upon the foremen's lack of respect for the intelligence and sense of responsibility of the workers. When the workers recognized that Tom Lloyd was seeking to integrate their knowledge with what he had learned in his formal education and experience, that source of conflict disappeared—only to reappear suddenly in the tri-isobutylene crisis.

On Tuesday, April 6, at 6:30 p.m., Tom Lloyd received a telephone call from the main office with the order to start the tri-iso-butylene run as soon as possible. He had known some time in advance that a product of this nature was to be made, but it was not until this time that he was given the exact specifications (initial boiling point and dry point temperatures).

Lloyd asked if he could start the run the following morning, but he was told that this was a rush order so that it was necessary to start work immediately.

Since Lloyd was not familiar with the detailed operations of the fractionating column, he telephoned Dan Benton, his staff engineer, and asked him to return to the plant to take charge of operations at once.

The fractionating column in which the product was to be made was under the direct charge of the fractionator operator, but, having had a good deal of fractionating experience, the hydro-stillman was naturally interested also, and both men normally worked under the supervision of the poly operator.

To this group were added Lloyd and Benton, who ordinarily spent little time within the plant. During the run, Lloyd spent most of his time at Hi-Test, consulting with Benton and the operators. He also took samples from the fractionating column up to the laboratory in order to run distillation tests on them. When he went home to sleep, he called in Catalyst Operator Thompson to do the distillations.

Benton was in active charge from Tuesday night until Friday morning. During that period, he was in the plant almost continually, getting only ten hours of sleep. At the start, he took over the No. 3 fractionating column himself and directed the fractionator operator in all changes. Since the plant was operating in a routine manner otherwise, there was little for the poly operator and the hydro-stillman to do except watch Benton and the fractionator operator.

Benton had certain definite ideas as to how the run should be started, and it appeared that by Thursday morning he had been successful. The product at that time tested to specifications, but by the time the test results were reported, the column had become flooded and was no longer making the product. Having been unsuccessful in this effort, Benton listened to the suggestions of the operators and tried out a number of their ideas.

At the start of the daylight tour (7 a.m. to 3 p.m. Friday) fractionator operator Kendall gave his opinion to Lloyd that no further progress could be gained along the lines then being pursued, and went on to outline his ideas as to how the fractionating column should be handled. Lloyd had a high regard for Kendall and therefore decided to turn the column over to him without restrictions or supervision. By now Benton was physically and mentally exhausted, and Lloyd sent him home.

At the end of Kendall's tour, he still had no results, but he was able to convince Lloyd that he was moving in the right direction. Lloyd ordered Kendall to work another eight hours, remaining in charge of the key column. Walling was poly operator on evening tour (3 p.m. to 11 p.m.).

Lloyd instructed Walling to pay close attention to the way Kendall was operating the column.

At the end of evening tour, the product was still to be made. Lloyd sent Kendall home and held Walling over for another eight hours, ordering him to take exclusive charge of the column. Early Saturday morning, twenty-two hours after Kendall began trying his plan, the product came over, and shortly the brief run was completed.

One operator expressed the general viewpoint of the workers when he said:

> It wasn't until they left it to the operator that they got the thing lined out. Sure, it would have gone much faster if they had made it that way in the first place. The operator knows these columns better than the technical man.

During the week of the run, Joe Sloan had worked Monday through Wednesday on graveyard tour (11 p.m. to 7 a.m.) as a hydro-stillman under Walling. Thursday through Saturday, he worked as poly operator, but when the product was finally being made, he found Walling held over to retain charge of the key column, so Sloan had nothing to do with the making of this experimental product.

Some weeks later I asked Sloan to tell me particularly about his reactions to the tri-iso-butylene run. He said it had not bothered him particularly. He went on,

> Now I don't have anything against Benton. I like Dan. But we hadn't been accustomed to having an engineer supervise operations like that. He was around all the time telling the fractionator man what to do. Lloyd was there most of the time too. He didn't really do anything. He would just talk to Benton and with the rest of us, figuring out what to do. Then he spent some of his time running distillations . . .

> One night when I was on tour, we had Thompson in there from the catalyst plant running distillations for Lloyd while he slept. We had never had a man from the catalyst plant work in there with us before. Thompson [a company union representative] and I got into a hot argument about the company union and the CIO. It didn't really amount to anything, but I didn't like to have Thompson around all the time. He has the type of overbearing personality that don't appeal to me . . .

> One night Tom Fitch [Lloyd's predecessor as foreman] called the plant at 2 a.m. He had something to do with the run from the main office end . . . Fitch knows the operations here a lot better than Lloyd . . . Lloyd was in the plant with us at the time. I asked him why he thought Fitch had called. "Oh," he says, "he probably just wanted to show he was interested in his job." I said to Lloyd, "Then why are you down here now? For the same reason?" He didn't have anything to say to that. (Whyte, 1961:209-11)

The long time required to produce a small sample of tri-iso-butylene must have been seen in the main office as evidence of incompetent local management. As I observed it on the scene, it also involved an at least temporary disruption of the relations between foreman Lloyd and the workers.

The foreman's past behavior had reflected high confidence in the intelligence and skills of the workers. Nevertheless, under pressure from the main office for immediate action, he fell back upon the conventional wisdom: calling on the professionally trained man to take control of the project.

Workers believed the project could have been completed much sooner if Lloyd and Benton had let them control the process. What might have been can never be known, but the arguments over what should have been done may help us to focus on the key issue.

In discussing the case with me later, Lloyd said it would not have been practical simply to turn over the problem to the workers. He knew it would take more than eight hours to shift over to this experimental project. Success would therefore require a consistent operational strategy from one tour (shift) to another. If he had simply turned the problem over to the operators, each shift change could have brought in a new approach, thus creating confusion and inefficiency.

Workers cast doubt upon this rationale. In effect, they argued that there were systematic differences between the operating strategies pursued by the chemical engineers and those practiced by the workers. Confronted by a new technical problem and guided by their scientific and engineering education, the engineers would take aim at the target and manage operations so as to reach the technical specifications by the most quick and direct route. Having learned from experience that this particular fractionating column never did operate in accordance with its engineering design, workers advocated a different strategy. They would have proceeded by successive approximations: aiming in the general direction of the target, taking a small step at the start, followed by a period of observation and testing, until the process stabilized at a new level. On the basis of what they had learned from observing the impacts of the initial changes, they would go on to the next stage, again followed by a period of observation, testing, and waiting for the process to stabilize. This way, it would take them longer to reach the target, but, when they got there, the process would be stabilized within required limits, rather than surging beyond that point.

The case does not prove to us that the workers were right and the engineers were wrong. It does focus attention on the need to integrate technical and scientific knowledge with experiential learning of those intimately involved in the work process.

My own learning of "what ain't so" was far from unique. Any field researcher who gained the confidence of workers picked up evidence of practical worker knowledge that was unrecognized by management. Robert Guest describes this case encountered when he was working on the project that resulted in *Toward the Automated Factory* (Walker, 1957):

> The opening of the National Tube division's new multi-million dollar tube mill in Ohio was delayed because the engineers had found a number of "bugs" during test runs. We had spent several months previously interviewing workers, foremen, and union officials to study how people adjusted to new technology. From workers, we kept hearing comments as to why the opening was delayed and why the test runs were not going well. They said they knew what was wrong but the "big shot" engineers, many of whom were out of the Pittsburgh headquarters, never asked the men or the foremen for their opinions. The comment from a piercer plug operator was typical. "If they don't treat us like intelligent human beings we'll be goddamned if we're going to tell them what's wrong. Let 'em stew in their own juice." Especially striking were their observations to the effect that the new mill had the potential of turning out steel tubing at a rate eighteen percent higher than the rate officially announced by the engineers! The union had also filed a complaint saying that the incentive plan was unfair and that the men would end up losing money.

> After a six month delay and much pressure from headquarters the incentive question was settled to the union's satisfaction. A worker called me one night at my hotel and told me that I might see something interesting if I came to the new mill at the start of the midnight shift. At precisely midnight a loud klaxon sounded. The lead man raised his arm and in a loud voice called out, "Let 'er roll!" The red hot billets spit out of helical rolls at a speed I had never seen before. There were no delays or breakdowns on the shift and within a month capacity had gone over twenty percent (beyond the engineers' estimates).

> Only later did we realize the significance of the incident, a phenomenon well-documented in later studies of worker participation. It illustrated the consequences of corporate decisions dominated by the technical experts who fail to make use of the "common wisdom" of rank-and-file employees at the shop floor level. (Guest, 1987)

Note that the common wisdom was backed up by impressively accurate projections of the capacity of the mill: eighteen percent beyond its rated capacity predicted, somewhat over twenty percent achieved with experience and increasing skill. This suggests that to a considerable extent experienced workers think and act like scientists. They do not carry out controlled experiments or articulate academically acceptable theories, but they do take actions and then observe their apparent consequences. If an action does not yield the desired consequences, they modify that action next time or else try something quite different. If the action yields the desired results or comes close, they take further actions along the same line, making adjustments to varying conditions, based on observations of the results achieved.

Recognizing that workers actually use their brains on the job is a necessary first step toward advances in theory and practice. Why should such an obvious lesson have been so hard for management people to learn? We can explain this managerial "resistance to change" only through placing it in the framework of the distribution of power and status within organizations and the hold on managerial minds of traditional cognitive maps.

Over the years, I had various opportunities to present to management groups my evidence that the theories of scientific management were not working out in practice. In general, I found little resistance to my stories from the factory floor demonstrating "what ain't so." In fact, managers seemed to enjoy tales of how workers were outwitting management or how management was failing to utilize worker knowledge and skill, and they often volunteered tales from their experience to support the same points. Nevertheless, I saw no evidence that tales on "what ain't so" were leading managers to think and act differently in their own work. The linkages between research and practice still remained to be established.

In the following chapters, we will examine the organizational learning processes that have begun to establish that linkage.

8. Social Research on Organizational Behavior in Industry

We begin here to trace the development of research and practice in the field earlier called human relations in industry and now known more generally as organizational behavior. We begin with the United States because most of the early research was done here, and American researchers dominated the field until around the middle of this century. These American studies were influential in shaping later research abroad, but until very recently this research had had a minimal impact on American management practices. In fact, it may be argued that this American research was more influential on practice abroad than at home—for reasons we will explore later.

WHEN AND HOW DID HUMAN RELATIONS RESEARCH BEGIN?

I trace the beginnings of behavioral science research in industrial relations to Elton Mayo and his colleagues at the Harvard Business School who worked on the Western Electric research program in the

1920s and early 1930s, culminating with the publication in 1939 of *Management and the Worker* (Roethlisberger and Dickson). Many sociologists prefer to trace the origins back to Max Weber, who indeed did make his important contributions decades before Mayo; but Weber's writings on bureaucracy did not lead directly to the development of a new field of study. It was the Harvard-Western Electric collaboration that launched research in the field first called human relations in industry.

I first became acquainted with the Western Electric program in a seminar with Elton Mayo in the fall of 1937. I read and discussed with him his books on the Hawthorne plant, which presented earlier interpretations than the more solid and systematic *Management and the Worker.* It was this experience with Mayo, reinforced by associations with social anthropologists Conrad M. Arensberg, Eliot D. Chapple, and F.L.W. Richardson, that led me away from community studies (Whyte, 1943) and into industrial relations.

In 1940 I moved from Harvard to the University of Chicago to study under social anthropologist W. Lloyd Warner, then known particularly for his Yankee City studies. As I learned later, while at Harvard he had led the Mayo group from the famous experiment of the test room girls in the Hawthorne plant to a study of a work group in its natural factory setting: the bank wiring room. This still seems to me one of the finest work group studies ever carried out. The test room experiments excited public attention because of the surprising finding that the young women continued to increase their production when the conditions of work were made more favorable or less favorable. Since Roethlisberger (1977) himself later offered seventeen full or partial explanations of that result, the scientific significance of the test room studies seems to me to have been greatly overrated. The bank wiring room study suggested the importance of examining a group of workers in its natural hierarchical structural working conditions—a line of research more compatible with social anthropology than with the psychological orientation of Mayo.

In fact, Mayo himself derailed these promising beginnings in what I have called a monumental misinterpretation of the practical implications of the Hawthorne plant studies (Whyte, 1978). I like to startle my students with the claim that, though there may be a phenomenon such as "the Hawthorne effect," it did not appear in the Western Electric research at the Hawthorne plant. The Hawthorne effect interpretation is based on the notion that the increasing productivity of the test room women was a response to the friendly interest in them and in their work by the research observer and therefore indirectly by management. As Arensberg (1951) pointed out, however, the men in the bank wiring room, like the women in the test room, were provided by management with a friendly and sympathetic observer and yet their productivity ran in a straight line throughout the observation period.

How can we explain these productivity differences? We can believe either that women are more gullible than men or (as I think more likely) that the explanation lies in the markedly different structural conditions in which the two cases were situated. The bank wiring room was designed to operate just like a regular department, with the constant presence of the observer being the only deviation from that norm. The men worked under the close supervision of the foreman and had frequent and predominantly negatively tinged interactions with their inspector. In contrast, no inspector was ever present in the test room, and the foreman only appeared to deliver materials and pick up the output. In today's terminology, the test room functioned as an autonomous work group.

Unfortunately, Elton Mayo never sought to explain the striking output differences between the two cases. The hypothesis of the Hawthorne effect to explain the results of the test room study was attractive to him because it fit in with his previously stated convictions that the human problems of industry arose out of boredom and obsessive reveries suffered by workers in repetitive jobs. The company and the workers, he believed, would benefit by the establishment of a personnel counseling program to enable individuals to achieve catharsis by unburdening themselves to sympathetic nondirective interviewers.

In effect, the inauguration of the personnel counseling program blocked off social research at Western Electric. Whatever benefits workers or the company gained through the twenty years and many millions of dollars Western Electric invested in personnel counseling, that program bore little resemblance to research. Social research had also been on the shelf in the Harvard Business School for a decade or more while the professors went about gathering case materials for teaching.

Revival came in 1943 under the leadership of two social anthropologists who formed the Committee on Human Relations in Industry at the University of Chicago. Picking up the neglected leads from the bank wiring room case, they committed themselves to studying industrial life in its natural settings. W. Lloyd Warner chaired the committee and

Burleigh B. Gardner served as its executive secretary until 1946, when he left the university to form his own research and consulting organization. Warner and Gardner were joined by Everett C. Hughes (Sociology Department), Allison Davis and Robert J. Havighurst (Department of Human Development), Frederick Harbison (Department of Economics), and George Brown (School of Business). In 1944 I joined the committee to direct a study on human relations in the restaurant industry, and I stayed on to become executive secretary from 1946 to 1948.

I believe the committee was the first interdisciplinary group of professors and students carrying out a research program in human relations in industry. The program was initially supported by six industrial companies providing $3,600 a year each. Shortly after the beginning, Sears, Roebuck and Company joined in supporting the committee, and small pieces of support were picked up elsewhere.

The Chicago initiative was followed up shortly by the Labor-Management Center of E. Wight Bakke and the Technology Project of Charles Walker at Yale and the work of Douglas McGregor and others at MIT.

EVALUATING HUMAN RELATIONS RESEARCH

As I look back on early human relations research, from the 1920s to the 1950s, I see major strengths but also important weaknesses. In this period, researchers went into the industrial plants as participant observers or to gain a close but detached view of work life through intensive interviewing and observation. Fieldworkers such as Melville Dalton, Donald Roy, Orvis Collins, Charles Walker, and Robert Guest gave us far more realistic descriptions of factory life than had existed previously in the academic literature. Hardly anyone is doing such fine-grained micro-organizational studies these days, even though the rapidly changing industrial scene would seem to demand a new generation of industrial explorers.

Our weaknesses stemmed in part from our history of building a discipline in opposition to "scientific management" or Taylorism. As pointed out in Chapter 3, we were busy discovering "what ain't so" in Taylorism. This can be a useful ground-clearing operation, but discovering "what ain't so" does not tell us what is so.

In our concern with describing patterns of behavior, we focused on what came to be called "informal organization." We demonstrated that the formal structures and work procedures of management did not determine behavior at work, yet we gave insufficient attention to those formal structures to be able to state how in fact they did influence behavior.

We did not completely neglect technology, but we did not know how to treat it as a variable in relation to the social system of the plant. Through the pioneering work of Charles Walker, Robert Guest, and Arthur Turner (Walker and Guest, 1952; Walker, Guest, and Turner, 1956) we recognized that the automotive assembly line was one of the most oppressive work systems that had ever been devised, but we assumed that it was so economically efficient as to make any other system impractical. We knew it would be economically impossible to go back to earlier methods in which craftsmen had built cars, but we did not see ahead to the more flexible systems of organizing work that developed years later. In other words, we treated technology as a constant rather than as a set of variables. (Nor did we learn until many years later the importance of treating ownership as a set of variables rather than as a constant.)

We did give some attention to the impact of economic incentives on workers in our studies of piece rates (Whyte, 1955) but we had no way of integrating the economics of the firm into our framework. We knew that the behavior of managers was influenced by the way they interpreted the numbers that purported to reflect the performance of the firm but, with few exceptions (Argyris, 1952), we did not focus on the point where economic analysis and behavioral analysis come together.

REACTIONS AMONG SOCIOLOGISTS
AND ECONOMISTS

This sudden opening of a new field of study attracted wide attention and enthusiasm among students. It was greeted with some apprehension, however, among our colleagues in sociology and economics at Chicago and elsewhere. Some sociologists concluded that they too should move into teaching and research in this new field, which they preferred to call industrial sociology. Tracing the origins of the field to

Max Weber, they focused attention on broad studies of management and labor, with emphasis on the macro-level or societal aspects.

Meanwhile, those of us pursuing human relations were involved in intensive fieldwork in factories and even with small work groups. Some sociologists and labor economists attacked us for being both unethical and unscientific. As we were then entirely supported by management, they claimed we were not really engaged in scientific pursuits but were rather creating a managerial sociology, helping management to manipulate workers and to undermine unions or avoid unionization. And as workers and union leaders knew that our work was supported by management, they would not talk frankly to our interviewers. Therefore, we could get only a one-sided and unscientific view of the topics we were studying.

We were also accused of disregarding the role of unions. When we did study rare cases in which local unions and management had resolved their conflicts and developed cooperative relations, critics claimed that our conception of cooperation meant simply having union leaders and workers agree to do whatever management wanted done. Our critics also charged us with believing that all conflicts between labor and management could be resolved through "good communications"—that panacea being offered by the management people who learned from our research.

ACADEMIC TURF PROBLEMS

Before the human relations boom, the field of industrial relations had been monopolized by labor economists and industrial psychologists, concentrating on the measurement of individual skills and aptitudes. As human relations opened up the new approach, many industrial psychologists joined the trend and began calling themselves industrial social psychologists.

Although some labor economists attacked the ethics of the human relations researchers, others were more puzzled than hostile. In fact, some of them—particularly Frederick Harbison and Charles Meyers—went out of their way to try to fit us in; and leaders of the Industrial Relations Research Association (IRRA) tried to encourage behavioral scientists to get involved with IRRA, which is still predominantly for labor economists.

The difficulty of fitting us in can be traced in part to the differing scale of studies on the two sides of the divide. In the 1940s and 1950s, when labor economists thought of doing a case study they would have had in mind something like labor relations in the steel industry. If they really wanted to narrow down the field, they might settle for a study of labor relations in U.S. Steel. In contrast, behavioral scientists approached the field with a much more micro focus. For us a case study was likely to be limited to a particular factory or even to a single department in that factory or a single work group. Instead of studying an international union as a whole, we were more inclined to do intensive studies of local unions (e.g., Sayles and Strauss, 1953).

The mixed reactions to what we were doing then were well expressed at a 1948 Cornell summer institute on industrial relations. When I had finished my report, a labor economist expressed his concern about the lack of a firm theoretical framework guiding our research: "You people in human relations are certainly doing interesting research, but do you know enough yet to teach courses?" I replied rather undiplomatically, "In your studies of labor relations you are constantly having to point out that the orthodox theories of economics don't apply. We are trying to build theory in the field from the ground up."

MANAGEMENT INDIFFERENCE
TO HUMAN RELATIONS

Many years later, perhaps it is possible to state with some detachment that attacks on our ethics were largely based on misinterpretations of management's interest in and utilization of our research, as well as on a misunderstanding of the way we went about our work. To be sure, the people who decided to finance our research must have thought their companies would get some benefits, but their initial expectations were both modest and vague. In a period of high profits during World War II, $3,600 a year was a trifling sum. Some executives who had intellectual and cultural interests beyond the bottom line may have been attracted by the part of the program that brought them together for dinner every six weeks with the professors to engage in high-level discussions of labor, management, and society.

If executives had an immediate practical interest in our research, it concerned the problem of absenteeism and labor turnover. In the very tight wartime labor market, they had difficulty filling orders because workers were not coming to work regularly or simply were leaving in search of openings elsewhere. Even that interest, however, did not at first open any doors for research. It was a year from the beginning of the committee on Human Relations in Industry before its members were able to gain permission for in-plant research from any of the six companies supporting the program.

There were two common answers to researchers' requests for permission to launch in-plant studies. One answer was that things were going so smoothly in the plant that management did not want any outsiders to come in and ask workers how they felt about their jobs because such probing might get workers to think about reasons to be unhappy. The other answer was that the situation was so tense that the introduction of any outsider could set off an explosion.

Lacking access to the plants, our researchers could learn about worker-management relations only through house-to-house interviews in working-class neighborhoods. The data collected in this way were miscellaneous, but at least the interviews did furnish stories that might have some bearing on what led workers to consider a job good or bad, a supervisor good or bad, and so on.

The breakthrough to in-plant studies occurred suddenly in one of the evening meetings shortly before I joined the committee. After expressing his frustrations about his company's labor relations, Walter Paepcke, chief executive officer of Container Corporation of America, said, "The situation in our 35th Street plant is so fouled up that no outsider could possibly make things worse. Why don't you come in and see what you can do?" Burleigh Gardner went through this open door and began the first of a series of field studies that was eventually extended to several of the other supporting companies. (It should be noted that Paepcke hardly conformed to the stereotype of the big business man, fixated only on the bottom line. Later he was to provide the money and the impetus to found the Aspen Institute, which became a center for high-level discussion of the arts, literature, and world affairs.)

Paradoxical as it may seem, in those years with the committee we found many workers and local union officers and even some international representatives more open and interested in what we were doing than were most managers. As we always told them at the outset about our source of support, they initially viewed us with suspicion. But once a skillful field-worker had spent time getting acquainted with workers on the factory floor and talking with local union leaders, and as they found there were no negative consequences from our presence in the plant, the barriers began to go down. Many workers came to express themselves freely and frankly. Why? Again and again we got the same explanation. Workers and local union leaders had tried to get management to take action on their problems. Either they could not get anybody in management to listen or else people listened but then nothing happened. So they would say to us, "You talk to the management. Maybe you can get them to understand our problems."

My entry into the program in 1944 was made possible by a $10,000 grant from the National Restaurant Association (NRA). That grant did not mean that members of the association had any strong interest in understanding human relations in their industry. They had approached the University of Chicago to establish a master's program in restaurant administration. George Brown reported to the Committee on Human Relations in Industry that the School of Business was prepared to accept financial support from the National Restaurant Association for such a program, but only if a small portion of the funds was set aside to support research. Brown reported that no one in the School of Business had any interest in research in the restaurant industry. Did the committee members have anything to suggest? Everett Hughes suggested that I direct a study of human relations in the restaurant industry.

Toward the end of our fieldwork I was invited to give talks to restaurant management people in several cities. For that purpose I focused on what I was calling "human elements in supervision," and that subject did evoke some interest. When the NRA members read the first draft of the manuscript, however, they were distressed by my discussion of the low prestige of the industry and the low status of waiters, waitresses, countermen, dishwashers, and so on. The most revealing comment on my manuscript was phrased in three blunt sentences: "I thought that the reason we wanted to work with the University of Chicago was to raise the status of our industry. If this book is published, it will have the opposite effect. Therefore it should not be published." If the university's contract with the NRA had not included a clause protecting the author's right to publish, I doubt that it would have been possible to arrive at any agreement for revisions of the manuscript that would have satisfied the NRA people and would have satisfied me and our committee.

In the early postwar years I saw no change in the general indifference or even hostility of most operating managers to our human relations research. To be sure, there were notable exceptions. For example, James C. Worthy (1950, 1984) of Sears, Roebuck and Company had a lively intellectual and practical interest in our research and worked with people from our committee in developing the Sears attitudinal survey program and on further projects. But such exceptions were few.

At first I attributed our failure to stir up more interest and support from managers to our inability to talk their language, but now I think that was a misdiagnosis. Some of us were able to speak and write in rather clear and simple terms. The problem was that top management people saw no need to change. These were the years following World War II in which our "great arsenal of democracy" had achieved an enormous international reputation. Productivity teams from all over the world were visiting the United States to learn the secrets of our know-how. As late as 1968, when Japan was already beginning to make serious inroads into our industrial dominance, the French journalist Jean-Jacques Servan-Schreiber published his best-seller in which he claimed that U.S. managers were so much more efficient than Europeans that the United States was taking over economic dominance of that part of the world (Servan-Schreiber, 1968).

Since top management people were being told by their admirers elsewhere that they had all the answers, why should they listen to people from the ivory tower who might point out problems they were not mastering? In that era we barely got to talk to a plant manager, let alone to any higher-level line manager. We had better access to personnel administrators, who were looking for gimmicks that might help them gain status in their companies. But then personnel administrators would say, "What we want you to tell us is how can we make the workers feel they are participating." We had to answer that we were not into impression management. When we explained that the way to make workers feel that they were participating was to open up opportunities for them to exert influence on decisions important to them, the personnel administrators lost interest in further discussion.

BEYOND THE 1950s: FROM HUMAN RELATIONS TO ORGANIZATIONAL BEHAVIOR

Attacks on human relations research, along with the increasingly acknowledged deficiencies in human relations theory, led eventually to abandonment of that label. Our field is now generally known as organizational behavior.

The change in labels should not suggest that a single new model or theoretical framework has emerged. At the risk of oversimplifying an active but disorderly field, I now see two competing lines of research, which I call the mainstream and the alternate stream.

For both streams in the 1950-90 period, I find that the intellectual discourse has become more international, with major influences on American research coming in from abroad—particularly from Great Britain and Scandinavia. These international influences are particularly marked in the alternate stream.

What has become the mainstream contrasts with the human relations approach in several important respects:

- a shift of emphasis from the micro to the macro—from interpersonal relations to formal organizational structures, technologies, and the impact of markets and other environmental factors on the organization;
- a shift from the study of patterns of relations toward the definition of variables and the specification of hypotheses to be tested by rigorous quantitative methods;
- a shift from intensive interviewing and observational studies toward questionnaire or survey research; and
- a sharp separation between theory and practice, with researchers generally avoiding any link of research to practice.

Mainstream researchers do not all share the same interests and methodologies, of course, but they have enough in common to be identified as a group by most scholars studying the development of organization theory.

There is also an alternate stream that groups together researchers concentrating on *organizational change*. In a sense, this stream arose out of the human relations approach instead of representing a sharp break away from it. Like those of us active in the 1940s and 1950s, the alternate stream researchers reject the separation of theory from practice, arguing that science can best be advanced when the two are linked together. The difference is that today's organizational change researchers have sharper action tools and better theoretical frameworks than we did in those earlier decades.

Although the mainstream and the alternate stream are clearly different in some ways, they also have certain interests in common. Researchers of both kinds accept the influence on organizations of formal structure, markets, and other environmental conditions, but the alternate stream researchers go on to study how organizational performance can be improved within those limiting conditions. Both streams have strong interests in worker participation, but they pursue that interest in quite different ways. Alternative stream researchers have welcomed opportunities to sharpen their theoretical and methodological tools through forms of *action research,* whereas mainstreamers have generally avoided getting involved in the action.

Until Joan Woodward (1965) came on the scene, the only theory of organizational structures was that handed down by the scientific management school: that for any organization of a given size there was just one best way of designing its structure. The studies of the Woodward group in the United Kingdom demonstrated that plants with different technologies and work processes require distinctively different organizational structures.

The Woodward studies set off a flood of research on organizational structures. Paul Lawrence and Jay Lorsch (1967) extended this analysis into the relations of the organization and its markets. Howard Aldrich (1979) went further to argue that the environment tended to select those organizational characteristics that best fit it.

Those developing the alternate stream (concerned with organizational change) picked up the Woodward lead on organizational structures to work on the theory and practice of changing structures, technologies, and social systems so as to fit them together more fruitfully. Having begun his research career in England long before Woodward, Eric Trist went on to formulate the concept of socio-technical systems (for an account of the evolution and utilization of the socio-technical framework, see Trist, 1981). The idea is basically simple: The most effective organizations will be those in which the technology and the organization structure and social processes are designed to fit together. If this seems obvious, note that it departs radically from past practice and most current practice. In the past, designers of organizations laid out the technology and assumed that work and social processes must be designed to fit the requirements of technology.

From England to Scandinavia and America, Trist and his socio-technical systems framework have had a great influence on the theory

and practice of organizational change. In Norway, Einar Thorsrud created and guided for many years the Industrial Democracy project, bringing together Norwegian and foreign social scientists with Norwegian
workers, managers, and union leaders to learn how to design (or rede-
sign) organizations to enhance both economic efficiency and the quality
of working life (Elden, 1979; Thorsrud, 1977). In Oslo in June 1987,
hundreds of social scientists and practitioners gathered to honor the
memory of Thorsrud and to discuss how best to contribute to the flow
of research and action on socio-technical systems.

That the mainstream and the alternate stream have diverged sharply
from each other can be readily demonstrated by picking up a textbook
from a mainstream social scientist. Consider, for example, Richard H.
Hall's *Organizations: Structure and Process* (1982), in which leading
figures in the alternate stream are almost completely overlooked. Eric
Trist is mentioned only briefly in reference to his earliest study, and
Einar Thorsrud and other leading figures in the alternate stream do not
even merit footnotes. Or consider the leading action researchers focusing on the problems of changing leader behavior in organizations:
Donald Schön (1983a) is not mentioned by Hall, and Chris Argyris
(1986) is only mentioned in connection with his critiques of mainstream research.

In America today, a large majority of organizational behavior researchers appear to be in the mainstream. I have the impression that
some eminent mainstreamers consider their stream the only habitat for
true scientists and regard the alternate streamers as (1) surviving relics
of the human relations movement or throwbacks to that movement, or
(2) people who may be doing interesting things but who basically are
just "storytellers."

Scientific questions, however, are not decided by popular vote. In the
long run, the academic competition between the two streams will be
decided by which stream proves superior in its contributions to science.
That the alternate stream offers more promise, not only for practice but
also for science, is a thesis that I will argue in subsequent chapters.

9. Organizational Learning Internationally

In this chapter I focus on the organizational learning process through which workers have come to play more active roles in changing industries. As the learning process evolved internationally, I first need to trace these international linkages, with particular attention to Scandinavia and Japan. Major participative changes first arose in Norway but were developed more widely in Sweden. Changes in the Swedish automotive industry have been influential beyond Scandinavia. Since World War II, Japan has carried out a revolution in manufacturing methods and industrial relations. The great and growing competitive power of Japanese companies has had and continues to have enormous influences on American industry.

Documentation on changes in those two parts of the world offer us unparalleled background knowledge. Here I draw particularly on the work of Robert Cole, who may well be the only American social scientist fluent in both Japanese and Swedish. For his doctoral thesis, Cole carried out a participant observer study in the Japanese automotive industry. In a later period, he studied participation in Sweden and Japan (see Cole, 1989).

SCANDINAVIA

Participative changes arose first in Norway and then spread to Sweden. Norway and Sweden share a long common border, and Norwegians, Swedes, and Danes speak slightly different but mutually intelligible languages. The three countries share ownership and management of their international airline. All these factors facilitate communication across national borders. Both in Sweden and Norway industry is highly unionized, with unionization in manufacturing being well over eighty percent, which makes it essential for unions to be strongly involved in initiating participatory changes.

The chief intellectual impetus toward participatory changes came to Norway through Fred Emery from Australia and Eric Trist and others at the Tavistock Institute of Human Relations in London. The leading actor in Norway was Einar Thorsrud, a social psychologist who had set up the Work Research Institutes in Oslo and Trondheim. Thorsrud was strongly committed to worker participation and to joint union-management projects.

Combining these commitments with the socio-technical systems framework he adopted and adapted, Thorsrud and his associates gained attention throughout Scandinavia, particularly with the program of participative changes in the shipping industry. This program arose in response to a combination of social and economic problems. The companies were facing increasingly severe competitive problems, because the wages and salaries of Norwegian seamen and officers were much higher than those paid by shipowners in developing countries. Also, Norwegian seafarers were becoming increasingly reluctant to spend so much time away from home throughout long careers. As Norway maintained a very low level of unemployment, it was becoming difficult for shipowners to attract and maintain ship crews.

Thorsrud and his associates, working with the unions and the management of a major shipping company, organized a participative socio-technical analysis of ship design and manning. The aims were to make the ships more efficient, operating with smaller crews, and at the same time to enhance the working lives of the seafarers. The program developed with joint study teams focusing their attention on the physical design of ships to be constructed and on the integration of that physical design with a new social system. (Thorsrud, 1977).

This program resulted in far reaching changes in the physical structure of ships and the social system involved in operating them. These changes, combined with some technological innovations, made it possible to reduce the size of ships' crews from over forty to fewer than half that number. The program also involved dramatic changes in the status systems of the ships. Traditionally, there had been sharp physical and social separation between ships' officers and crew and also between the deck crew and the engine room crew. The new ships provided common space for eating and recreation as well as upgraded sleeping arrangements for crew members. The organization at work also changed to provide for cross-training of deck and engine room crew members so that to some extent they could perform each other's functions. This also enhanced the marketable skills of deck crew members, who previously had very little relevant work experience to offer employers on shore. Members of the deck crew could more readily apply what they learned about engine operation and power systems to shore occupations.

By the mid-1960s, these changes in Norway had gained attention in Sweden and were to have major impacts in many other countries (Walton, with Allen and Gaffney, 1987; Walton and Gaffney, 1989). In 1966 the Swedish Employers Confederation (SAF) set up a technical department on work reorganization and small groups. The industrial engineers starting this department had already gained some familiarity with organizational behavior research and action in other countries and were particularly familiar with Norwegian developments.

According to Cole (1989:91),

> Three of the key events that served as a transmission belt from Norway to Sweden were a visit to Norway in 1966 of a Swedish union and management team led by Reine Hansson, who was close to Thorsrud's research; the translation of Thorsrud's research into Swedish in 1969 under the auspices of a joint labor-management publication company . . . ; and the "halleluja conference" held at the Museum of Modern Art in Stockholm in 1969 with Thorsrud as the featured speaker. The conference was sponsored by the technical department of the Swedish Employers Confederation (SAF) and attended by officials of major companies, as well as by selected union officials.

The conference was attended by leaders of industry and government. The planners had not initially invited union leaders but did so on Thorsrud's urging.

Up to this time, the leaders of the main union of blue-collar workers (known as LO) and the white-collar workers' union (TCO) had displayed little interest in work-place democratization. The national leadership had been concentrating primarily on negotiating industrywide agreements in various fields and on influencing national legislation.

Since World War II, Swedish workers had had representation on works councils that theoretically could influence shop-floor work systems, but surveys in the 1960s indicated that workers felt they were gaining little from this institution.

Union leaders had become somewhat involved in 1966 when they responded to an invitation from SAF to form the Development Council for Cooperation Questions and its research subgroup, the Development Council Working Group for Research, which came to be known as URAF. Nevertheless, it took a well-publicized strike to motivate union leaders toward active involvement in rethinking and reshaping industrial work. According to Cole (1989:256),

> Clearly, the strongest galvanizing force that gave new impetus to union support of direct worker participation in the workplace was the 2-month wildcat strike at the LKAB iron mine in December 1969. The well-paid miners were concerned about poor working conditions and their loss of wage advantage compared to other occupational groups. . . . It would be hard to convey in a few sentences the impact of this strike on the Swedish public, government, management, and unions. It attracted enormous media coverage, with surveys showing some 70 percent of the public in sympathy with the strikers. But this was hardly simply a strike against management, for the LKAB mine was state owned. Moreover the local union officials were portrayed as both powerless and totally unresponsive to rank-and-file demands. The strike and the public support that ensued were thus as much attacks on insensitive government and union bureaucracies as they were against traditional management. The LKAB strike was followed by a wave of wildcat strikes throughout the country in 1970 and 1971.
>
> These strikes set in motion a national debate on the meaning of work, the proper role of trade unions, what employees had a right to expect from work, and the possibility of restructuring work and authority relationships. Media coverage was intense.

Beyond the backing and guidance of the SAF and LO for the movement toward employee involvement, the change program developed at Volvo was especially important because the auto manufacturer was the most prestigious and strongest international competitor in Swedish industry. Volvo's involvement arose in response to increasing concern with the problem of keeping Swedish workers on the assembly line. With full employment and ample job opportunities for Swedish workers, Volvo and other industrial companies had had to rely increasingly upon foreign workers, and Volvo was experiencing serious absenteeism. Here the events in Sweden were influenced to some degree by U.S. social research several decades earlier, particularly by *The Man on the Assembly Line* (Walker and Guest, 1952, p. 5).

Years later the coauthor of that book established this idea-action linkage (Guest, 1987):

> In the late 1960s the Volvo company in Sweden became concerned about high absenteeism and poor performance in its plants. Young people especially were not attracted to assembly line work. Pehr Gylenhammer, Volvo's new young president, sought out sources of information that might explain the causes which in turn would lead to solutions. He turned to his medical director for some ideas, who explained to me later what happened. He said, "I searched out many sources of information from medical journals and particularly from the psychiatric literature without too much success. But when I came upon your book it was a revelation. It not only identified the basic problems, but it pointed the way to solutions."

Note that the Walker and Guest book did not offer any solutions to the social problems of assembly-line work. At the time all of us in human relations research were unconsciously committed to the idea of technological determinism: the notion that the automotive assembly line was so economically efficient that it would be impossible to devise another system that would be economically viable as well as socially satisfying. It was only when social and psychological problems on the assembly line made it difficult to attract workers that Volvo was moved to consider ways of humanizing assembly work. Nevertheless, Walker and Guest's pioneering work did serve to focus attention on what needed to be changed in order to humanize work in Volvo. This set off a search for ways in which the social and psychological needs of human beings could be met through a different technology that would nevertheless be economically efficient.

In the Kalmar plant, built in 1974, Volvo moved ahead boldly, reorganizing the work so that the vehicle was put together by several groups of workers following each other in sequence. According to the current president of Volvo (Holtback, 1988, p. 4),

These innovative work methods, along with a philosophy that took into account the workers' culture, have worked nicely. After six years, we had 40 percent fewer faults, and the total man-hours per car had been reduced by 40 percent. Kalmar still maintains lower absenteeism rates, personnel turnover, and assembly costs than other plants. We are applying what we learned at Kalmar to other plants.

I might add that the emphasis on using technology to serve humans and create a balance between the physical and intellectual content of jobs applies to other industries in Sweden as well.

At Uddevalla, Volvo has implemented still more radical restructuring of automotive assembly, described in this way by President Roger Holtback (1988, p. 5):

The innovations at Uddevalla will be as dramatic as those at Kalmar, we believe. A work team of eight or ten people will have the capability of building an entire car, although that may not happen at first. The work-place will represent a return to the values of skilled, experienced crafts-people who take pride in their product.

For instance, work teams will have greater responsibility, and work cycles will be increased. There will be fewer repetitive tasks, and team members can rotate tasks. Each team member will take his or her turn as group leader. Each group will have access to financial data, production results, and will be able to check supplies instantly via computer. Blue and white-collar assignments will be integrated, and each group will reflect a mix of sexes and ages. For over a year we have been training workers in the new technology and processes they will utilize when the plant opens this summer (1988).

The result is a group stronger than the sum of its individual members. We will continue to use this concept in the future. . . .

Another giant step we have taken at Uddevalla is to get together with the workers and labor unions from the start. I gave management and labor union representatives about the same authority to influence the decision making process. And we were able to quickly arrive at guidelines for this new factory.

These changes considerably enriched the jobs of workers, as they learned to perform a variety of tasks. The new designs also had a great advantage in flexibility over the conventional assembly line in that workers could move back and forth to different jobs according to what was needed at any time. The rigidity of the assembly line had caused serious problems when workers were absent. A company always had to employ more workers than were actually required on the line so as to have people available to step in for those absent. In contrast, in the new design plants, when one member of the work team is missing, other members can fill in the gap. This reduces the output of the group but avoids the breakdown in operations that could happen on the conventional assembly line.

The new design also introduced radical changes in the role of the foreman. He or she is no longer responsible for monitoring and controlling the activities of each individual worker, but instead becomes responsible for several work groups. The foreman is supposed to help the individual members to form an effective team and, beyond that, to leave the internal management of the team to its members while he or she ensures a steady flow of parts and supplies to the work stations and arranges for regular preventive maintenance.

In Volvo, both types of worker participation are illustrated. Worker representatives have been actively involved influencing managers in working out the organizational and work designs, and workers have taken over decision making in their new work stations.

JAPAN

The Japanese program emphasizing small group activities in the late 1960s and early 1970s should be seen in the context of "an increasingly tight labor market as the economy grew rapidly and the agricultural sector could no longer serve its historic function of providing surplus labor" (Cole, 1989:56). This labor market change was occurring while educational levels were rising markedly, which led high school graduates to react against simple and repetitive jobs. Cole (1989:56) notes also firms in industries that had the greatest recruitment problems, such as auto and steel, took the lead in introducing small group activities.

Japanese firms were investing heavily in technological advances, but, in contrast to the United States, these changes were seen as requiring increasing attention to the orientation and training of workers qualified to operate the new and more complicated technologies.

It has been widely claimed that Japan learned about worker participation and quality circles from the United States. This is a half truth.

To be sure, there was an international learning process going on, but the Japanese introduced their own models of participation.

Throughout its history, Japan has been active in examining practices and structures in other countries and importing and adapting ideas. This search and application process was greatly intensified after Japan's disastrous loss of World War II. Japanese students in the United States were attracted to the human relations literature of the 1940s and 1950s, and books of the leading exponents of this line of work were translated and sold in Japan. For example, Robert Guest reports that the Japanese edition of *The Man on the Assembly Line* sold over 10,000 copies.

The American human relations movement appears to have had a much stronger impact on practitioners in Japan than in the United States. In fact, the Japan Human Relations Association (JHRA) was founded by Hideo Kawabuchi following his return to Japan after a year of study of industrial relations at Cornell in 1951-1952. JHRA continues an active program of training, conferences, and publications to this day.

The birth of quality control circles (QCCs) has been credited to an American, W. Edwards Deming, a U.S. expert on statistical methods for monitoring and improving the quality of manufactured products. He indeed made an important contribution with his lectures in Japan beginning in 1951. Leaders of Japanese industry and the Japan Union of Scientists and Engineers (JUSE) eagerly reached out to Deming because they recognized that Japan would never be able to gain international markets with its pre-World War II reputation for poor quality. So important did the Japanese see Deming's contribution that they established in his name the highest national prize to be awarded to a quality control circle.

Without minimizing the importance of the Deming contribution, we should recognize that he thought he was instructing Japanese managers and engineers in statistical process control, and it was the Japanese themselves who made a quantum leap to involve workers directly through quality control circles. In the QCCs, groups of workers generally meet weekly, with or without their supervisor, to discuss and study quality and other operational problems. To complete the process, they present their conclusions and proposals for improvement to management.

In contrast to the later American experience (described in the next chapter), quality control circles were introduced only several years after major Japanese companies had carried out campaigns to decentralize their manufacturing operations. Insofar as possible, this passed decision-making responsibilities to the workers themselves. To support that change, managements had developed intensified training programs to enable workers to understand the fine points of judging factors affecting productivity and quality.

The QCC movement has spread more widely throughout industry in Japan than in any other country. Cole (1989) reports that in Japan every two and a half days there are local, regional, or national QCC meetings in which teams of circle members from various companies report on their achievements and compete for recognition and prizes.

The leading Japanese companies manage these local, regional, and national QCC conferences, rotating among themselves so that a single company is responsible for each conference. The Japanese companies have also been able to agree on the "best practices" for organizing and directing quality control circles and to organize training courses and publications based upon these best practices.

In Japan QCCs are a management-dominated movement. Unions play no role in the program, but they do not oppose it. The unions have been concentrating on wages, benefits, and particularly on employment security. There has been an implicit trade-off: In return for ceding to management great freedom in managing the work place, the unions have won much greater employment security—at least for major companies—than unions have achieved in most other countries.

Whereas American participatory programs have spread unevenly in a variety of forms, Japanese programs are far more standardized nationally and are present in well nigh all major Japanese companies.

10. Organizational Learning in North American Industry

To understand employee involvement in North American industry, we need to place it in a time perspective. I see employee involvement (EI) evolving through three distinct stages: 1) the 1940s through the 1960s, 2) the 1970s, and 3) the 1980s, with the pace of change accelerating from the second to the third stage.

Stage 1: The 1940s through the 1960s. In this stage employee involvement (or worker participation in decision making, as we then called it) was of interest only to a few professors and students. If we looked around, we could find cases where maverick managers and union leaders were encouraging worker participation and seemed to be getting some interesting results. Our reports on these cases attracted practically no interest from American management and labor. In fact, Japanese management people evinced far more interest in this literature than did their American counterparts (Whyte, 1987).

Stage 2: The 1970s—the quality of work life (QWL) movement. In this stage interest in EI extended beyond the academic world into the ranks of labor and management. In fact, Irving Bluestone (vice president of the United Auto Workers (UAW) and director of its General Motors (GM) division) was one of the very few labor leaders to speak up about employee involvement before 1970, and early in the 1970s his negotiating team secured a contract clause requiring UAW and GM to set up joint programs in this field. Also in this stage a Japanese import, quality circles, became something of a fad in many American companies.

Typically, the 1970s had two characteristics. First, this period was focused on efforts to humanize work life, giving little up-front attention to productivity. Management people assumed that an improvement in job satisfaction might yield concrete benefits in labor peace, lowered absenteeism, and turnover, and thus indirectly increase productivity. Recognizing that management's past efforts to get labor support for increasing productivity had been interpreted as speed-ups, leaders of labor and management avoided any direct emphasis on productivity.

Second, programs were focused narrowly on shop-floor problems. According to the prevailing ground rules, EI groups were not to consider any topics covered in the labor contract or in the policies and prerogatives of management. This made it possible to sell EI to labor and management as a low-risk enterprise, but it drastically limited what could be achieved.

Stage 3: The 1980s—toward the integration of employee involvement and collective bargaining. In response to greatly intensified international competition and organizational learning regarding the limitations of the 1970s models, a small but growing number of labor and management people set aside the 1970s ground rules and began to engage in more basic restructuring of their relations.

Before we consider examples of this basic restructuring, let us go back to view the forces that moved the parties from the first stage to the second and then from the second stage to the third.

EI: FROM STAGE 1 TO STAGE 2

The late 1960s marked the beginning of change, moving worker participation from academia into the world of practitioners in industry and labor. This was an era of social ferment and activism on the university campuses, and this activism led to increasing concern with the problems of workers and work life.

One event, early in the 1970s, focussed public attention on worker demands for improvements in the quality of work life.

> The collision came at Lordstown, Ohio, a Chevrolet Vega plant at General Motors' new assembly division, in February, 1972. The plant was billed as having the most advanced engineering design, made to suit the workers, but the Lordstown strike became one of the most famous walkouts in recent American labor history. The issue was not wages or the right to organize, but the quality of working life itself. The workers were angered at the pace of an assembly line where Vegas moved past at 101 per hour, giving each person 36 seconds to complete his or her appointed task. "You just pray for the line to stop," one worker said. Workers had responded with high absenteeism and sabotage before they went on strike for twenty-two bitter days. (Simmons and Mares, 1983:44)

The strike was widely attributed to the characteristics of Lordstown's work force, predominantly drawn from younger people with higher levels of education and aspiration than the older generation. Infected by the social ferment of the times, these workers were not willing to accept conditions their elders had tolerated. Whatever the influence of age and education, these were hardly major factors. One GM executive commented that "in the ten other corporation consolidations to form the new Assembly Division nine strikes had occurred" (Simmons and Mares, 1983:44).

As Irving Bluestone has commented,

> I was Director of the UAW General Motors Department at the time of the strike at Lordstown and entered the negotiations to settle the strike. The news media hype describing the situation placed major emphasis on the younger average age of the work force and the "youth" rebellion. Actually, age, extent of education and other comparisons with older plants were by no means the key factors in the strike. Essentially, this was a strike against speed-up, management's insistence on high speed production with insufficient manpower. . . . It was but one of many other strikes which resulted from the then recently created General Motors Assembly Division. . . . (Subsequent to the brief Lordstown strike, the longest strike in the history of GM occurred at one of its oldest assembly plants at Norwood, Ohio, over essentially the same issues as at Lordstown.) (personal communication)

In terms of public perceptions and concerns, the media misinterpretations of the causes of the Lordstown strike were much more important than any research-based explanation of that event. Lordstown came to symbolize the rising of a new generation of workers who were not willing to put up with the dehumanizing conditions of work tolerated by older generations. The event focused public attention on a perceived need to improve quality of work life.

Shortly thereafter *Work in America* (HEW, 1973) was published. This was the outcome of a project sponsored by Eliot Richardson, Secretary of Health, Education and Welfare. It was based on surveys indicating substantial worker dissatisfaction with their work lives. The fact that it was authorized and produced by leading officials of the Republican administration of Richard Nixon signaled to the public that concern for the quality of work life was no longer a fringe issue of concern only to radicals and academics.

Out of this same stream of development arose the Work in America Institute, established by Jerry Rosow in 1975. Rosow had been a personnel executive in Exxon and an assistant secretary of labor. Beyond public pronouncements and publications and media discussions of quality of work life, some of the first steps toward implementation in a major industry developed in the automotive field, spurred by UAW. In 1972, Irving Bluestone worked with maverick industrialist Sidney Harman, chief executive officer of the Jervis Corporation (later Harman International Industries) to establish the first joint union-management employee involvement process in its Bolivar, Tennessee, plant. Behavioral scientist Michael Maccoby served as consultant in this case. According to Bluestone, "The experience gained at Bolivar was helpful as we proceeded to introduce the first QWL processes in a few of the GM plants" (personal communication).

Through pushing the issue in bargaining over several years, in 1973 the UAW was able to secure a company commitment to set up at the highest level a joint labor-management committee to stimulate and guide participatory activities in GM plants. Later a similar clause was negotiated with Ford, the main difference being in the name given to the program. GM called it Quality of Work Life (or QWL) whereas Ford used the title Employee Involvement (EI).

It was not until nine months after the signing of the GM contract that management appointed its members to the joint committee. Perhaps the

GM executives assumed that Bluestone would be content with a symbolic victory, but he kept after GM to make good on its QWL agreement.

The spread of interest in worker participation in the late 1970s and early 1980s is reflected in a 1981 *Business Week* report titled "Quality of Work Life: Catching On":

> One sign that a theoretical concept is taking root in everyday life is a conference at which practitioners outnumber theorists. In 1972 the first international conference on improving the quality of work life met at Harriman, N.Y., and included only 50 advocates, mainly academics, with no union officials and few managers. The second international conference, which ended on Sept. 3, attracted more than 1,500 delegates to Toronto, and the 200 unionists and 750 management people—the real practitioners—far outnumbered the academics, consultants, and government officials.
>
> The conference was an indication that the quality-of-work-life movement—which includes many forms of new work organizations and which is increasingly referred to as "QWL"—is expanding rapidly, albeit from a small base. In the U.S., where the concept generally means involving workers in shop-floor decisions through problem-solving committees, QWL is far from being institutionalized in industry. It faces many obstacles, as debate at the conference indicated, but the perception is growing that QWL could form the basis of a new industrial relations system.

In this stage, QWL spread rapidly in a variety of forms, perhaps the most popular model being imported from Japan. On discovering the extraordinary spread of quality control circles in Japan, many Americans concluded that we needed to try this social invention. Americans did make one symbolic change: dropping the word "control" from the name because the word sounded too undemocratic. Otherwise, quality circle activities were simply tacked on to existing structural and social process arrangements. In contrast, in Japan the quality circle movement arose following a major drive to decentralize responsibility to the lowest levels possible in industrial organizations. This meant allocating much greater responsibilities to work groups.

As management reached out to bring in quality circles, there arose a rapidly increasing number of consultants in this field. In the early stages of the participation boom, two organizations, one old and one new, attempted to promote and guide the development of quality circles. (My account of this period is based primarily on Cole, 1989.)

The older and more established organization was the American Society for Quality Control (ASQC). As Cole (1989) points out, ASQC was unable to give effective leadership to the movement because its growth and development had been based on a struggle to gain higher status for the engineers responsible for quality. This meant establishing professional standards, which militated against democratizing the activities through involving workers and other nonengineers.

Recognizing the inability of ASQC to lead the quality circle movement, consultants began organizing what became in 1978 the International Association of Quality Circles (IAQC). The aim was to reach out to all those interested in quality circles without demanding formal professional qualifications. By the end of 1987 IAQC had grown to a total of 5,503 members. While this growth in a ten year period sounds impressive, IAQC was plagued by serious organizational and policy problems throughout its existence.

There was constant tension between consultants and members working in industrial companies. Consultants had created the organization and they had the strongest personal interest in its activities. At the same time, they were involved in a well-recognized conflict of interest. Each consultant or consultant group was attached to its own training methods, and the consultants naturally resisted the standardization of an officially adopted program.

This conflict of interest also had an impact on training programs. Company members favored development of an active training program organized and directed by IAQC whereas consultants were concerned that such an emphasis would cut into their own training contracts. In effect, the consultants won out as participation in IAQC training programs steadily declined over the years, leaving the organization with the primary functions of holding conventions (at which consultants could display their wares) and publications.

IAQC was also plagued by the problem of developing a stable and efficient administrative structure for an organization that was guided and controlled primarily by volunteers. This tended to maximize the influence of consultants, who were more able and willing to commit their time to IAQC activities than were those employed by companies. This did not necessarily mean that company members placed a low value upon IAQC activities but simply that their ability to participate depended on decisions of their superiors. If the superior officer believed strongly in IAQC, the member could participate actively;

but turnover in that superior position could remove the subordinate from the program.

Consultants themselves were concerned about the weak support IAQC was receiving from companies. Consultants could hardly advocate that IAQC be an organization run by consultants because that would raise the question, which consultants? In fact, on several occasions IAQC reached out to offer leadership to company executives, but there were so few willing and able to assume these roles that the IAQC was at the mercy of whoever was willing to accept.

There was a continuing problem in the relations between the board of directors, composed of individuals who devoted time to IAQC mainly at board meetings and conventions, and the executive director, who held a full time position. It was difficult for the board to monitor and control activities. On one occasion an executive director was charged with exploiting the organization for his own purposes and was brought to court and convicted of these charges.

Under its new name, Association for Quality and Participation, IAQC has survived and continues to hold conferences to promote participatory activities in industry. Throughout the 1970s, other organizations arose to serve the same mission. The Organizational Development (OD) Network sponsors the Ecology of Work Life conferences; locally based labor-management committees seek to promote and guide joint union-management programs; and various universities have been developing educational and applied research programs along this line. In Canada the Ontario Centre for Quality of Work Life served as a focal point for promoting and guiding joint union-management programs until it was disbanded in 1987.

As the Japanese learned from Americans regarding worker participation but then went on to develop their own distinctive model, so Americans have borrowed from Japan but have then developed models that differ from Japan's in program structure, organization, and control.

Promotion of the spread of participatory programs. In contrast to the American pattern, the Japanese program has been controlled by the leading companies, which were able to get together to agree on the "best practices" and to organize training courses and publications based on those best practices. Here an important cultural difference may be involved. Throughout their history the Japanese have reached out beyond their own country to learn the best practices in any field; once this learning has been adapted to Japanese conditions, the Japanese have encouraged everyone to adopt those best practices. In contrast, American culture places a much higher value on creativity and individual initiative, which leads us to encourage everyone to "do their own thing." Over all my years of listening to management people, one endlessly repeated statement sticks in my mind: "Our company is unique." From that proposition, it naturally follows that each company must develop its own unique system of worker participation. This cultural tendency places a drag on any movement to diffuse new systems across companies, although it may well stimulate creativity within individual companies and plants.

Integrated development versus parallel structures. Japanese practice and U.S. models of quality circles and other EI activities present a contrast between an integrated organizational program and the development of parallel organizations. Japanese quality circle programs developed following substantial emphasis on decentralization of authority and responsibility to the lowest possible levels, so Japanese managers and supervisors found that quality circles supported decentralization through training for worker involvement in decision making on shop-floor problems. In the United States, quality circles were generally introduced without any prior commitment to decentralization of authority and responsibility. This fostered a situation in which employee involvement activities ran afoul of the powers and prerogatives of supervisors and middle managers.

Restrictive ground rules versus flexibility. The employee involvement activities that spread rapidly in many American companies developed within important limitations: The groups were limited to shop-floor problems and were not allowed to consider issues covered by the labor contract or by managerial prerogatives. But such limitations did not affect quality circles in Japan. In the first place, Japanese labor contracts never had detailed work rules typical of American practice. It appears that the Japanese unions allowed management considerable freedom in making and changing work rules in exchange for guarantees of employment security. And the Japanese were not as concerned as Americans were with defending managerial prerogatives because the Japanese had not been making the sharp distinctions between labor and management characteristic of American industrial relations culture.

Management control versus joint control. The Japanese program is controlled by the companies, without any direct involvement of union leaders. The American programs of greatest interest to us are those jointly controlled by union and management.

EI: FROM STAGE 2 TO STAGE 3

Movement from stage 2 to stage 3 was stimulated by two main factors: greatly intensified international competition and organizational learning gained through experience during the 1970s.

When competitive pressures were threatening mass layoffs and plant shutdowns, the interests and needs of managers and workers shifted drastically. With the survival of factories and jobs at stake, there was little enthusiasm for efforts to improve the quality of work life. In some cases where union and management had been working together on QWL, managers now openly called on the union to help increase productivity. Union leaders were now more willing to respond to this challenge, as they recognized that saving jobs depended on the competitive strength of their work place.

Organizational learning involved a recognition of the inherent limitations of the EI cases, under the ground rules of the 1970s. Typical experience could be divided into two time periods. At first, workers and local union leaders responded with enthusiasm because management was finally going to pay attention to long-standing worker gripes and was recognizing that workers could contribute with brains as well as with physical skills and stamina. In this period, many shop-floor work problems did get resolved, but, after the easier problems had been taken care of, the EI groups ran up against the ground rules. Many of the problems facing workers and managers could not be resolved without changing work rules (covered by the contract) or by changing management policies and prerogatives. When the ground rules did not change, the EI groups tended to lose the support of both labor and management and become dormant.

Increasingly the competition crunch and organizational learning are pushing aside the 1970s ground rules. Now EI groups can propose changes in work rules and in management policies and prerogatives. This does not mean that what is tentatively agreed on in an EI group automatically becomes policy and practice. In most cases, when work rule changes are recommended, union and management negotiators must see whether they can work out the new contractual language. When an EI group proposes a change in management policies or prerogatives, making the change must involve considerable discussion within management. In most such cases, EI and collective bargaining remain separate but become closely linked.

We illustrate the shift from stage 2 to stage 3 with a case representing some of the most far-reaching change we have encountered: the case of Xerox Corporation and the Amalgamated Clothing and Textile Workers Union (ACTWU).

For years Xerox and ACTWU had gotten along reasonably well, but the intense collaborative relationship did not develop until—in the face of Japanese competition that was sharply reducing the Xerox market share in copiers—top management sought to respond with a new EI program. Management directed the personnel department's organizational effectiveness unit for the Webster, New York, plants to design and implement this program.

Planning began in 1978. According to Dominick R. Argona (personal communication), current chief of that unit, the planners began by canvassing what was known through social research and from the experience of other companies regarding what does and does not work in employee involvement. Xerox has a joint venture in Japan (Fuji Xerox), so they had ready access to Japanese information and ideas on quality control circles. However, their surveys of U.S. experience with this social invention indicated to them that about seventy-five percent of American quality circle programs were petering out after only a few years of experience. This suggested the need to find a better model.

By the early 1980s, with the assistance of consultants, the parties had established a joint union-management EI program within the ground rules prevailing for the 1970s cases.

Well into the second year of the EI program, the parties encountered a crisis that led to a breakthrough beyond the conventional limits of worker participation. Management announced to the union a plan to shut down the wire harness department, lay off 180 workers, and buy the wire harnesses from a vendor. This followed a management study determining that it was possible to save $3.2 million a year through outsourcing. The shutdown would take place within six months.

This outsourcing plan sent shockwaves through not only the wire harness department but throughout the production plants in Webster, New York. Union leaders recognized that this would not be the only department to be shut down as the company continued its competitive benchmarking and found cheaper vendors in the United States or abroad. The announcement also posed a serious threat to the EI program. How could employees be encouraged to help management to achieve higher productivity when at the same time management was planning major layoffs?

At this point, consultant/facilitator Peter Lazes assumed a leadership role in urging the parties to find some alternative to layoffs. He spent several weeks going back and forth between top union leadership and key management personnel and industrial relations officials in search of a new option. Out of that discussion process emerged the social invention we call the *cost study team* (CST), whose purpose would be to determine if it would be possible to make savings in this department that would bring its costs down to the level offered by the vendor. Lazes presented the idea first to the union leaders. Managers believed that the task would be impossible, but, in order to maintain cooperative relations with the union, Xerox accepted the union initiative. Furthermore, in order to give "the impossible dream" every chance of success, Xerox provided extraordinarily strong support for the project.

The parties agreed to establish a CST composed of six workers in the wire harness department, a staff engineer, and the supervisor of the department. Management also designated an accountant and a technical expert in manufacturing to be on call from the CST for advice and information. The CST was given six months (full-time work on company payroll) to do its study and report to management. Xerox also paid travel expenses to permit team members to visit domestic and foreign vendors.

At the same time, the parties agreed to set aside the 1970s ground rules. The CST could consider changes in work rules. Management allowed the CST full access to relevant financial and operating figures and allowed the CST to consider changes in management policies and prerogatives.

Toward the end of the six month period, the CST presented a report documenting how Xerox could save over $3.6 million, well beyond the $3.2 million target. The greatest savings were projected in changes in work rules; the second greatest savings came from a proposed reduction in production control and divisional overhead of $582,000. This latter reduction was achieved through persuading management to set aside its conventional formula for allocating overhead costs and, rather, to base such figures on overhead support services and facilities actually being used by the wire harness department.

There is, of course, a difference between projected savings and savings actually achieved. As might be expected in such a new type of project, the implementation of the plan took longer than the CST had hoped, and the actual savings fell short of the projected figure. Nevertheless, when the changes were put into place, management calculated that the team had achieved at least the $3.2 million target initially established.

Decision makers in top management of the reprographic division were not only surprised at the results of the wire harness project but also sufficiently impressed to recognize the potential of these emerging new models of management and labor relations. They moved quickly, in consultation with union leaders, to establish CSTs in three other production units that had been noncompetitive with products offered by vendors. In the following year, all three of these CSTs reached the required savings target or else came so close that management was happy to settle for the results—which for two of these teams came to savings of up to forty percent of annual costs. These experiences convinced management and union leaders of the value of extending participatory management and union-management cooperation throughout the division.

The changes even involved the restructuring of research and development and the design for construction of new plants. In the conventional R&D program, the development engineers work out a basic design for the product and turn that over to the industrial engineers, who work out the details of how the product is to be produced and determine the number and qualifications of workers involved at each point in production. Then they turn those more detailed plans over to the foremen and plant superintendents, who are responsible for moving the project from the pilot stage into production. When the process is carried through in this fashion, with each specialized group doing its own thing and then passing the project on to the next group, often the company has to recycle the process several times. The plans developed at a previous stage often prove impractical at the next stage.

Xerox has now completely reshaped the process by including production and maintenance workers and production foremen in the design team so that those who will be responsible for producing the product will be involved early. This enables them to help the team to anticipate problems that occur at later stages. Management estimates that this new design for R&D is reducing by sixty percent the time it takes Xerox to move a new product or model from the drawing board to actual production (Allaire and Rickard, 1989). In today's highly competitive economy, the profit or loss on a new product or model often depends on when it reaches the market. Although the total benefit from streamlining the R&D process is impossible to calculate, the gain in future revenues is potentially enormous.

Similarly, in designing a new plant, management departed from the conventional style of turning the project over to architects and engineers. In the case of the toner plant, workers who were going to be responsible for production were involved in planning from the outset.

It now seems obvious that it is more efficient to involve workers who are going to produce the product or operate the process in the design stages so as to avoid problems that inevitably arise when the machines are installed in ways that provoke friction and inefficiency. Such involvement runs counter to conventional ways of managing.

These achievements were accompanied by two interrelated changes that served to institutionalize the Xerox strategy for achieving cost reductions and employment maintenance. First, management agreed that, before outsourcing any component, Xerox would create a union-management cost study team. If the CST developed a sound plan to meet the price of the vendor, the work would remain in-house. Then, in the 1983 labor contract, Xerox committed itself to guaranteeing employment to all workers who had been with the company for at least three years. No individual jobs were guaranteed, but this meant that a worker whose job was eliminated would be employed elsewhere within Xerox. This clause was also incorporated into the 1986 and 1989 labor contracts.

Xerox was able to make this extraordinary employment guarantee only because management now had confidence that the participatory and collaborative relationship with the union provided the means for balancing technological and structural changes with employment security. Furthermore, even as a company operating worldwide, Xerox was committed to a policy of retaining at least 50% of its manufacturing employment in the United States.

SIGNIFICANCE OF THE XEROX CASE

The Xerox case is important in several respects.

It provides an impressive model of organizational learning, showing how the parties devised a new problem solving strategy to discover alternatives previously unavailable and even, in some cases, unimagined. After devising creative solutions to immediately pressing problems, in many cases the parties revert to business and labor relations as usual. This suggests that, although the immediate problem was solved, organizational learning did not take place. With Xerox, we have seen how the CST experience led directly to structural and process changes in research and development and in the design of a new plant.

In this case, instead of following what was then the conventional wisdom of keeping collective bargaining and managerial prerogatives on one track while trying to develop employee involvement on the other, at Xerox the parties discovered creative ways of merging one track into the other.

Another important feature of this case is the parties' development of an innovative model of participatory action research (PAR); a methodology in which practitioners are actively involved with behavioral scientists in designing research, gathering and analyzing data, and reporting research findings for action. The nature and significance of this unfamiliar methodology will be examined further in this book's final chapter.

Our analysis of the evolution of EI in three stages should not lead us to assume that, from one stage to the next, there was a well nigh universal shift in ground rules, practices, and participatory processes. At this writing, there are probably still far more companies and unions engaged in the 1970s stage 2 models than there are participants in stage 3 methods. In this analysis, we are not concerned with the actual number of stage 2 or stage 3 cases in existence at any time but rather in the trend of change. Where union and management have been working effectively together, increasing numbers of cases manifest stage 3 characteristics: integration of EI with collective bargaining.

The logic of this analysis is the same as one would apply to national studies of changes in manufacturing technology. In that field, one is not concerned with simply describing the most prevalent technologies; one looks for "leading edge cases" in which companies apparently have achieved important technological advances. If these new technologies then prove economically and socially successful, we assume that companies that have been left behind will learn that they have to move in the same general direction in order to survive and prosper.

UNION OR NONUNION

We have been examining advances in social technology, which have similar prospects of diffusing through our economies. We have limited our analysis, however, to EI processes in unionized situations.

As I have not studied any EI cases in nonunion plants, I cannot apply this analysis to those cases on the basis of research. However, our findings in the union-management cases raise questions about a common assumption that, in facing intensified competitive pressures, it is advantageous for management to maintain a union-free organization.

If we accept the now common assumption that competitive effectiveness depends in important respects on active employee involvement, then unionization may be advantageous. I do not mean to suggest that it is impossible or even extraordinarily difficult in a nonunion plant to develop EI effectively but only that the unionized plant may have certain built-in advantages.

In a nonunion plant, even where top management makes a sincere commitment to participation, I see certain built-in limitations. In the first place, effective participation depends on workers feeling free to express ideas and present information fully and frankly; but this is not the only requirement. We should not assume that a "good idea" from workers is automatically accepted. Often a good idea will involve technical problems, which make it easy for management to reject it. Effective participation requires the development of the kind of dialogue that will allow thorough exploration of a good idea in order to solve the technical difficulties. Furthermore, an effective participation program depends also on the willingness of worker members to argue with managers. In some cases, arguments lead to constructive resolution of an issue, resulting in the improvement of a flawed idea or the joint development of a new idea.

When workers are not represented by a union, their fate on the job depends on their superiors. Workers naturally hesitate to criticize management, and may hesitate to argue with managers; and they may go along with managerial ideas even if they have serious reservations. Going along may not be simply a function of worker anxiety regarding relations with superiors; many workers hesitate to voice their objections because they lack sufficient confidence to articulate what they have learned from experience when meeting with management people who have had much more formal education, are on their own turf, and have the conceptual apparatus of business administration at their command.

In unionized situations, shop-floor workers have potential support of their local officers (who may even serve on a full-time basis in large plants) and of international representatives who can guide and stimulate the process and provide protection against reprisals, backed up as they are by the labor contract.

Finally, in a nonunion plant, when a plant manager committed to an EI program is succeeded by a manager who has neither the values nor the skills needed to support such a program, that is the end of employee involvement. In many unionized companies, turnover is rapid in plant management positions whereas union leaders are likely to remain in their positions through many changes in managerial personnel. Where effective joint programs exist, both management and union informants tell us that it is the union that drives the process. When, as is generally the case, the new manager has received from management little or no orientation regarding the practices and organizational culture of joint programs, union leaders provide the institutional memory and seek to persuade or pressure the new appointee to fit into the joint problem-solving methods. (For further analysis comparing participatory programs in unionized and nonunionized firms, see Hecksher, 1988, and Herrick, 1990.)

11. Coping with the New Manufacturing Organization

Had I written this book just a few years ago, the present chapter would not have been included. It now seems necessary because I have become aware of such major changes that are so major as to justify reference to "the new manufacturing organization." The transformation under way is having major impacts on employee involvement and collective bargaining. Before these effects can be understood, we need to understand the nature of the emerging new manufacturing organization (NMO).

I begin with a discussion of the logics underlying the NMO. This is drawn from several sources: the writings of industrial engineers and students of production management and of industrial relations; and the experience of my colleagues in Programs for Employment and Workplace Systems as they seek to help management and labor to develop participatory strategies to cope with the NMO.

My discussion concludes with coping strategies: how practitioners of employee involvement attempt to deal with the challenges of the NMO. Here I examine the interrelations of the NMO with employee involvement (EI) and collective bargaining. Some of this analysis may apply also to nonunion plants, but I shall concentrate on the problems and opportunities involved in union-management relations.

THE NEW MANUFACTURING ORGANIZATION

I aim to provide a preliminary framework to make sense out of the new manufacturing organization. I am not claiming that the principles to be described are represented in fully developed form in large numbers of companies here and abroad, but the worldwide trend is clearly in the direction of putting these principles into practice.

The new manufacturing organization aims to bring together a number of new elements (systems, procedures) integrated together with some preexisting elements. Its emergence has been spurred by intensified international competition, particularly from Japan, which no doubt has the most companies that approximate the design of the new manufacturing organization to be described below.

The NMO comes along symbolized by acronyms representing some of the principal new elements: JIT (just-in-time), SPC (statistical process control), TQC (total quality control), and CAD-CAM (computer-aided design, computer-aided manufacturing). Some of the new elements have become known by their original Japanese names—for example, *Kaizen,* which means continuous improvement.

As it is much easier to implement the NMO in a greenfield site, where the spacial design, the technology, and the people involved all make a fresh start, here I concentrate on the problems of moving from the old manufacturing organization (often described in terms of the scientific management principles of F.W. Taylor) to the new manufacturing organization.

The main elements of the NMO are mutually dependent, so efforts to introduce one element without considering its impact on the existing manufacturing organization are bound to be counterproductive. This does not mean that all of the new elements should be introduced at the same time, which would be a recipe for disaster. It does mean that the planners for introducing each new element must undertake to anticipate how it will work with or clash with elements of the current manufacturing system as well as with those new elements that are to be introduced later. When we say that these elements are mutually dependent, that means that the principles shaping them are interrelated. Therefore, some framework is needed to guide the transformation process.

Understanding the principles underlying the design of the NMO should enable practitioners to go beyond mere mechanical imitation of elements that appear to work in other companies and in other countries. The principles are intended as a guide to a process of analysis to determine how specific elements should be designed and adapted to meet the unique conditions of a particular factory.

A cognitive framework is designed to provide a theoretical map of the territory within which the planners seek to operate. The guiding principles to be described below are designed to link operational objectives with methods for achieving those objectives in pursuit of longer-run goals, such as increasing the company's competitive strength and enhancing employment security. I describe the underlying principles for the new manufacturing organization in the context of how they contrast with preexisting elements of manufacturing organizations.

From Vertical (Command/Control) to
Horizontal (Work Flow/Sequential) Orientation

The old manufacturing organization was designed in vertical terms, establishing a chain of command to direct the work operations in detail and to provide the maximum possible control from the top down. Under the old model, in order to work out the inevitable discontinuities and imbalances, coordination between departments in the work flow had to be managed through the exercise of authority and problems between departments were appealed to higher authority for decision.

In the new model, the horizontal orientation is designed to facilitate the flow of materials and work processes according to the sequences in which the work actually gets done—from the receipt of materials and parts into the plant through the initial production operations, to sub-assembly, on to final assembly, and then to the shipping department to be moved out to customers. The driving force behind this principle is known as just-in-time (JIT): a system for organizing and managing the flow of parts and materials into the plant from suppliers through the various departments of the plant and finally out to the market.

The old model was supported by large buffer stocks (parts and materials stored and waiting to be used). It was as if the old model was designed to enable each department to operate independently from the departments preceding and following it in the work flow.

JIT is sometimes thought to be a system for reducing inventory costs. It does make possible enormous savings in buffer stocks, but its impacts are more far-reaching. Where buffer stocks are drastically reduced, down-time in one unit can quickly lead to downtime in immediately related units, and then the paralysis can spread throughout the plant. This apparent disadvantage can be converted into an asset. Under the old model, deficiencies in operations could readily be overlooked, their sources buried from view under the pressure to get on with production. Under the new model, the source of an operating problem becomes immediately apparent not only to the worker but also to staff engineers and supervisors who converge on the spot to work with the operators to solve the problem. Furthermore, the necessity for fine tuning the work flow leads management to train workers to observe indications of impending problems so as to avoid breakdowns. This discipline is reinforced by the development of mechanical and electronic devices monitoring operations in order to give advance notice of potential breakdowns. In general, problems located at their source and acted on immediately are much more likely to be solved than are those that can be set aside while the work goes on.

The horizontal orientation is reinforced by a related principle often phrased as "meeting customer requirements." The customer is not visualized simply as the buyer of the products but rather as the next work station in the work-flow sequence. Whereas the old model emphasized controlling workers in order to achieve the standards of performance determined by management, the new model requires those in each work station to look to their counterparts in the next work station to determine whether they are carrying out their operations in such a way as to satisfy the requirements of that unit.

As JIT requires minute-to-minute coordination at the interfaces between units in the work flow, the system cannot be managed effectively from above. The operators themselves must make decisions about their own operations. This shift of responsibilities to operators must be supported by providing them with a flow of accurate information so that they themselves can monitor their own performance.

The decentralized model also involves major changes in the roles of supervisors. Under the old model they gave orders and served as policemen to coerce compliance. Under the new model, they have become boundary managers and providers of resources, making sure that the operators have the parts, materials, and tools needed to perform in such a way as to meet the requirements of the next customer in the work flow. As the operators take over responsibilities previously lodged with management, far fewer supervisors are needed than before. Under the old model, ratios of first-line foremen to workers of between 1 to 10 and 1 to 25 were common. With the new model, we see ratios of 1 to 50 and 1 to 100 or more.

The horizontal principle applies not only to work flow on the shop floor but also to the linkages between suppliers and manufacturers and between manufacturers and customers.

The same principle of organization by work flow is being applied increasingly to reshape relations in research and development and between R&D and the production organization. Writing in *Business Week,* Otis Port (1987) provides the following description of the old organization and its problems:

> A high wall has always stood between design and manufacturing, with designers essentially ignorant of how their creations are translated into finished products and not in the least eager to find out. Well-manicured designers toss their ideas over the wall, and leave the nitty gritty details to the dirty-fingernail types in the factory.
>
> . . . Juran and other experts assert that no more than 20% of quality defects can be traced to the production line. The other 80% is locked in during the design phase or by purchasing policies that value low price over the quality of purchased parts and materials.

The old model created an adversarial relationship between the design engineers and the production managers. As the production people received designs that created problems in manufacturing, they either had to struggle with difficult designs or challenge the design people to go back to the drawing board and make changes. These conflicts and incoordinations substantially increased the lead time from the initiation of the design process to the beginning of production and also imposed major problems in coordination.

Under the new model, American companies are increasingly forming "design for manufacturing" teams. As noted before, Xerox has gone beyond incorporating production management and engineering people into the joint team in order to include operators who will eventually produce the product and also maintenance workers who will service the machines.

From Rigid to Flexible Organizations

The old manufacturing strategy appeared to be based on one principle: Get it structured right and keep it in that groove. The ideal was to have long production runs so as to minimize time lost in setting up the equipment for the next production run. That strategy is no longer practical. Customers are demanding higher quality and a greater variety of products and models, and America's competitors are meeting that demand.

Because each product or model may require a different combination of work operations, it is no longer practical to operate with the rigid job classifications established by management and then negotiated into labor contracts. As the plant shifts back and forth among products and models A, B, C, . . . X, inevitably the work operations needed for product B will be different from those required for product A, and so on. Maintaining the old system of job classifications would thus require employing many extra workers so that some would be standing around until a changeover that requires their operations. Due to the fact that each product or model may require a different combination of operations, multiskilled workers are required.

It is inefficient to have the determination of who does what, when, and where controlled by management, so work teams are taking over these decisions.

The NMO has produced dramatic reductions in set-up times. These have been accomplished simply by focusing study and experimentation on setup technology. If you are going to run one product or model for several weeks, then it adds little to unit costs if it takes eight hours to set up this production run. If the production run is limited to eight hours, an eight-hour setup time would be ruinous.

Here again the Japanese have led (Suzaki, 1987), but American companies are pushing hard to catch up. The new models of setup methods involve carefully programmed teamwork among production and maintenance workers and engineers built on technological innovations designed to reduce downtime to a level hardly imaginable years ago.

Economies in the Utilization of Resources

In the 1960s, a Cornell graduate student set out to do a doctoral thesis comparing Japanese, German, and American automotive assembly plants in Peru. His strongest impression of the Japanese plant was the crowding of so many people and machines in such a small space. At the time, we just passed this off as a peculiar characteristic of Japanese culture.

It was not until years later that we recognized the economic significance of what we had seen: enormous economies in the utilization of space. To Japanese industrialists, the typical American manufacturing plant of the 1970s must have looked as if it had been designed by lift truck and automatic conveyer system salespeople. The Japanese discovered that, if they located work stations in sequence close together, no special mechanical equipment and no additional operators were needed to move the parts and materials from one work station to the next. The items processed at one station were placed on trays mounted on carts to be rolled a few feet to the next work station.

How much can be gained through this basic economizing strategy? Schonberger (1982:121) cites a case in which a Ford Motor Company official compared the designs for a plant from Japanese designers and American designers. For the same project, the Japanese design called for very much the same technology as the American design—but for forty-one machines compared to thirty-nine for the American plan. Even so, the Japanese designed a plant of 300,000 square feet compared to 900,000 square feet for the American design.

Due to this economical use of space, in recent years Japanese firms have spent about half as much in interest on bank loans as have American firms. If this cost advantage is compounded further by allowing Japanese firms to build plants at about one-third the cost of American plants, the cost differential becomes overwhelming. A comparison of modern American and Japanese plants in the same industry shows that the Japanese have very little advantage in technology. Their advantage is rather in more efficient use and maintenance of that technology and also in the more effective integration of human work and machine operations.

Schonberger (1982:57-58) cites a Toyota plant called "probably the most efficient engine plant in the world" that was still using twenty-year-old American-made machine tools and transfer lines. Of course, they had been superbly maintained and also upgraded from time to time.

Advances in technology should not be limited to new machines.

According to one report, in 1980 the majority—about 60 percent—of Japanese equipment spending "was devoted to upgrading the capabilities of *existing* equipment and processes." In contrast, the report says, most

U.S. companies spend 75 percent on additional capacity and replacement of old machines. We would be much more content to upgrade the old if we did not allow it to deteriorate. (Schonberger, 1982:71-72.)

Reduced investment costs are not the only advantage. When you buy a new machine, you only know how it is *supposed* to perform. There are substantial expenses involved in moving old equipment out, installing a new machine, and in the inevitable debugging of a new machine's operations; and then it may not live up to expectations. In contrast, operators, supervisors, and staff people know how the old machine performs and are likely to have good ideas on what could improve it. Furthermore, if one of those changes proves to be impractical, it can be eliminated without inordinate expense.

The new model also achieves substantial economies in the fuller utilization of human resources, as work teams take over the organizing of their own work.

From Productivity to Quality Emphasis

Under the old model, responsibilities for productivity and for quality were functionally separate. In management rhetoric, production supervisors and operators were responsible for quality, but, as many foremen told us over the years, they were driven by superiors to strive for high production, giving little attention to quality. The assumption was that quality would be taken care of by inspectors, checking the products before they left the plant.

According to the old model, high quality meant "conformance to engineering specifications." In effect, these engineering specifications never established exact measures to be achieved to make a product acceptable. There was always a range of variance permitted. Under the old logic, if the products met these engineering specifications, then this constituted perfect quality.

This logic was shaken when engineers discovered that some Japanese products enjoyed a higher-quality reputation than did the "perfect" products produced by the American plant. As they studied this puzzle, they discovered that comparable Japanese parts had substantially less variance in their measurements than the American parts.

The principle governing the old model was expressed in the often quoted maxim "If it ain't broke, don't fix it." In other words, if the current level of performance is satisfactory, make no changes. The Japanese competitors have countered with a principle that could be paraphrased in these words: "Even if it ain't broke, make it better." No current level of quality is good enough for the future. Each year the quality record must be superior to that attained the year before. This principle is not implemented simply by a rhetorical emphasis on high and improving quality. The new model firm emphasizes keeping systematic records of quality defects, finding out where and how they occur, and tracking down the sources of problems.

The new model deemphasizes the importance of final inspection in order to place the responsibility for quality particularly with the operators at each work station. Operators are also responsible for recording the occurrence of each quality defect, along with some notation on its possible cause.

This process has come to be called statistical process control (SPC). The ultimate responsibility for analyzing the quality data may rest with staff specialists, but operators provide most of the basic data and help to figure out how to make improvements.

From Staff Initiative to Staff Responsiveness

In theory, the mission of staff people is to assist line officers in managing operations. Under the old model, they are very involved in planning, monitoring, coordinating, and controlling operations. This leads to an accumulation of staff specialists in central offices and in management offices in the plants. As students of production management have pointed out,

> To guarantee production in such an environment required lots of buffer inventories, rework stations, and expediting. Because all those expediters tended to get in each other's way, companies tried to maintain order by hiring coordinators. They piled staff on staff (a phenomenon that has been called "staff infection") until they had three or four overhead personnel for every production worker, and top management became increasingly removed—both physically and psychologically—from the production line. (Hayes, Wheelwright, and Clark, 1988:17)

The new model thins out the central staff and plant office staff and locates remaining people close to work operations. They are now in a position to respond quickly to problems brought to their attention by the operators and as they observe the functioning of the machines.

Under the old model, the staff specialist was expected to be the professional expert, telling operators and supervisors what to do. Under the new model, the staff specialist becomes a member of the team of workers and supervisors who come together to discuss and analyze a problem and arrive at a plan of action. A change in the physical location of staff facilitates this role change. When the staff specialist was located in a remote office and was rarely seen on the shop floor, operators naturally saw this person as someone who claimed expert knowledge they did not possess. When his or her work station is located close to the work flow, the interactions between operators and staff people that inevitably occur make it much easier to get people together for problem solving, divorced from questions of power and authority.

From Technology Planning to Socio-Technical System Planning

In the 1970s, Robert Cole had the opportunity to sit in on a discussion of Japanese executives about the American response to the Japanese challenge. The question was, Should we worry that the Americans will respond by wiping out our competitive advantage? And, if so, what should we do about it?

At the end of the session, the Japanese reached the following conclusion: "Not to worry. Americans think machines are the answer" (Cole, personal communication). Although the aphorism, "There is no quick fix" has now become accepted as conventional wisdom, American executives still tend to seek the quick fix through investment in hardware—and, the bigger the problem, the bigger the technological fix that seems to be needed.

In contrast, our Japanese competitors do not believe in the technological fix or in any other quick fix. Rather than seek quantum jumps from one organizational state to another, they strive to make continual incremental improvements in technology and work systems.

Reforming Accounting Concepts and Methods

Just as the NMO requires drastic changes in the measurement and evaluation of quality, so also does it require a major shift in the way industrial accountants measure product costs. Accounting developed in industry primarily to serve two purposes: to provide stockholders with financial figures on the operation of their company and to provide the Internal Revenue Service with figures required for tax purposes. In figuring the cost of producing a product, it was not customary to make a study of what that product or model required beyond direct labor in such overhead items as staff services, research and development costs, marketing costs, and the like. The usual practice was to allocate indirect costs in proportion to direct labor costs or in terms of some other arbitrary standard.

What happens when such accounting conventions are practiced?

> We know one high-tech company whose overhead costs add up to almost ten times its direct labor costs, which come to roughly ten dollars per hour. Managers in this company are motivated to buy a part from an outside vendor, if at all possible, instead of making it internally because in so doing they reduce the costs for which they are responsible (which include the allocated costs) by $(1+10) \times \$10$, or \$110, for each direct labor hour saved. Managing an increasing volume of subcontracting, however, requires additional overhead personnel. Therefore, this company finds that its direct labor costs are decreasing, while its overhead costs are increasing—which drives up its overhead allocation rate for the remaining products and motivates its managers to subcontract even more. While extreme, this company is not atypical of many today that are being driven in unanticipated directions by the apparently innocuous mandates of their accounting systems. (Hayes et al, 1988:138)

This analysis suggests that the "hollowing out" of the American corporation has not occurred simply in response to inexorable economic and technological forces but is driven in part by the supposedly rational application of accounting conventions. Following the conventional logic of accounting leads to irrational outcomes from the standpoint of those concerned with maintaining employment and the economic health of American manufacturing companies. Fortunately, the economic distortions caused by conventional accounting practices are coming to be recognized by researchers, and some day companies may reform their accounting systems to reflect this research (see for example, Cooper and Kaplan, 1988; Kaplan, 1988).

HOW DO YOU GET THERE FROM HERE?

How do you get from the conventional manufacturing organization to the NMO, while maintaining production and preserving the strengths of the old organization?

Let us consider a case illustrating how it should not be done. This involves the introduction of a total quality control (TQC) program into factories that already had well established and much admired employee involvement programs, jointly led by managers and union leaders.

According to the experts who have developed programs to be administered by consultants, TQC must start at the top, with the chief executive officer being trained to analyze the quality aspects of his own work. The program then "cascades" down the management hierarchy, with each level (in association with the consultants) involved in training its immediate subordinates until at last the program reaches the workers at the bottom.

As union leaders have no place in the management hierarchy, does this mean they are excluded from TQC—unless they push their way in? Consider this description of how TQC reached the production plants, according to a personnel man who was playing a key role in the company's EI programs: "TQC came down on us in the plants like a freight train speeding down a track, without an engineer at the controls."

In this case, the union leaders blew the whistle, halting TQC before it got started in the plants. The union had a right to block the new training project because the labor contract stipulated that management could not undertake any new training of workers without union concurrence. The union leaders explained that they wanted to work with management to improve quality, but they had to know how TQC was supposed to relate to EI. When the TQC consultants were unable to answer the question, local managers and union leaders got together to retrofit TQC into the culture and work organization of the plants. As the union and management enjoyed a good working relationship, they were able to accomplish the retrofit without major problems. Nevertheless, management's failure to provide in advance for local plant participation in the introduction of TQC created frictions and delays in the implementation of TQC.

The point is that smooth progress in developing the NMO depends on integrating the technical and social aspects of each new program with each other and also integrating that new program with preexisting programs.

The same principle can be illustrated with the problems of introducing JIT. As already pointed out, for JIT to yield its potential benefits, management must delegate responsibility for organizing the work to work teams composed of multiskilled workers who assume major responsibilities for quality as well as for production. These changes also involve a substantial reduction of the number of supervisors and a redefinition of the supervisory role. All of these changes require not only extensive planning but also the development of new training programs for workers, supervisors, and managers.

A leading expert on manufacturing management expresses the challenge in these words:

> First, management must recognize that the changes required . . . demand a completely new architecture, and a new set of guiding principles. It is not simply a matter of changing a few things; almost everything must be changed and changed dramatically. These changes will affect how materials are stored, tracked, and allocated to the factory floor; how production processes are organized and linked; how accounting systems monitor performance and allocate costs; how the work force is trained and assigned; how information systems are altered and improved; how engineering defines its role; and how facilities are designed and upgraded. Such extensive and pervasive changes require changes in the forces that drive those detailed actions. It is not enough for management to intervene on a case-by-case basis and modify individual proposals. (Hayes et al., 1988:204-205)

In effect, the authors are calling for major changes in organizational culture—changes that must be guided by extensive involvement among those who will be working under the new systems. Considering that workers themselves have the expertise needed to anticipate the effects of changing their work, they should be involved in planning and implementing processes. Where a union has been active in an EI program, local union leaders can make important contributions to the development of the NMO through organizing and guiding worker participation.

THE NMO IN RELATION TO EMPLOYEE
INVOLVEMENT AND COLLECTIVE BARGAINING

The new manufacturing organization has been developing in the 1980s during a period of major changes in employee involvement and collective bargaining. To understand the industrial relations scene today, we therefore need to focus our attention on the interrelations of NMO, EI, and collective bargaining (CB).

Changes in EI and CB were already in progress before the NMO process was well advanced in many American plants. In the 1970s, characteristically EI focused on problems of what was then called quality of work life. Once a week or every two weeks, groups of workers would meet off the job with a member of management to discuss shop-floor problems. Under the ground rules then generally prevailing, EI could not be used to address any issue covered in the labor contract or embedded in managerial prerogatives. Furthermore, EI programs focused little direct attention on productivity problems, in order to discourage any suspicion that QWL was just a disguised form of speed-up.

By the 1980s these ground rules were breaking down in the face of intensified competitive pressures leading to mass layoffs as management tried to cut labor costs. With the survival of plants and jobs at stake, the parties could generate little enthusiasm for discussions of quality of work life. If EI was to continue, they could no longer avoid discussing problems covered by the contract (work rules, for example) or managerial prerogatives. In some cases, this led to a two-stage process: The EI group would work out a tentative agreement on changes to be introduced, accompanied by and followed by discussions among union officers and within management; then the changes would be implemented in a side agreement between union and management or in clauses in a new contract (see, for example, Klingel and Martin, 1988, and Whyte, Greenwood, and Lazes, 1989). In some cases, EI and CB were almost completely integrated (Rankin and Mansell, 1986).

The development of the NMO has ushered in major changes in the organization of work and therefore in industrial relations. With the sharp reduction in supervisory personnel, developing the NMO involves substantial delegation of work management duties to teams of workers. The stress on manufacturing flexibility calls for multiskilled workers. This is accompanied by a marked reduction in the number of job classifications. As the emphasis shifts from pushing production in each work unit to organizing a smooth flow of work from unit to unit, individual piece rates no longer fit into management strategies.

For abandoning familiar territory, what do workers get in return? For piece rates, the pattern is reasonably clear. In a unionized plant, management cannot simply decree the elimination of its incentive program. The parties bargain to substitute an increase in hourly pay.

This does not mean that no incentive plan is compatible with the NMO. Broad-based plans such as gain sharing or profit sharing are increasing in popularity. In a multiplant company, profit sharing on the basis of total company performance is likely to have little motivational impact at the plant level, although it may be regarded as an attractive fringe benefit. Gain sharing can have a much stronger motivational impact, but note that under such plans workers share in not only the gains but also the risks. Union leaders may argue against the substitution of the uncertain payoffs of gainsharing for payoffs much more under the direct control of individual workers. They may be much more likely to accept gain sharing in addition to increased hourly pay upon abandoning piece rates (see, for example, Ross, Hatcher, and Ross, 1989).

As unions accept sharp reductions in number of job classifications, and as workers become multiskilled and take on increasing responsibilities for managing their own work, they can no longer be treated simply as cogs in a machine. As their value to the company becomes more obvious, negotiating for employment security becomes an increasingly practical objective for union leaders. In the 1980s we have witnessed major gains for some unions on this issue.

Through the development of NMO, do the workers also gain in the human dignity accorded their work and therefore in increasing respect from management? In some cases, this seems to be happening. Here and there we see elimination of time clocks, reserved parking spaces for top management, executive dining rooms, and other indicia of status distinctions between workers and managers. However, it can be argued that as management moves away from tight personal control, workers remain tightly controlled by the technical systems of the NMO.

Under the NMO, EI changes in form and, in one dimension, is intensified. The introduction of the NMO tends to shift the emphasis from parallel structures (discussion groups meeting away from the job) to EI that is integrated into the actual job operations, as workers assume responsibility for organizing their own work.

Does this mean that the NMO leads to a democratization of work? That depends on how we define the term. As Janice Klein (1989:61) points out, the NMO places systems limits on the scope of worker decision making: "The reform program that ushers in JIT and SPC is meant to *eliminate all variations within production* and therefore requires strict adherence to rigid methods and procedures."

Furthermore, while the logics of the NMO require worker involvement in decision making at the shop-floor level, the technologies themselves do not require worker participation in decision making on issues transcending the shop floor. Whether or not workers and union leaders get involved in discussing and negotiating on issues traditionally covered by managerial prerogatives depends on the decisions of managers and union leaders in each particular case.

An issue currently being debated in various automotive locals is reflected in the words "management by stress" (Parker and Slaughter, 1988a, 1988b): the claim that the NMO greatly increases the psychological stress placed on workers, not to mention other employees. The argument is based on the fact that the NMO is a tightly strung system with very little slack. Under the old model, departments could function more independently due to the ample buffer stocks.

As old-model automotive assembly plants have long been known as high stress environments, this is hardly a new issue. Comparing the old model with the NMO, probably different types of stress are involved. However, measurements of different types of stress will not solve practical problems. In local union elections, workers may continue to press this issue in their votes for officers.

EQUITY AND SOCIAL POLICY ISSUES

Will advances toward the NMO save American manufacturing? Although there have been impressive gains in productivity in an increasing number of factories, we should not overestimate what can be accomplished at that level.

Here we should note an alarming decline of interest in the management of industrial production among higher-level executives and in our leading business schools.

In many of our business schools, manufacturing management has been losing its appeal to students, professors, and administrators as courses in finance and accounting grow ever more popular. The same trend has been noted among well-established executives. A leading authority on manufacturing management, Robert H. Hayes, reports,

> The written summary reaction of participants to a course on manufacturing management that he taught to high level general managers of American companies in the mid-1970s: "you did very well with a subject that unfortunately has limited appeal." (Hayes et al., 1988:17)

Will workers and managers in the plants struggling to improve performance get the necessary support and understanding from those who control the company's strategic decisions?

Akio Morita (1987), Chairman of Sony Corporation—a leading Japanese firm with important facilities in the United States, gives this answer:

> Unfortunately, American industry is now being distracted by a game called mergers and acquisitions. America's brightest managerial talent is engaged in takeover moves and empire building. The best students do not study engineering but become MBAs or lawyers and, eventually, professional money makers. This is not a productive enterprise. . . .
>
> America must return to fundamentals, to making things of real value. A business organization's real asset is its people—their good will, their enthusiasm and their creativity. But how can you expect your people to be motivated to work when they are traded like merchandise? A nation's economy is only as strong as its manufacturing base, and this base is chipped away by every mindless merger and by every decision to shift production to a newly developed country only to save on labor. (Copyright © 1987 by the New York Times Company. Reprinted by permission.)

12. Analyzing an Organizational Culture

The chapter on the NMO introduced the concept of organizational corporate culture, a notion that has become popular in management circles in the 1980s. In this chapter, I illustrate the use of the concept through a study of the culture of that most extraordinary set of organizations, the Mondragón cooperative complex in the Basque country of Spain.

The chapter also provides another example of the uses of participatory action research (PAR). What began in 1975 as a conventional field study later evolved quite unexpectedly into a major PAR project. The transformation began in 1983 toward the end of the second study visit I made with Kathleen King Whyte. Simply as a token of reciprocity for the help we had received from our Mondragón informants, I offered to present our impressions to a group of people who might be interested. In that session, José Luis González, personnel director of FAGOR, responded enthusiastically and asked, "Why don't you send us a proposal for further research and a budget?"

That took me by surprise. At age sixty-nine and having recently wound up a long and ambitious research program in Peru, I could hardly consider such a major commitment. Nevertheless, I was impressed by González's response, and I was fascinated by Mondragón. On returning to Cornell, I sought the advice of Davydd J. Greenwood, director of the

Center for International Studies. A professor of anthropology, Greenwood had previously conducted research in the Basque country that had won him recognition as a leading authority on that culture and society, and he knew far more about Spain than did the Whytes. Greenwood suggested that we seek support from the Spain-United States Committee on Educational and Cultural Exchange to set up a broad-based cooperative program linking Cornell with FAGOR. With González, we worked out a joint proposal, which evolved into a three-year program supported initially by the committee.

For present purposes, I limit myself to description of only those aspects of the joint program focusing on the study of organizational culture as it evolved into a PAR project. That program led me to extend my Mondragón research involvement beyond 1983. It also led Greenwood to develop a PAR project on the study of the culture of FAGOR. While I played only a minor role in the PAR project jointly led by Greenwood and González, the Whytes' research became integrated with that project in ways to be described. Thus the PAR project substantially enriched our own research.

INTRODUCING THE
MONDRAGÓN COOPERATIVE COMPLEX

Our Mondragón research ranged widely over the cooperative complex but concentrated particularly upon FAGOR, the largest and oldest group of cooperatives within the complex.

Mondragón is an important case not only for its extraordinary success in the face of widespread disbelief in worker cooperatives as viable forms of organization but also for what it can teach us regarding the creation of organizational culture. The case is particularly instructive because what developed from the Mondragón project describes a new organizational culture for a set of organizations without parallel anywhere in the world.

Worker cooperatives have been well known in the literature of the cooperative movement, and they also have frequently occurred in Spain and particularly in the Basque country. Mondragón, however, is neither a single cooperative nor a simple aggregation of worker cooperatives. The complex links together a network of about 100 cooperatives with second-level support and development institutions: a cooperative bank, educational institutions organized along cooperative lines, a research and development cooperative, and a social security cooperative.

To understand the growth and dynamics of the worker cooperative complex, it is useful to divide its evolution into five time periods, along the following lines.

1941-1955: Laying the foundations. The story begins with a young priest, José María Arizmendiarrieta, who was known to his friends and followers as Arizmendi or as Don José María. In 1940, Mondragón was a small city (about 8,000 population) with some tradition of industrial work. In the Spanish Civil War (1936-39), most Basques either fought with or sympathized with the republican side against Franco and fascism and ended up on the losing side. In the early postwar years, Basques saw themselves as a conquered people, with the military forces of Franco controlling their destiny. These early postwar years were known locally as "the hunger period" because the people were desperately poor. Mondragón at the time was crowded into old and inadequate housing, and health problems were widespread.

At the time, any gathering of more than five people had to be registered with the government authorities—with a single exception: meetings under the auspices of the Catholic church. As a result the Catholic church was used as a reasonably safe haven for educational as well as religious activities.

In his seminary studies before coming to Mondragón, Arizmendi had devoted his attention not only to religion but also to social and economic problems. He was particularly concerned with finding alternative ways of organizing the economy that did not fit either the standard capitalist approach or orthodox Marxism. He had done serious reading regarding the cooperative movement with special reference to worker cooperatives. He was familiar with the negative judgment of Beatrice and Sydney Webb regarding the prospects for the development of worker cooperatives: "All such associations of producers that start as alternatives to the capitalist system either fail or cease to be democracies of producers" (Coates and Topham, 1968:67, quoting the Webbs). Arizmendi was also well aware of the common problems of worker cooperatives that had led the Webbs to this opinion, but he did not accept their conclusions. He thought there must be other ways to reconcile the interests and needs for economic development with those of social justice, and he devoted his life to finding these new ways.

Don José María devoted his early years in Mondragón to teaching and community organizing. His teaching took the form of dialogue with blue-collar youth, the segment of society to which he devoted particular attention. One of the members of the group later reported that from 1941 to 1956 "we counted more than 2,000 circles of study that he conducted. Some for religious and humanistic orientation; others for social orientation" (Whyte and Whyte, 1988:32).

From 1941 on, Arizmendi conducted at least one study session every 2.7 days (not counting holidays and vacations) in addition to teaching in the technical school that he helped to organize. As one of his former students commented, "He taught classes in religion and sociology—and really his religion classes were mainly sociology."

Being unable to persuade the leading private firm to expand its apprenticeship program beyond the sons of its own workers, Arizmendi worked with blue-collar youth and their parents to establish the Escuela Politécnica Profesional providing education first to boys from 14 to 16 primarily in technical subjects related to industrial development. That school, renamed for him after his death in 1976, expanded over the years both in numbers of students (including increasing numbers of young women) and in the level of education it provides until today graduates of the school have completed approximately three years of what we would consider an undergraduate program.

In community organizations, Arizmendi also worked with youth and their parents to establish a community health program, focusing first on testing citizens for tuberculosis, which was quite prevalent in this era. He also helped to organize and encourage the young men in the creation of the sports club, including a community support campaign to provide the youth a field on which they could play soccer.

In all of these activities, Arizmendi believed that the social and psychological impact on the young community activists was at least as important as the physical outcome of their efforts. In spite of the extreme poverty and the sense of hopelessness that pervaded the community following the victory of Franco, he saw possibilities for the young people and their parents to better their lot. He also recognized that, as they were successful in one organizing activity, they would gain not only valuable experience but also confidence in their own abilities to change the world in which they lived.

1956-1969: Launching into a period of rapid growth. This was an era of autarchy, as Spain was cut off from the rest of Europe through high tariff barriers. At the same time, consumer demand was rapidly growing in Spain, so that any manufacturer who could produce a reasonably acceptable product could count on an expanding national market.

In 1956, five of the students who had entered the first year's class of the escuela got together with Arizmendi to create the first of the Mondragón worker cooperatives: Ulgor, a firm devoted first to the production of space heaters. Following the completion of their educational program in the escuela, the five had gone to work in private industry. With the encouragement of Arizmendi, they determined to continue their own education, enrolling in a college program in industrial engineering at the University of Zaragosa, outside of the Basque country. As these young men came from poor families who could not support them away from home, Arizmendi arranged for them to study in absentia, appearing at Zaragosa only to write examinations at the end of each term.

For its first two years, Ulgor was legally a private firm, but the founders were committed to making it a collective enterprise. Frequently they met with Arizmendi after working hours to discuss technical, social, and organizational problems. This period allowed them to learn from experience at the same time as they were learning from continuing discussions with Arizmendi.

This was a period of rapid growth as new cooperatives came into existence through Ulgor or other sources and as support organizations, particularly the cooperative bank, were created.

1970-1978: Slower growth and rising conflict. This was a period marked particularly by the oil shocks of 1973 and 1975, when the Organization of Petroleum Exporting Countries (OPEC) enforced enormous increases in the price of oil. Not being an oil-producing nation, Spain was hit particularly hard.

This was also a period of increasing political turbulence. Dictator Franco died late in 1975, but he was known to have been in poor health for many months before his death. By the 1970s, even under Franco, the tight controls on independent political and union activities had been loosening. It seemed that the whole society was trying to orient itself to major changes that were bound to come with the dictator's death.

The 1974 strike in Ulgor provided the most serious labor dispute in the history of the complex. In comparison with strikes in private industry, this was a very small event. Just over 400 worker members out of the 3,500 in Ulgor went out and the strike lasted only a few days. Nevertheless, because it represented such a contradiction between reality and cooperative ideology, the strike attracted intense interest around Mondragón even outside of the cooperatives and became a topic of considerable political debate.

Following preparatory efforts within the escuela, Ikerlan, an applied industrial research cooperative, was founded in 1975 and soon became a major engine for change and growth.

1979-1983: Coping with the recession. The worldwide recession affected Spain particularly severely, beginning earlier than elsewhere (in 1979) and producing unemployment figures over twenty percent in Spain and over twenty-five percent in the Basque provinces.

The rate of profits for the cooperatives had been falling through the previous period, and now the challenge was no longer managing expansion but rather preserving the existing cooperatives. In 1983, one out of every three of the Mondragón worker cooperatives was in precarious condition, in need of technical and financial assistance from management consultants as well as emergency intervention to prevent failure.

The struggle to save failing enterprises and preserve jobs was long and hard but, in the end, extraordinarily successful. According to the way we estimate unemployment percentages in the United States, in 1983 the number of members of the Mondragón cooperatives unemployed at any time never exceeded 0.6 percent.

1984-present: Renewed dynamism and accelerated expansion. In 1987, Mondragón's cooperative employment increased by 500, and the number of jobs increased by 1,050 in 1988. In 1988, the total sales of the Mondragón cooperatives had increased by nearly fifteen percent over 1987.

ETHNIC AND ORGANIZATIONAL CULTURES

Analysis of the culture of the Mondragón firms must begin by distinguishing between organizational cultures and the broad community culture in the Basque provinces. Some critics have attributed

Mondragón's success principally to the Basque culture. This interpretation would rule out drawing any general lessons from the Mondragón experience because the Basque culture cannot be reproduced elsewhere.

Obviously, one cannot deny that there is some connection between the Basque community culture and the organizational cultures arising within the Mondragón complex, but it is easy to overinterpret such connections. For example, Basques themselves speak of "our associative tendencies," but, in the traditional culture of the Basque community, these tendencies led to the formation of small groups or work guilds with high internal solidarity but closed to the outside world. From the outset the Mondragón complex has been an open system, designed for inclusion of anyone who wished to work and had the abilities needed, without regard to ethnic, religious, or political orientation. It is estimated that at least 25 percent of the members of the Mondragón cooperatives were not Basques in their community of origin and in their family and community social orientation.

The Basques' associative tendencies may help us to understand why worker cooperatives are so common in that region. In the mid-1980s, it was estimated that there were far more worker cooperatives outside of the Mondragón complex than in it. These outside cooperatives were isolated units, whereas Mondragón had built a strong network of supporting and collaborating organizations.

We may assume that ethnic culture has some relation to the growth and development of the Mondragón cooperative complex, but, in contrast, it must also bear some relationship to the political-terrorist organization known as Eta. If ethnic culture can give rise to such drastically different phenomena, it should be clear that any assumption of cultural determinism is bound to be misleading.

ORGANIZATIONAL CULTURE

I based my analysis of the culture of the Mondragón cooperatives on the following definition:

> For our purposes, the culture of a people is a system of widely shared beliefs and values and a set of characteristic behaviors used in organizing

social processes. The culture includes an ideology, a cognitive map or
framework within which people explain their own characteristics and their
relations to others of different cultures. (Whyte and Whyte, 1988:254)

As sociologist Everett C. Hughes commented, "The most important elements of the culture of peoples are the things they take for
granted." This means that much of the culture is not apparent to outsiders or even fully articulated within the community or organization. To
penetrate fully into the world of the "taken for granted," ideally a participant observer should spend many months inside the community or
organization. This was not possible in our case. Beginning with a two-
week visit in April 1975, we next spent three weeks in Mondragón in
October 1983 and had three more visits during 1985 and 1986—a total
of about twelve weeks in the field over an eleven-year period. Our
knowledge of Mondragón was greatly expanded through the work of
Ana Gutierrez-Johnson, a Cornell graduate student, who accompanied
us on the first trip and remained for seven weeks and later returned on
two occasions for extended fieldwork.

Although we had very limited opportunities to observe cooperative
organizations in action, we were able to carry out intensive interviews
with a large number of the key figures in this cooperative development
and we had full access to very rich documentary sources. The reports
of the units involved in the governance of the cooperatives provided
especially rich sources of data as they report not only the decisions
made but also, for all controversial questions, what the arguments were
for or against the actions taken.

We begin with the *cognitive framework* guiding the cooperative. We
see the framework consisting of basic values, objectives, and guiding
principles regarding how people should behave in relation to those
values and objectives. Combined with the cognitive framework, we find
shaping systems that maintain or change policies and structures.

The Mondragón cooperatives manifest the *basic values* of equality,
solidarity, dignity of labor, and participation.

The Basques recognize important distinctions in social class position,
but they try to minimize the impact of these structural elements on
behavior, emphasizing instead the idea of equality as it is represented
in democratic politics and also in the rights and obligations of citizen
members of worker cooperatives. After an initial brief period when
voting was weighted in relation to the job classifications of members,
membership and voting have been on the basis of one member, one vote.

While recognizing the need to offer higher pay to more skilled and better trained people in the ranks of workers and managers, the equality principle serves to minimize the distorting impact of differential pay. For many years following the beginning of the cooperatives, the ratio between the starting wage and the salary of the top executive never ranged above 1 to 3. Later, to recognize the need for greater financial incentives to individuals with particularly important talents and abilities, that ratio was increased to 1 to 4.5.

Mondragón's Cooperative Congress held its first meeting in October 1987. In a hotly and closely contested issue, the congress voted to permit individual cooperatives with special needs to increase the ratio to 1 to 6. So far only a few cooperatives have gone beyond the 1 to 4.5 ratio.

Even a 1 to 6 ratio is extraordinarily narrow for organizations in highly industrialized nations. For example, an analysis of the pay differentials in 500 of the leading U.S. corporations indicated a ratio of 1 to 94, comparing the average wage of workers with the pay of the top executive (AFL-CIO News, May 13, 1989). Note the difference between using as the index number the *starting* wage for unskilled labor in the Mondragón complex compared with the *average* wage in the U.S. ratio. If the U.S. ratio for these 500 firms had been based on the starting wage, the ratio would probably have been close to 1 to 200.

The solidarity value discourages zero-sum games. Members of the same cooperative are supposed to rise or fall together; one group is not supposed to exploit the other. The same solidarity principle is applied to relations between cooperatives: One cooperative does not exploit another but, rather, cooperatives seek to develop mutually beneficial relations. The same principle is extended somewhat more weakly to relations between the cooperatives and the community. It is believed that the community has provided cooperative organizations with sources of strength, so cooperatives should in turn contribute to strengthening the community.

The dignity of labor is another basic value. Basques believe that all honest work should be accorded dignity. Of course, they recognize status and prestige differences among jobs, but they do not draw class distinctions nearly so sharply as is common in the south of Spain.

Participation is one of the most important values within the complex. The leaders believe that members not only have the right to participate fully in the governance of their firm but also that they have an obligation to participate.

We see the Mondragón cooperatives committed to the following five *objectives:* job creation, employment security, human and social development of worker members, autonomy and self-governance, and economic progress.

At the time of the creation of Ulgor, there was an extreme shortage of jobs in the Basque region. Opportunities for working-class children to find any job at all were limited; and, further, those who were employed were working in firms controlled by a social elite, which meant that the able worker had little opportunity for advancing beyond the bottom ranks.

Employment security involved a commitment to create new jobs while old jobs were being phased out. Human and social development meant that work places should provide a humane environment in which people could develop their talents and interests.

Autonomy and self-governance means building independent organizations that govern themselves.

Economic progress is recognized as an important means to achieving the other objectives. The leaders of the movement recognized that economic progress was required to enable them to achieve the social values to which they were committed.

Mondragón's *guiding principles* are the ground rules according to which cooperative leaders and members are supposed to behave. We find nine guiding principles which fall naturally into three groups of three. One group safeguards *diversity and individual rights,* another group supports *solidarity,* and a third group guides *decisionmaking.*

The diversity set includes openness: The cooperatives are open to membership by anyone with the required skills and training, without regard to ethnic background, religious belief, political party, or any other affiliation. It is estimated that at least twenty-five percent of the total membership is composed of individuals that were not born and raised in the Basque provinces. The cooperatives are committed to political pluralism. In contrast to worker cooperatives in some other countries (notably Italy and Israel) the Mondragón cooperatives are not linked to any political party and include members of various parties. To support the rights and obligations of the individual member regarding participation, the cooperatives provide extraordinary freedom of information. With a bare minimum of restrictions, any information available to management is available upon request to individual members.

The solidarity set covers principles applying at three levels. At the first level, we find the principle of size limitation. The cooperatives have sought to build organizations of the minimum size necessary for manufacturing and marketing efficiency, with the objective of keeping the firms small enough so that their management and governance can be handled by members who know each other. This means that when a firm grows to the size and complexity where it is possible to spin off a new and independent cooperative, that separation is carried out.

At the second level, we observe the principle of the creation of cooperative groups: firms that band together to share general management services, with the aim of securing economies of scale but without sacrificing the independence of the individual cooperatives.

At the third level, we find the principle of intercooperative complementarity: Whenever it can be done without sacrificing the interest of one of the parties to the transaction, Mondragón cooperatives buy from and sell to each other. It was recently estimated that in the FAGOR group, including the oldest and largest cooperative, nineteen percent of the parts and materials purchased came from Mondragón cooperatives.

The set guiding decisionmaking includes the principle of balance. The principle is expressed repeatedly in writing and in discussions with the word *equilibrio*. The word refers to the requirement of achieving a balance between the economic requirements of the firm and the socioeconomic interests and needs of individual members, between the technical requirements of the technology and the social interests and needs of the members, and so forth. The same principle applies to relations between the various cooperatives. They do not play zero-sum games in which one unit takes advantage of another. The interests and needs of both units must be weighed and balanced in decision making.

The founder stressed future orientation, and this has been built into the cooperatives' guidance system with considerable force. The leaders are not to consider satisfactory any current state of affairs; they must always strive for a better future state.

Finally, the cooperatives place great emphasis on organizational self-evaluation. Leaders are not expected to limit themselves to discussions and actions on current problems. They are also expected to develop a group process for evaluating the current performance of the organization in order to achieve improvements.

The *shaping systems* refer to certain major policies and to the structures for governance and management.

A critically important policy governs the rights and obligations of members. Democratic governance of the cooperatives is based on the principle of one member, one vote. Voting rights are independent of capital ownership. No stock is issued to members or nonmembers. The capital of the cooperative is built on a capital account for each of the members. The initiation fee and initial capital contribution are treated as if they were loans by the members to the cooperative. When the cooperative is profitable, those profits are divided every six months (according to a formula established by management) between a reserve fund remaining with the firm and the members' capital accounts, with ten percent going to community social and economic development projects independent of the firm.

The capital account of the member is not considered a personal retirement fund, as the cooperatives make other provisions for retirement, but the capital account cannot be drawn on by the individual until retirement or until he or she leaves the firm. Although none of the profits are paid directly to the members in cash, every six months they do receive an interest payment on their capital accounts.

Since no stock is issued to members or outsiders, the structure of ownership makes it impossible for outsiders to gain control of the organization—unless it goes bankrupt or the members vote to sell it. This contrasts with the common situation in worker cooperatives that are based upon stock ownership. Even if the original distribution is democratic, with each member purchasing one share of stock, as a worker cooperative becomes successful and expands, members are likely to submit to what we call "collective selfishness," recognizing that the financial interests of the original members can be enhanced if they take in new workers as hired labor rather than as members. History is replete with cases where successful worker cooperatives have eventually been converted into privately owned firms.

In the Mondragón complex, the structure of the organizations and the ground rules they follow provide for a much more complete separation between governance and management than is characteristic of U.S. private firms. In such private firms, generally the board of directors includes the chief executive officer and, frequently, one or more other top operating officials in addition to board members who do not work full time for the company. In the Mondragón complex, what we call the governing council (to distinguish it from a board of directors) includes only elected members of the cooperative and excludes the chief executive officer, who serves the council with voice but not vote. The manager of the cooperative is appointed by the governing council for a three-year term and may be reappointed following review of his or her performance, but reappointment is not taken for granted. The governing council also appoints for three-year periods the other members of the top management team, known as the management council.

As with other cooperatives, established according to the Rochdale principles, there is also an audit council—sometimes known as a vigilance council—of elected members whose sole responsibility is to provide a yearly review of the legal and financial operations of the cooperative and report to the membership.

The Mondragón complex has one organization that is a social invention and it is of vital importance for the operation of some of the guiding principles. The social council, like the governing council, consists of those elected by the membership, but on different bases. Members of the governing council are elected at large. Members of the social council are elected to represent particular groups of worker-members according to the nature of their work and location. The social council provides a means for representing the interests of members as workers, whereas the governing council can be considered an organization designed to represent the interests of members as owners.

As all members are also workers, why have two different organizations to represent owner and worker interests? As a member, each individual would like to maximize the long-term financial strength of the cooperative, whereas, as a worker, he or she would be more concerned with immediate financial rewards and with the quality of working life. When each member has to balance these competing interests individually, this necessarily creates ambivalence, and ambivalence is not a good stance from which to make decisions. The invention of the social council resolves this ambivalence problem, providing two organizations to deal with the competing interests and needs. Over the years, at least in the FAGOR group, the social council has become the chief organ for carrying on organizational self-evaluation and for developing channels of communication through which members of management are advised and informed regarding views of the membership.

One of the great strengths of the Mondragón complex is its organizational network. Students of worker cooperatives have recognized that an individual cooperative, isolated in a sea of private enterprises, has poor prospects for success and long-run survival. Mondragón provides not simply a large aggregate of worker cooperatives but rather an integrated network through which individual cooperatives are linked together in groups, and through which individual cooperatives and groups are linked with a cooperative bank (the Caja Laboral Popular), a cooperative research and development organization (Ikerlan), a cooperative social security and support organization (Lagun Aro); and all of these organizations remain closely linked with the educational institutions from which the earliest cooperatives sprang.

INTEGRATING THE FIELD STUDY WITH PAR

The Greenwood-González PAR project proceeded in two stages from 1985 to 1987. Following a planning study visit in the spring of 1985, Greenwood spent the month of July in an intensive working seminar with fifteen members of FAGOR's personnel department or of that department in member cooperatives. This stage focused on a study of the organizational culture of Ulgor, the oldest and largest cooperative in the complex.

The second stage, beginning in 1986 and concluding in 1987 with the writing of a book on participatory action research in FAGOR (Greenwood and González, 1990), focused more broadly on FAGOR itself. Here again the major discussion and work was concentrated in the July 1986 seminar led by Greenwood.

The July 1985 seminar consisted of three sets of activities: lectures on and discussions of field methods and theory, led by Greenwood; a critical review of the research literature on Mondragón; and then the joint writing of a 116-page monograph on the culture of Ulgor, focusing on two particularly stressful periods in its history.

It was at this point that the integration of the Whyte research with PAR occurred. Draft chapters of our book on Mondragón (Whyte and Whyte, 1988) were included in the PAR research review. The proposed focus of the project on organizational culture moved me to write my own preliminary interpretation of the culture of Mondragón cooperatives. Greenwood found this useful, and a member of the study team translated it for the group. In this way, what began as a conventional field study became integrated with the PAR project, to our mutual benefit. A member of the study team undertook a painstaking reading and critique of the draft manuscript, pointing out to me a number of factual errors, suggesting alternative interpretations of some points we made, and also providing significant additional information and ideas. The study team's interpretation of their organizational culture then fed back to us, reshaping and strengthening our own interpretation of their culture.

Data for the 1985 project came primarily from documentary research and a review of the members' experience with Ulgor; the 1986 project involved field interviews with cooperative members at various levels and departments of the cooperatives and culminated in group discussions on topics selected by the research team with members selected so as to represent a broad range of status, function, and experience. The selection of topics for these group discussions provides evidence of the extent to which team members were establishing ownership of the PAR process. Both Greenwood and I suggested topics, but the team chose three of their own making, which proved to be highly useful for both their purposes and ours.

The involvement of the personnel group in PAR led José Luis González to secure a top management commitment to incorporate participatory action research into future budgets of the FAGOR personnel department. Thus, a program that began with external funds (principally grants from the Spain-United States Committee on Educational and Cultural Exchange) is now becoming a recognized part of the FAGOR personnel program.

Following completion of the 1986 book project, members of the personnel team began to develop mini-PAR projects focusing on specific problems that had emerged in the overall studies.

Perhaps of greater long-run practical importance but impossible to measure have been changes in concepts and orientations among members of the personnel group. One motivation for such studies was a general concern that rank-and-file participation in decision making was not as active as cooperative ideals would require. Before this program, the prevailing interpretation of this phenomenon was member apathy: Most members simply did not care enough about their firms to become actively involved. Involvement in the PAR process convinced members of the study group that this interpretation was flatly wrong.

Particularly in the July 1986 discussion groups the members persuaded the study team that they cared deeply about the cooperatives and had many constructive criticisms to make, but did not find the formal structures provided for participation functioning so as to meet their needs and interests. This reorientation shifted the attention of the personnel team from a fruitless search for how to conquer member apathy to a potentially fruitful examination of how formal and informal structures functioned so as to facilitate or inhibit discussion of member needs and interests.

The PAR process also served to bring the concept of organizational culture down from the clouds of large abstractions to the level of recognizing and specifying particular elements of culture important in orienting behavior within FAGOR.

A MONDRAGÓN MODEL FOR APPLICATION ELSEWHERE?

In any culture, organization creation and development has to be guided in terms of the particular culture in which the organization is based, but nevertheless there are certain lessons we can draw from the most highly developed and successful complex of worker cooperatives that the world has ever known. The structure of ownership and control devised by Mondragón protects the cooperative from the fate that has led to the degeneration of worker cooperatives everywhere else in the world.

It is significant that the Mondragón movement was created within an educational institution and that educational institutions have continued to play a guiding and stimulating role. The network of mutually supporting organizations is clearly of vital importance. Elsewhere, we cannot expect such a network to be developed fully and rapidly, but in the United States and in some other countries we are observing the creation of not-for-profit organizations that have been specifically designed to support and guide worker cooperatives.

The cooperatives are also based on a rich organizational learning experience that has provided the leaders with an understanding of the culture of their organization and a well-understood set of guiding principles.

INTERPRETING ORGANIZATIONAL CULTURES

What does this analysis tell us about the study of organizational culture? Such an analysis should lead us toward a more realistic conception of the nature of organizational culture than we could get from a set of guiding principles handed down by management. Also, our analysis suggests the importance of not seeing organizational culture—

particularly in a large and complex organization—as one homogeneous whole. The culture of Mondragón provides ample room for diversity, controversy, and conflict. The organizational culture should provide for some broad agreement on general principles, but that does not ensure agreement on actions taken in response to those principles. In various situations, the same principle can be argued to support quite a range of actions, and we have observed Mondragón members discussing and arguing these options.

Finally, we should not think of culture as something static that changes little over substantial periods of time. The culture may be regarded as in a constant state of flux, with periods of stability punctuated also by periods of change. The culture at a given time provides some general limits or parameters regarding the way disputes should be resolved and decisions should be made, but this culture is constantly being reshaped by the interplay of forces described above.

13. American Diffusion in Industrial Participation

The evolution of participatory systems in industrial relations has been accompanied by and supported by a major conceptual shift regarding the role of workers. In the tradition of Taylorism, workers were regarded as passive agents to be controlled and manipulated by management. Today they are coming to be regarded as active collaborators who contribute not only physical effort and skill but also information and ideas required to achieve high performance. To be sure, the conceptual shift is not universal in the United States. There are still many managers who adhere to the Taylorism model and probably many more whose espoused theory fits the new framework but whose behavior is closer to the old model. Nevertheless, the direction of the trend is unmistakable.

What moves people toward a major conceptual shift? The record indicates that the initial impetus for change arises out of the recognition that the old ways of thinking and acting are not resolving pressing problems. As we see in reviewing the experience of Japan, Scandinavia, and the United States, the impetus for change in different countries may arise from either similar or different sources. In this chapter, we will review briefly the Japanese and Scandinavian experience and then concentrate on the American experience.

In Japan, the catastrophic loss of World War II created a widespread recognition that the old ways were no longer viable and reinforced a traditional tendency to look abroad for ideas and information that the Japanese could adapt to serve their new objectives. In this period the Japanese did not have to look far for foreign ideas and practices because some major changes were imposed by the U.S. occupying forces. The labor codes were rewritten so as to support a system of collective bargaining similar to the U.S. pattern. There followed a period of substantial industrial conflict, which moved leaders of management to search for ways of integrating workers into their firms more effectively.

In the same period, Japanese leaders recognized that,although their armaments industries had been producing at high quality levels, Japan could not hope to gain a strong position in industrial exports without overcoming its prewar reputation as the maker of products that were cheap but of shoddy quality. This opened Japanese minds to the enormous impact of W. Edwards Deming and of other foreign teachers and missionaries of statistically based systems of quality control. As noted before, however, the Japanese made a fundamental change in the methods of applying these systems. Deming thought he was simply teaching engineers and managers how to implement his systems, whereas the Japanese proceeded to enlist workers as active participants in the quality improvement drive. Long before the Americans, the Japanese recognized that high quality goals could only be achieved through active worker involvement. In Japan, worker participation was fostered in two complementary ways: through decentralization and the delegation to work groups of many responsibilities for making operational decisions, and through the development of nationwide programs of quality control circles (QCCs). These changes provided workers with substantial influence in shop-floor decision making.

Judging from the leading change cases, which were widely studied and admired nationally and internationally, the impetus to change came from somewhat different sources in Norway and Sweden. The Norwegian shipping project arose in response to the recognition that this industry, so vitally important to the nation, could not survive without major changes in the face of competition from national fleets with much lower wages and labor costs. In Sweden, Volvo's problems were only indirectly economic. In a full employment and generally prosperous economy, Volvo was finding it increasingly difficult to attract Swedish workers to its assembly lines—and keep them there. As Volvo was becoming increasingly dependent on foreign workers, leaders of management searched for ways of redesigning work so as to enhance the quality of work life.

THE AMERICAN EXPERIENCE

The American shift started later than in Japan or Scandinavia primarily because of the enormous prestige gained by American industry's feats of production during World War II. When so many foreigners were coming here in search of U.S. industrial know-how, few American managers perceived any need for change. The initial impetus arose in response to concern over union-management conflict in the 1960s. This concern in government and management circles stimulated the growth of meetings and in-plant activities under the general heading of quality of work life (QWL). AS QWL interest grew in the 1970s, Americans became aware of Japan's quality control circles and many companies sought to imitate the Japanese model; but they eliminated the word "control" from the name and also did not engage in prior efforts to delegate more work methods decisions to work groups.

In Chapter 9 we followed the only partially successful efforts of the International Association of Quality Circles to promote the spread of this Japanese social invention in the United States. In this chapter we focus particularly on the experience of individual companies and unions. (For a broader overview of this trend, see Hecksher, 1988; Herrick, 1990; and Kochan, Katz, and McKersie, 1986.)

In general, participatory programs in the 1970s were focused exclusively on shop-floor problems; managerial prerogatives or matters covered in the labor contract were not open to discussion. As America's loss of strength in international competition was becoming painfully apparent to leaders of management and labor, in case after case they got together to set up new structures and processes of participation transcending the limitations of scope and organizational level that prevailed throughout the 1970s.

An effective participatory program does not automatically spread from one company to another or even from one plant to other plants in the same organization. In the Xerox case, we followed some steps in the diffusion process among the major production plants in Webster, New York; and in Chapter 11 on the new manufacturing organization we focused on the emerging framework into which participatory processes must fit. Here let us focus on interorganizational learning as it facilitates the diffusion of participatory structures and processes.

In the United States participatory processes increasingly have the stated support of top management, but usually this involves just the authorization for local plant management to develop something along this line. Top executives of leading companies have not given much attention to the problem of diffusing participatory processes within their own companies and have taken no steps to stimulate development of a national program to support the diffusion of participatory structures and processes.

The diffusion challenge has been taken up by not-for-profit associations and institutes. As the leaders of these organizations have not agreed on the best practices that should be promoted, the field has been taken over largely by competition among private consultants and their firms.

Does this mean that the United States is at a disadvantage in competition with Japan in the diffusion of participative systems? If we consider only the extent of diffusion across all companies, then the disadvantage is clear and obvious. If we make the comparison in terms of standardization versus variation and organizational creativity, then the answer is not so clear-cut. By 1990 most American firms that had initiated quality circles had abandoned that model and were seeking to develop their own model.

If we limit our comparison to unionized firms—the only types that I feel confident in judging—then we should recognize two major differences between Japan and the United States. First, American firms generally develop participatory systems jointly managed by union and management. In Japan the systems are entirely management driven. Second, Japanese QCCs focus their attention almost exclusively on shop-floor problems. America's most advanced systems involve the union and workers in decision making on strategic business problems. For example, for Japan we have encountered nothing comparable to Xerox's cost study teams, with their penetration into traditional management domains of cost accounting systems and decisions regarding outsourcing products versus maintaining production within the firm.

The comparison may be made in terms of tentative generalizations regarding the national and organizational cultures of the two nations. The Japanese tend to be more effective in communicating and initiating action up and down the organizational hierarchy than are Americans, but this pattern is shaped by the hierarchy and strongly channeled within it. Americans tend to be more freewheeling in creating structures and processes that escape the boundaries of hierarchical levels and bring together for discussion and action organizational members at the bottom and at the top of the hierarchy in a particular factory. This freewheeling can lead to structures and processes that yield disappointing results, but these days such outcomes do not generally lead companies to abandon a commitment to participation. Rather, they lead labor and management to change a system that is not working in order to solve its particular problems, or to invent or adapt a new system. American organizational culture thus seems to offer more scope for creativity and flexibility in the development of participatory systems.

This comparison should not be interpreted to mean that the Japanese are simply not creative in devising new organizational systems. Americans have learned methods of just-in-time manufacturing and total quality control primarily from the Japanese. In participatory systems also, the Japanese must be credited with the breakthrough of first involving workers on a large scale in decision making on shop-floor problems. Having done that, however, and having developed a participatory system that seems to work well for them, the Japanese have concentrated on standardizing and diffusing that system rather than on searching for new and better participatory systems.

It would be pointless to argue which nation has the better participatory systems. The Japanese system works exceedingly well for Japan. In the United States some of the more advanced systems work spectacularly well, but the spread of participatory systems in industry is not nearly so extensive as in Japan. How best to build on organizational creativity to diffuse this type of organizational learning more widely and rapidly is the challenge we now address.

Consultants have been playing both positive and negative roles in diffusing participatory systems. We see the negative side among consultants who seek to sell to industry their standard package program, without being skillful or interested enough to help labor and management to develop a system that is well adapted to a particular organizational culture. We also note cases where a consultant helps the firm to establish a system that appears to work well and yet fails to help organizational members to develop the skills and understanding needed to maintain and strengthen that system. There have been many cases where a participatory system has disintegrated shortly after the consultant who installed it left the firm.

On the other hand, we have also noted cases where a consultant has worked with organizational members on a highly participative basis, helping them to devise and install their own system and also to gain the skill and understanding needed to maintain and strengthen it. As more consultants learn to do what we may call participative consulting, we may expect even greater contributions from consultants in the future.

The diffusion process is also supported by conferences and publications of agencies dedicated to this mission, such as the Association for Quality and Productivity, the annual meeting on the Ecology of Working Life, and conferences sponsored by the U.S. Department of Labor as well as the *Briefs* published by that department on outstanding cases.

My own experience suggests the importance of building interpersonal and interorganizational networks to stimulate and guide the exchange of information and ideas among practitioners in management and organized labor. I have been serving on the Academic Advisory Committee of the Work in America Institute, a not-for-profit organization supported (in 1990) by fifty companies, eighteen foundations, several unions (including the AFL-CIO), and government agencies. In addition to carrying out its own policy studies and publication program, Work in America organizes and manages several networks based on identifying outstanding cases of cooperative and participative programs. The plants where these programs are being carried out then become focal points for site visits and discussion between the visitors and the local management and union leaders.

Practitioners attending these site visits often report that they have returned home with ideas and information they want to try out in their own plants. Generally the visitors from a particular firm include union members as well as managers, so discussion of the practical back-home implications begins during the site visit and provides a strong impetus for participatory changes in their own plants.

As research director of Programs for Employment and Workplace Systems (PEWS) in Cornell University's New York State School of Industrial and Labor Relations (ILR), I have had the opportunity of observing at close range the New York State Network (but without any responsibility for that program). Founded in 1984 with annual funding by the state (increased in 1990) and supported equally by research and technical assistance contracts, PEW's mission is to help labor and management to maintain employment through improving the effectiveness of their organizations.

Since it was first organized by Donald Kane in 1988, the New York State Network has been concentrating on manufacturing organizations and has included membership from sixteen companies and seven unions, whose members participate in three meetings a year. While there is some change from meeting to meeting in those representing their organizations, there has been enough continuity so that members from different organizations have gotten to know each other rather well and often contact each other outside of the meetings to compare experiences.

The 1989-1990 series of meetings provided a most impressive demonstration of the power of such a network for the diffusion of ideas and information in our field. Here we follow organizational learning from Xerox and ACTWU to the Blank Company and the Blank union. (The company and its people are not identified because at this writing the parties are not yet ready to "go public" with their experience.)

For our purposes, the sequence of meetings began with one in which the Corning company and its union made the main case presentation. This was the first network meeting attended by John Torre, manager of one of the Blank Company plants. In a later discussion session, John Torre's presentation of his efforts to revitalize a failing plant gave the impression that his participation strategy involved seeking direct contacts with workers without any union involvement. Network members challenged him on this point and wanted to know why no local union officers had accompanied him to the meeting. Torre replied that he had suggested their participation, but relations had been so adversarial—three strikes in the last four contract negotiations, covering his plant and three neighboring Blank plants—that the union officers had been unwilling to risk going anywhere with management.

Responding to these network prods, before the next meeting Torre urged two of the stewards in his plant to attend. The union leaders advised against going, but said that the stewards were free to do so, and they did.

The next meeting featured a presentation of the Xerox-ACTWU case reported in part in this volume. Chief presenters were Dominick R. Argona, Xerox manager of organizational effectiveness, and Anthony J. Costanza, vice president of ACTWU (and previously general shop chairman for the Webster, New York, plants).

The February 1990 meeting was attended by a larger Blank union group, including the top local officers and the business agent in addition to the two stewards. The outside speaker on this occasion was Edward

Cohen-Rosenthal, who has worked particularly with unions and has strong union credentials. He particularly emphasized ways in which unions could work with management in advancing union objectives, and this seemed to reassure the Blank union people. As the meeting broke up, the Blank people got together and asked each other what to do next. They agreed to meet for further discussion back at the plant.

That network meeting was late in February 1990. It took them until mid-March to schedule their first joint meeting, but, after that, events moved rapidly. In that meeting, they agreed to establish a union-management committee to explore ways of working together. Recognizing the barriers posed by a history of conflict and mistrust, they also decided they needed an outside facilitator to guide subsequent discussions.

At the February network meeting, Sally Klingel of PEWS had consulted with the Blank union representatives about her project to develop training materials for union leaders on the new manufacturing organization. Union and management people now agreed to invite Klingel to play the role of facilitator. As she told us, because both John Torre and the union business agent were highly articulate people, one of her main tasks was to hold them in check so that the two top people did not dominate discussions. (In the June network meeting, both union and management speakers credited Klingel with playing the essential role of keeping them "on the track" in working out an effective relationship.)

In the meeting featuring the Xerox-ACTWU case, the Blank union stewards had been particularly impressed with the social invention of the cost study team (CST). They had been concerned about products that the company had recently outsourced and about imminent future outsourcing. They persuaded their local officers to set up their own adaptation of the CST idea, which they call the Keep the Work Here Committee.

At the suggestion of Sally Klingel, PEWS invited the Blank union and management people to make the featured case presentation. They accepted and prepared very seriously for this event. Such a joint presentation was a new experience for both parties and also a difficult and complicated assignment. They were allotted an hour for the presentation, to be followed by an extended discussion period. That meant dividing the time between union and management as well as determining who would present what for each party.

At the June meeting, Torre began the presentation. In reviewing the plant's problems, he avoided pinning any blame on the union and acknowledged management's deficiencies. At one point he said, "We did a lot of communicating, but we didn't really listen." His personnel manager reported that he had had a staff job in this plant earlier and was happy to get away from it. When he was to be reassigned there, he tried to avoid it, but now he was clearly enthusiastic about the joint program.

The leaders for the union in this plant led off for their group. They stressed hostile feelings and mistrust that had prevailed in labor relations and said that union officers in the other plants had advised them against getting involved with management and PEWS. Still, they acknowledged that fighting was not solving their problems, so they were willing to try a new approach—but still very tentatively.

They then turned over the presentation to the two stewards who had initiated and led the Keep the Work Here Committee. As I learned later, in a formal sense this had been exclusively a union operation, but informally management had participated in providing facts and figures as requested and in providing technical assistance on cost accounting and engineering.

The stewards described eight cases in which success meant bringing back outsourced products or avoiding outsourcing that management had earlier planned. For each case, they provided figures for dollars saved and also made clear the impact these projects had on job security. The figures were truly impressive, and these gains had been achieved between mid-March and the end of May in a program launched out of a history of conflict and mistrust.

Having followed the Xerox-ACTWU case closely over several years, I could have told the Blank people the basic substance of that story. But I would not have had the credibility with the practitioners that the principal actors in that case had. Furthermore, I would not have been able to answer many of the questions the Blank people wanted to ask about what Xerox and ACTWU people had learned from their own experience.

My experience with these three network meetings reinforced my conviction that there are better ways to diffuse the knowledge gained from such cases than having the professor report his conclusions and recommendations to the practitioners. In the final chapter of this book I will extend this discussion of better ways.

PART III

Theoretical Foundations

14. Why and How Do Participatory Practices Work?

How do participatory processes and structures work? And why do they work? For my purposes, "work" means increasing both organizational productivity and member commitment to the organization.

The "why" question involves motivation, which will be discussed in the next chapter. The "how" question involves explaining the impact of participation. Basically, when participatory systems work well, they produce results because they apply to problems a much wider range of information and ideas than are involved in decision making in more conventional organizations. It is often said that those who know most about any job are those who are performing that job. Participatory systems work through integrating this experiential expertise with formal and scientific knowledge. In industry and agriculture, how can that be done?

I have given a preliminary answer to that question in the preceding chapters, and I will summarize my conclusions later in Chapter 20, "Theory and Practice in Agriculture and Industry." I have also noted that for industry the research literature shows generally a correlation between participation and members' favorable attitudes toward their work situation but shows no consistent pattern regarding the relationship between participation and productivity. I have then argued that the latter finding can be attributed to misguided research designs and problems with defining and measuring productivity.

Those seeking to arrive at global conclusions regarding the participation-productivity relationship have thrown together cases ranging from small-group laboratory experiments to large-scale field projects, without regard to differences in technology, tasks, formal structures, or the actual nature of participatory processes. The general tendency has been simply to ask organization members whether they *feel* they have been participating in decision making and then try to correlate their responses against changes (if any) in productivity following the introduction of activities that were intended to be participatory. Why should anyone believe that, under all circumstances, any form of participation structured in any way and implemented skillfully or incompetently should yield gains in productivity? I prefer to assume that in some cases participation works and in some cases it does not, which poses the research problem of discovering the differences between successes and failures. In this book I have discussed a number of cases in which participation has clearly worked, and furthermore I have traced the organizational learning processes that have made it work.

In industry, the definitional and measurement problems arise out of the common tendency to measure productivity in terms of the output only of those directly engaged in producing the product. In many cases, where direct labor accounts for less than ten percent of total product cost, it is irrational to assess productivity solely in terms of direct labor.

Related to this problem is a general failure to distinguish between two different forms of participation in decision making (noted in Chapter 1) which I call *decision freedom* and *upward initiation of action.*

Decision freedom is observed when low-ranking people are free to make certain decisions about how to do their work, without having to secure the approval of their superiors. This condition is often observed where management establishes or encourages the development of semi-autonomous work groups. In agriculture, small farmers often—but not always—have such freedom. Sharecroppers may have some of their decisions controlled by their landlord. As we have seen in the DIGESA case, extension policies that control access to inputs the farmer needs can sharply reduce this freedom.

Upward initiation of action occurs when workers make complaints or suggestions or otherwise propose changes and management responds favorably to such worker initiatives.

The relationship between the definitional and the measurement problems can be seen if we note one major effect of the introduction of semiautonomous work groups. Where workers are free to make many decisions previously reserved to supervisors, fewer supervisors are needed. In fact, we have noted in American industry a widespread shift in ratios between workers and first-line supervisors; a plant that just a few years ago had one supervisor for every 15 to 20 workers may now have a 1 to 50 ratio, and we have even seen ratios beyond 1 to 100. In such a situation, a shift to decision freedom participation can reduce total company costs substantially without this change necessarily being reflected in the physical output of direct labor. Therefore, I argue that it is more realistic (and scientific) to relate changes in worker participation to changes in *total factor productivity* rather than to changes in the physical output of production workers.

Chapters 15 through 19 aim to provide the theoretical foundations for enhanced member motivation and increased organizational commitment. I summarize my answers to the "how" question in Chapter 20.

Both these questions must be answered if we are to understand the potential effects of participation. Highly motivated but incompetent members cannot be expected to perform well, and the same conclusion holds for highly competent but unmotivated members. Competent and highly motivated members can still fail to improve organizational performance if they work in an organization that does not provide supporting structures and social processes.

15. Motivation in a Socioeconomic Context

In this chapter, I focus on motivation in a socioeconomic context, imbedded in structures of interpersonal relations and involving costs and benefits. In this approach I use two theoretical frameworks, that seem to me seriously flawed but offer useful bases on which to build a better theory. The two frameworks are B.F. Skinner's theory of operant conditioning and the economic man concept underlying orthodox economic theory.

Skinner (1971) claimed that future attitudes and behaviors are shaped by the consequences of past actions. Favorable outcomes provide positive reinforcement to the behaviors that led to them and increase the likelihood of similar behavior occurring in the future. Unfavorable outcomes provide negative reinforcement, decreasing the likelihood of similar behavior occurring in the future. Furthermore, Skinner argues that positive reinforcement is more effective in shaping behavior than negative reinforcement—in other words, that it is more effective to induce actions through potential rewards than to penalize people for actions one wishes to prevent.

To put Skinner's framework in commonsense terms, which we will use hereafter, he is focusing on the impact of rewards or penalties on future actions. That rewards and penalties do have impacts on behavior is undeniable, but we need to go beyond that simple proposition to build a useful theory for human beings.

The economic man concept is similar to Skinnerian theory in its focus on rewards and penalties but differs in two respects. Economists focus primarily on material rewards and penalties, generally expressed in monetary terms in industrial societies. Economists assume that, in reaching decisions, insofar as he has access to relevant information, man estimates the potential costs and benefits of various alternatives, and selects the option that promises to be most materially advantageous to him. (Those propounding this doctrine were not concerned over its sexist implications and so did not consider using "economic man/woman" or "economic person." To avoid confusion, we will retain the wording established in the literature many generations ago.) Whereas the economic man concept focuses on calculation of future consequences, Skinner is not concerned with what goes on inside people's heads as they decide to act. He considers these mental processes scientifically unknowable and therefore not worth studying. He is only concerned with establishing the impact of contingencies (outcomes of past actions) on future actions.

Economists recognize that humans are not motivated exclusively by anticipation of material rewards or penalties, yet the importance of economic incentives cannot be denied, particularly as we study organizations in which people work for a living. Our aim therefore is not to discard economic man but rather to build on him toward a socioeconomic man framework.

Before building a better theory, let us explore further the deficiencies in the two frameworks on which we intend to build, beginning with Skinner (for a more comprehensive critique of Skinnerian theory, see Whyte, 1972).

What I call the "one body problem" is one of Skinner's principal weaknesses. In his classic experiments with pigeons, Skinner is unconcerned with his relations with the pigeons. He directs us to focus exclusively on the behavior of the pigeon, how the pigeon first pecks at random until it happens upon a spot that releases a pellet of corn. Eventually the pigeon becomes conditioned to the linkage between the spot pecked and the appearance of the corn so that the random pecking is eliminated.

To apply these findings to humans, we have to recognize not only that humans are smarter than pigeons but also that most of the rewards and penalties experienced by humans are generated in interaction with other humans. Thus the reward or penalty rarely appears in pure form but rather linked with other individuals, groups, or organizations that shape such contingencies. The meaning of the reward or penalty must therefore be interpreted in a social framework.

FOCUSING ON INTERACTIONS

The search for such a framework took me back to where I came in, theoretically speaking, with the interaction framework, developed in the 1930s by anthropologists Eliot D. Chapple and Conrad Arensberg (Chapple, with Arensberg, 1940; Chapple and Coon, 1942). The interaction framework directs our attention to the observation of interpersonal relations: the frequency and duration of the interactions among persons A, B, C . . . N and the pattern of the initiation of changes in activities.

Years ago one professor expressed surprise that "Bill Whyte has managed to get so far with such a simpleminded set of ideas." While I have increasingly recognized the insufficiency of these initial ideas, I was nevertheless operating with some powerful tools that were then, as now, generally neglected by my more sophisticated colleagues.

Sticking largely to this interactional focus, I was able to chart the organizational structure of informal street corner gangs and show the relation between this structure and the athletic performance and mental health of members of these groups (Whyte, 1943).

BEYOND INTERACTIONS

I recognized the insufficiency of the interaction framework in 1950 when I was at Bethel, Maine—the Mecca for converts to the gospel of group dynamics. Building on the interaction framework, George Homans had proposed a relationship between interaction and interpersonal sentiments: Up to some point, the more frequently that Person and Other interact, the greater their liking for each other will be (Homans, 1950). After observing for two hours a day for two weeks a twenty-person group whose interactions were associated with growing tensions and hostilities, I found it necessary to reformulate the Homans proposition as follows: Up to some point, the more frequently persons interact with each other, the more intense their personal feelings will become. I can illustrate what I mean by intensity by pointing out that, during the course of these two weeks, even when the total group was not in session and members were conversing in twos and threes, everybody seemed compelled to focus attention on what was happening in the group, and we all seemed completely oblivious to the Korean War, which was getting underway. In positing a correlation between interactions and intensity of sentiments, I left open the question of whether those sentiments would be positive or negative. It occurred to me that frequency of interaction will be positively correlated with favorable interpersonal sentiments more often than not simply because, whenever people are free to do so, they tend to terminate interactions with people they come to dislike. This was not permitted at Bethel; you could push your chair back from the table (and some people did sometimes) but you were not allowed to leave the room. Similarly, workers in an organization generally find that they have to interact with certain other individuals in order to get the job done, whether they like it or not.

In order to go beyond the interaction-intensity relationship and predict positive or negative sentiments, some additional element had to be added to the equation. I found myself grasping for notions of rewards and penalties or psychological reinforcements.

It was years later before I came to recognize the second important gap in the interaction framework. It worked exceedingly well with street corner gangs, where the group was an end in itself and the activities of the group consisted primarily of trying to make life more exciting and interesting for each other. For such a social group, there are no tasks that have to be systematically performed, in standardized ways, leading to some required output. I was dealing with a pure social system. When we move into the study of a work organization, we necessarily have to deal with a socio-technical system.

Parts I and II of this volume illustrate a socio-technical approach to the analysis of organizational behavior. In Chapters 16 and 17, I present my way of linking motivation and interaction through the delineation of types of transactional relationships.

Before building further on Skinner, let us examine what I see as the other weaknesses of his framework.

EXTENDING THE SKINNER CRITIQUE

Here I focus first on *the cost-benefit ratio and the social comparison process*. Laboratory experimenters, from Pavlov with his dogs to Skinner with his pigeons, could disregard the costs of the action to the actor, for they were trifling compared to what the animal received through its action. That is not generally the case with humans. The important rewards a person seeks usually involve substantial effort.

We must also consider the costs to the other party in the interpersonal relationship: the one who controls the rewards. Here we must consider not only the magnitude of the rewards offered but also how their distribution is managed. I explored such questions in greater detail in *Money and Motivation* (Whyte, 1955).

In general, we assume that workers will produce more if rewards are linked to their output, but establishing this direct linkage to the individual worker poses serious practical problems. Individual piece-rate systems depend on time and motion studies or other administrative measures to determine a baseline beyond which incentive rates will be paid. In unionized situations, the alleged unfairness of such rates is likely to produce a large volume of grievances and to increase friction and distrust between labor and management. Even in nonunion situations, workers find ways of resisting management through restricting output so as not to tempt management to change job methods or to justify restudies of the job and a cut in the rate.

Piece-rate systems also generate problems of perceived inequities. Skilled maintenance workers, whose output cannot be directly measured, will protest when they find that semiskilled production workers are being paid more than they receive, and union leaders will press for substantial pay increases for skilled workers.

To some extent, management can solve these social comparison problems by raising the compensation of the agrieved parties, but this tactic may simply shift the locus of protest to other groups of workers who now see themselves as disadvantaged. Also, of course, buying labor peace through yielding to all claims of inequities can be so expensive as to jeopardize the existence of the plant or company.

We must also consider what I call *time lag and trust*. In operant conditioning experiments, the animal gets the reward immediately after a given action. Few of a person's actions generate immediate rewards. In work life, there is often a lag of days or months between actions and rewards. Persons therefore must assess the probability of receiving promised rewards in the context of their experience with those offering the rewards. If they feel they have been cheated in the past by those offering the rewards, then they will not believe promises of future rewards.

Time lag is also important in a related context: the nature of the reward offered in relation to the *personal objectives* of the person offering that reward. In the pigeon and dog experiments, rewards were not only immediate but also concrete. The rewards offered humans are often presented in symbolic terms, in the words stated or written by those controlling the rewards. Persons must therefore judge from symbols the nature of the rewards being promised. People do not make these judgments in a mental vacuum. Through their social and intellectual experience, they develop *cognitive maps,* ways of viewing the world around them, which shape how they interpret and respond to potential rewards. Their responses are also influenced by the culture of the organization and of the society in which they work and live.

A focus on personal objectives leads us to another weakness of the Skinner framework. In Skinnerian terms, persons are treated as passive subjects, responding to the reinforcements derived from past actions. From that stance, it is impossible to explain how it is that many individuals remain committed to certain objectives over a long period of time during which they receive little or no rewards and encounter many frustrations.

To explain such commitment, we have to make two assumptions: that humans are not simply passive subjects but rather active agents, and that they become especially strongly committed to the objectives they set for themselves—or at least play an active role in setting. It is one of the great strengths of an effectively organized participation program that it allows and even encourages organization members to play active roles in determining their own objectives. In contrasting authoritarian and participatory organizations, Richard Walton (1985) writes of the shift from control to commitment in the workplace. Experienced organizational consultants and internal facilitators stress the importance of the *ownership of ideas.* Regarding potential organizational change, members are more likely to respond to ideas for which they have some sense of ownership. And that sense is more likely to arise for ideas they have had some part in developing than for ideas imposed on them.

CRITIQUE OF ECONOMIC MAN

In *The Moral Dimension,* Etzioni (1988) makes a powerful argument to demonstrate the limitations of economic factors in influencing behavior, but he does not go on to discuss other limitations of mainstream economics that seem to me equally important.

Economics was initially built out of a study of markets, where individuals or organizations are actively engaged in buying and selling and where some of the main costs and benefits involved are immediately observable. In organizations and communities, few economic incentives or disincentives have as immediate and direct an effect as they do in the market. They have to be interpreted in a social and organizational structural context.

One of the most serious limitations of orthodox economics is its failure to distinguish the economic interests of the firm from the economic interests of the individuals who make or influence decisions. In legal theory and in our courts, the corporation is treated as if it were an individual. Economists tend to treat this legal fiction as if it were a fact.

To be sure, decision makers argue that their actions are shaped solely by their concern for the economic welfare of the firm. Thus the chief executive officer who persuades his board of directors to provide him with millions of dollars deferred compensation as a "golden parachute" in case of a hostile takeover will argue that such financial security enables him to perform more effectively for the company, but do we really believe that is what motivates him?

Consider also the popular practice of "taking the company private." A group within top management arranges to borrow enormous sums from a bank to finance their purchase of their company's stock and thus take it off the public market. As the price paid may be 50 to 100 percent higher than the current market price, the private company emerges from the transaction with an enormous debt that may have negative consequences for its future performance. Nevertheless, unless the company later goes bankrupt, the organizers of the transaction are likely to gain large financial benefits. It may be more to their advantage to hold large pieces of a struggling company than to hold much smaller pieces of a more profitable company.

For economists to go beyond the world of legal fiction and deal with realities in the economics of the firm, we need intensive studies of actual cases in which key decision makers make decisions ostensibly in the interests of the company but also involving their own personal interests.

Another deficiency in economics is its failure to integrate industrial accounting into economic analysis. Researchers have recently been concerned about the way practitioners in industry use accounting formulas to assess the levels of profit and loss among their various products and models and, on the basis of the accounting figures, make decisions to phase out or expand production. In a modern factory making several products, what is assumed to be the cost of each product depends to a very large extent on the way *indirect* costs are allocated—and that is determined by the accounting system in use.

Customary methods of allocating indirect costs to products can cause enormous distortions of economic realities, leading companies to abandon products that are profitable while continuing to produce those that lose money. A growing research literature points to the urgent need to reform accounting methods to bring them more in line with economic realities (see particularly Cooper and Kaplan, 1989). If economists really wish to study decision making in industry, they need first to develop a sophisticated understanding of the problems and potentialities of industrial accounting.

In agriculture as well as in industry, we have to place economic rewards and penalties in a context of how they are *socially structured.* I illustrate this point from field studies in Latin America (Whyte and Williams, 1968).

We have found that different types of change projects have different social requirements and different consequences in the distribution of costs and benefits. We have described four distinct types, as follows:

Individual direct. The individual farmer bears all of the costs and gains all of the benefits, as when he tries out new seeds, fertilizer, and so on. His costs and benefits are not affected by what others may do—except in the extreme case where a large number of farmers may adopt a high-yielding variety at the same time and thus flood the market so that no individual profits from the innovation.

Individual through group, with equitable sharing of costs and benefits. Here the project cannot be carried out without the collective labor of others who are to benefit from it, and the success of the project may depend on the ability of its organizers to achieve perceived equity in the distribution of costs and benefits.

Unequal distribution of costs and benefits. In such a project, regardless of the skill of the change agent, some people are bound to gain more than others or some may gain whereas others actually lose.

Controlling individual interests in favor of group interests. If the community as a whole is to benefit, individual members must be restrained from doing what might otherwise be rewarding to them and their families. Such cases are often found in the field of animal husbandry, when the community faces problems of overgrazing with a need to reduce the size of the herd and increase the food consumption efficiency of the animals through introducing superior stock. Here the community as a whole stands to benefit from the project, but it is to the advantage of each individual family to keep as many animals on the range as possible.

If potential projects are analyzed in socio-technical and economic terms, it becomes obvious that each type of project poses a different set of organizational problems and therefore requires a different organizational strategy.

For theory and for practice, it is fruitless to debate whether or not economic rewards or penalties influence behavior. Obviously they do, but we need to determine how and through what social channels these influences operate.

16. Costs and Benefits in Elementary Transactional Relationships

To realize that motivation must be analyzed within a socioeconomic framework provides us with a general orientation yet leads us into a wide and complex field of analysis. To go beyond this point, it would be helpful to utilize concepts that enable us to link together human interaction and motivation in observable behavior. I presented such a framework earlier (Whyte, 1969) and summarize it here.

The framework can best be understood as applied to interpersonal or to intergroup relations—the relations between A and B, between two groups or two organizations such as the union and management. Each type represents a distinctive combination of human relations with rewards and penalties.

This is a typology of what I call *transactional relationships*. This chapter is limited to discussion of what I call elementary types because each one can occur by itself, although each one can occur in association with other elementary types or with one of the complex types. The complex types can only be observed in association with one or more other types.

After defining each elementary or complex type, I go on to a general assessment of the potential costs and benefits that each party to the relationship might expect to experience.

I classify the elementary types as follows:

- Positive Exchange,
- Trading,
- Competition,
- Negative Exchange, and
- Open Conflict.

The complex types, discussed in the next chapter, are

- Authority,
- Joint Payoff, and
- Resource Allocation/Conflict Resolution.

In my framework, rewards and penalties are motivators toward actions; costs and benefits involve the assessment—by a researcher or by the parties involved themselves—of the results of the actions. We are asking whether the parties are likely to be satisfied with the benefits received in relation to the costs expended. In most cases, the costs incurred and the benefits received cannot be fully measured in monetary terms; yet the actors do make judgments of what they consider favorable or unfavorable outcomes, and those judgments affect future behavior.

POSITIVE EXCHANGE

What is now called exchange theory had its inception many years ago in the publication of *The Gift* by French social anthropologist Marcel Mauss (1954). The contributions of Alvin Gouldner (1960), George C. Homans (1961), and Peter Blau (1955) have brought the analysis of interpersonal reciprocities to the forefront of behavioral science theorizing.

There are four fundamental characteristics to what I call Positive Exchange:

Alternative form. A and B do not act out both sides of the relationship simultaneously. A does a favor for B and, at a later time, B does a favor for A.

Implicit weighing of values. Both parties understand the importance of the favors given or received and the obligations acquired or discharged in the exchange, but they do not talk openly about the magnitude of the favors being exchanged or the obligations involved. That is, if we observe A and B openly discussing whether each one has met his obligations in the positive exchange relationship, this is a good indicator of serious deterioration in the interpersonal relationship (Whyte, 1943).

Direct reinforcement. In positive exchange, A is rewarded by B, and B is rewarded by A, directly. This is in contrast to what I call the Joint Payoff relationship, in which A and B (and possibly others) carry out certain activities jointly and receive extrinsic rewards from others who are not engaged in producing the activities. That is, A and B may gain intrinsic satisfactions from working together, but the extrinsic rewards are extracted from the environment.

Balance or imbalance in exchange. There are two distinct subtypes of the Positive Exchange relationship.

(1) Unbalanced exchange: A does more for B than B is able to do for A in the same terms. B thereby becomes obligated to A. B discharges this obligation by doing what A wants him to do.
(2) Balanced exchange: A does a favor for B, and B reciprocates with a similar favor of approximately equal value.

Costs and Benefits

To assess costs and benefits to the two parties involved and to their organization(s), we need to separate unbalanced from balanced Positive Exchange. We consider first the unbalanced form.

In this form, the transactional relation can serve usefully in establishing patterns of informal leadership in organizations. In his classic study of *The Dynamics of Bureaucracy,* Peter Blau (1955) showed how the more expert agency officials did favors for the less expert by advising them how to handle difficult cases. As the more expert did not turn to the less expert for advice, the unbalanced exchange established the more expert officials as leaders in group activities.

Frequent occurrence of unbalanced Positive Exchange relations between the same two parties tends to build a dominance-dependency relationship. Blau notes that the less expert agents limited the frequency of their requests for advice so as not to accentuate their dependency, and the more expert did not encourage these calls for advice so as to have more time to do their own work.

In political organizations, these informal restraints are not likely to be so strong. A major way in which political leaders build up their power is through doing favors for constituents that the voters can only pay back through voting for the leader and doing what he asks to support his campaign. (If the constituent offers to trade money for what the politician does for him, this act—commonly called bribery—is not Positive Exchange but rather Trading.)

Important as it is for politicians to do favors for constituents, the gains to be achieved through such actions are not unlimited. For the politician, the time, energy, and resources available tend always to run short of the demands for favors from organization members and constituents. He is plagued by the citizen who claims, "You ain't done nothing for me lately." There are always more votes needed than there are favors to be given out by the leader and his lieutenants, so the leader must contend with charges that the distribution is inequitable—as well as with the attacks of outsiders who question the morality of the patronage system.

It is only in rare cases that there appears to be no limit to the potential of positive exchange for acquiring and maintaining power. Kuwait, for example, has a small population in relation to enormous reserves of oil. As long as the oil lasts, the ruling family has well nigh unlimited possibilities to control the population through an unbalanced exchange relationship. Loss of power would be much more likely to occur through factional rivalries within the ruling family or an international conflict than through the breakdown of the exchange relationship.

In industry or business, establishing a dominance-dependency relationship through heavy reliance on unbalanced Positive Exchange is likely to work against operational efficiency and the ability of the firm to expand.

This is a common problem in developing countries. When the level of interpersonal trust is low, the entrepreneur is likely to limit his associates in a business or industrial venture to a few close friends and relatives. If the business expands substantially, the entrepreneur soon runs out of close friends and relatives to put into the new positions. We are then likely to observe a split between the few key members of management in whom the entrepreneur has confidence and those others who do not have his confidence and therefore must be closely watched. The owner may find that he is putting so much time and energy into controlling those he does not trust that the essential tasks of operating the company are not adequately performed. The crisis may come even before the entrepreneur has run out of close friends and relatives to put in key management positions. Some who come to these positions through having discharged their obligations satisfactorily in past Positive Exchange with the owner may simply not have the talent or the motivation to perform adequately those tasks on which the success of the firm depends. The firm may then run into such difficulties that it is no longer able to extract from the environment the resources necessary even to maintain the preexisting network of Positive Exchange relationships among relatives and friends.

Balanced Positive Exchange does not support development of dominance-dependency relations. It can strengthen social solidarity—an important contribution—yet it does have inherent limitations.

The burden of reciprocity was brought home to me when I was a member of the Rotary Club in the village of Trumansburg. We met for dinner every Thursday evening at 6:15. From about 5:30 on, the members would gather for drinks at the bar of Gregory's Restaurant. From time to time, I felt that I would enjoy a drink before dinner, but I rarely feel like two drinks before dinner.

So as to allow time for a drink, I tried arriving at about six o'clock. The bar then would be rather fully occupied, so that it would take me some time to make my way through the crowd and reach a point where I could get the bartender's attention. By this time, the bartender was already pouring my drink—courtesy of a fellow member. I considered this a heartwarming gesture at first, but as weeks went by and I found myself sponging on my friends, I became increasingly uncomfortable.

At first I tried to sneak up to the bar unnoticed so that I could buy my drink before somebody bought it for me. Since I was the tallest man in the club, it was difficult for me to elbow my way through the crowd without having someone notice me and beat me to the order.

I then decided that I would have to invest more time in the pre-dinner ceremonies, arriving early, before the bar was fully occupied. I would then keep watch for the arrival of one of the several men to whom I was indebted for past drinks. As soon as he came through the door, I would call out the order for his customary drink.

That stratagem did not work either. Since I was now starting the ritual earlier, my friend and I would finish our drinks still fifteen to twenty minutes before the dinner gong. At this point, my friend would bang his empty glass down on the bar and order another round of drinks—one for himself and one for me. In this way, reciprocity was achieved. But I ended up having to drink (and pay for) two drinks, when I would have been much happier if I could have limited my before-dinner drinking to one.

I solved the problem only when I moved to Ithaca and left Gregory's bar and the Rotary behind me.

While this may seem a trivial case, it nevertheless illustrates a very common problem that tends to arise with Positive Exchange. Under certain circumstances, the maintenance of reciprocity can become a real burden to at least one of the participants. In such situations, he comes to feel that he is not "breaking even" with the transaction and would prefer to avoid it altogether.

Positive Exchange also has the disadvantage of inflexibility. Once the relationship is established, there is just no way of terminating it without embarrassment—unless the parties to the exchange become physically separated so that both recognize the impracticality of continuing the relationship. While there are individual differences in this regard, there is a limit to the number of Positive Exchange relationships that an individual can maintain. Let us assume that A has such relationships with B, C, and D. He finds himself enjoying his relationship with B less as time goes by, and he enters into Positive Exchange relationships with E and F. As these new relationships develop, A finds that he no longer has the time and energy to maintain the relationship with B. He therefore on some occasion fails to reciprocate, and the relationship with B deteriorates. A feels uncomfortable and B feels resentful.

This sort of problem typically arises in cases of social mobility. Such social mobility involves not only getting a better job, moving into a better house, and buying a better car; it also involves associating with new friends and reducing one's interactions with old friends who have not similarly risen in the social structure. The mobile individual often feels uneasy because he does not like to think of himself as disloyal to his old friends, but, if he is to fit into the new social circle at the status level he is reaching, he simply cannot maintain past relationships.

Those former friends who are left behind say to each other that Joe used to be a really good fellow until he got to be too "high hat" for them—or express their resentment in more colorful terms. Joe can avoid this only if he leaves the community.

TRADING

This type appears in several forms. In primitive or peasant situations, the transaction can be carried out on a barter basis, one type of goods being exchanged for another. In our society, trading usually involves the transfer of goods or services for money. Within a business organization, money can be involved in an accounting sense, credits or debits being transferred from one unit to another. Trading does not need to be limited to transactions involving money or other concrete resources. Services may be performed by the parties for each other without resources being transferred.

Trading is like Positive Exchange in that the receivers of the acts anticipate plus values. It differs in three respects:

(1) This type of transaction is simultaneous in temporal form instead of alternating. That is, the parties arrive at the same time at an agreement as to what each is to do for the other or give to the other, although the actual performance of the services or transfer of the resources may take place at different times in the future.

(2) The values to be transferred are stated explicitly, at least in major part. That is, while the parties presumably make no attempt to discuss the intrinsic satisfactions they are going to get out of the transaction, they do make explicit the extrinsic values that are to be transferred.

(3) In Trading, the values that are transferred are always different. That is, in Trading, A may agree to give B $200 for a typewriter, but A does not agree to give B $200 in order to have B give him $200. While Positive Exchange sometimes involves transfers of different types of values, Positive Exchange often involves the passing back and forth of the same type of value: A gives a gift to B and B later reciprocates by giving a gift of similar value to A; A buys a drink for B and later B buys a drink for A.

Trading is, of course, one of the main ways in which surpluses are brought into the organization. On the assumption that both value more highly what they get than what they give, the transaction produces a surplus (or profit) to each of them.

Trading often occurs within an organization, particularly among individuals responsible for tasks that are at least in part interdependent and where none of the participants has the power to give orders to the others.

Leonard Sayles (1964:61) describes these transactions in the following way:

> In effect, there is a wide variety of "terms of trade" to negotiate: what, when, how, and for how much the work will be performed. Often there are efforts by "buyers" to improve the terms once they are negotiated, e.g., by asking for a few "extras" or an earlier completion date. The buyer not only supplies a budget or an approved activity (which will justify the existence of the seller), but he may also be called upon to supply waiting time, special manpower, tools, space, even good contacts with supply sources of one kind or another, or special informal favors in the area of organization politics. All are analogous to a market place.

In the buy-sell relationship, each side tries to improve its own position within the larger organization. For example, the manager of the selling unit recognizes that he raises the value of his unit to the company by being able to sell more, and that furthermore he can improve performance of his unit by concentrating on those items that the unit can produce especially well and at low cost. If he makes such gains, he can increase the satisfactions of members of his own unit.

The buyer also has an interest in negotiating the terms of trade. If she can get the needed item at lower cost, receive faster delivery, and get better quality, she can improve the performance of her own unit, improve the position of her unit in the company, and increase the satisfactions of unit members.

While both buyer and seller have something to gain from working together, the problem for the negotiators is to arrive at an agreement that will provide a reasonable balance of advantages and disadvantages to both parties.

Those who are skillful in developing these Trading relationships invest substantial time in preparing the way for their transactions. The manager needs to get around to gather information on potential buyers and sellers and what they need or have to offer. Such social circulation is also a means of spreading information about the capabilities and needs of his own unit. Sayles (1964:64-65) provides these illustrative statements from individuals successful in the buy-sell relationship:

> (A potential "seller"): I never miss a chance to go out to lunch with a department head who may be able to use our services. You've got to keep telling people what you can do for them if you expect to build up the reputation of your department and its activities.

> (A potential "buyer"): You can't rely on written memos or reports to keep up with what's going on in the company. Many times some group is working on something which could be very useful to you, if you knew about it. So whenever I have some free time, I wander around to keep current. Then when we have to farm out something or have some difficult problem, I know where to go and, just as important, *who* to go to, who can help us.

To predict the behavior accompanying Trading relationships, we need to distinguish between the balanced and unbalanced relationship between the parties. In the balanced relationship, both parties believe that they have roughly equal chances to gain or lose in the transaction, and they feel that they have equal freedom to withdraw from the transaction and to seek a different Trading partner. We do not have to measure to determine that the two parties actually are dealing on a basis of equality. It is what they perceive that is important, and it is not difficult to get people to tell us whether they see the relationship as balanced or unbalanced. Of course, we assume some correspondence between reality and perceptions of reality. If, in order to get what he wants, A has no alternative other than Trading with B, he is not likely to believe that he does have other alternatives.

In a balanced Trading relationship, we assume a continuing inclination of the parties to interact and, as interactions continue, a strengthening of favorable interpersonal sentiments—provided that the transactions yield the anticipated results.

The unbalanced Trading relationship occurs when one or both of the following two conditions are present:

> A can get what he wants from B, C, D, or E, etc., whereas B can get what he wants only from A.
> A does not want what he can get from B as much as B wants what he can get from A.

In the unbalanced relationship, the sentiments of the disadvantaged participant can only be predicted if we know to what extent the partner to the transaction is exploiting his or her monopolistic advantage. If A exploits this advantage to the full, as long as B has no alternative means of getting what he wants, he will continue Trading with A, but he will develop or maintain hostile sentiments toward A and limit his interactions and activities with A to those necessary for Trading. B will also be inclined to search for alternative Trading partners and other means of reducing the power differential between himself and A.

At the other extreme, let us say that A offers B terms that are close to what B could get if he had alternative Trading partners. B recognizes that A is acting more favorably toward him than is necessary. This behavior of A tends to generate favorable sentiments toward him by B. We may describe B as being "grateful" to A and speak of the general relationship between them as "paternalism." In this situation, B appears to be "loyal" to A, even though an observer might feel that A is not giving B nearly as much as he should.

Furthermore, B manifests this loyalty by refraining from doing what A does not want done and responding when A asks him to do something. The same point holds for Positive Exchange. As A does more for B than B can do for him in return, we say that B is under "obligations" to A, remains "loyal" to A, and is ready to respond when A asks him to do something.

Applying this analysis to rural development in Peru, I concluded that empowerment of downtrodden individuals depended in large measure on opening up *alternative* courses of action so that these people could make key decisions for themselves. As long as anyone or any organization exercised full control over the material and informational resources on which their progress depended, they would remain in an extremely dependent position. In that situation, economic gains could come to them only through what those holding power gave to them. In a desperately poor country, whatever its political ideology, no government can be expected to do much *for* the poor.

COMPETITION

This type resembles Negative Exchange and Open Conflict in that those involved are opposing forces but it differs because Competition always involves a third party who determines who has won or at least serves as referee or umpire regulating the competitive activity.

Interpersonal and intergroup competition can unleash powerful forces in social, economic, and political affairs. To assess the impact of competition on interpersonal sentiments and on the creation of surpluses or deficits, we must distinguish between *zero-sum* and *independent outcome,* with gradations in between. We illustrate with the following hypothetical cases:

Athletic contest. A (or team A) wins by defeating B (or team B).

High school examination competition. Prizes are offered to the members of a given high school class for those who make the best scores in an examination. B knows that if A wins first prize, B cannot win that prize. On the other hand, there is nothing that B can reasonably do to prevent A from winning—in contrast to the situation in type one. (Conceivably B could prevent A from winning by disabling A so that he would not be able to appear for the examination, but that would invite severe penalties on B).

Statewide or national examination. In this case, the members of our hypothetical high school class are competing with hundreds of thousands of other high school students in their state and perhaps the nation in a contest where, let us say, the top five percent of students may be rewarded. Here, for all practical purposes, the outcome for A is completely independent of the outcome for B. That is, if A makes it into the top five percent, his winning lowers the probability of B winning by such an infinitesimal amount that we can consider the two outcomes independent of each other, and they will be so considered by the participants.

The first type is generally known as zero-sum competition, meaning that if A wins, B necessarily loses, and vice versa. (Let us say that A gets +1 for winning and B gets −1 for losing.) If we go beyond simply noting who wins and who loses, however, we find that zero-sum does not always hold as perceived by the participants and their supporters. Let us say that team A is thought to be vastly superior to team B and team A does indeed win but by a narrow margin in a hard-fought and well-played game. In such a situation, it is often said that B has won a "moral victory." The closeness of the score does not necessarily detract from the prestige of team A or from the satisfaction of its members. In fact team members may gain in both prestige and satisfaction through having withstood an unexpectedly severe challenge.

The inverse is also true. There have been occasions when two profes-sional boxers have fought such a dull and sluggish fight that winner and loser both have been resoundingly booed by the spectators.

These illustrations indicate that, when we take perceptions and ex-pectations into account, even a clear win-lose contest may yield a total sum of values for the two parties that is either greater than or less than zero.

Subject to this qualification, we still must recognize that the three types of competitive relationships described above tend to yield quite different patterns of interactions, activities, and sentiments.

The first type is likely to generate hostile sentiments, as B recognizes that A is directly responsible for his defeat. In athletic contests, these hostile sentiments are supposed to be suppressed by "good sportsman-ship" but are often expressed openly. Such hostile sentiments tend also to spill over to the fans supporting the two teams. Some years ago an athletic contest between the national teams of Honduras and El Salvador precipitated "the soccer war," and more recently in Europe soccer matches between national teams have been followed by riots.

In the second type of situation, losers may be envious of winners and make derogatory remarks about them, but, as the winners have not taken any direct action against the losers, negative sentiments are not likely to be nearly as strong as in the first type of case. On the other hand, in the second type of case, we would not expect to find students helping each other in preparation for the examination because each one recog-nizes that the help he gives another can reduce his own chances of winning.

In the third type of case, we expect negative interpersonal sentiments to be at a minimum because no participant can unfavorably influence the outcome for another participant. In fact, if the participants get together to help each other in preparing for the examination, each one's chance of victory may be increased. We may even say that this type of situation lends itself to cooperation. If the prospective participants in the examination do not initiate collaborative efforts, the teacher should have little difficulty in stimulating them to work together.

Another case of competitive independence occurred in a research project carried out in the 1960s by Julio Cotler in the Peruvian high-lands. He was directing two three-man teams. They were working on the same problem in the same general geographical area but in two different communities, and they met only from time to time with Cotler in the city of Cuzco. In these reporting and discussion session, Cotler had the impression that members of each team were taking great pride in their own work and hoping to outperform the other team, and yet he observed no evidences of interteam hostility. In this situation, neither team had any way of adversely affecting the performance of the other nor did Cotler's judgment of good performance on the part of one team depend on his judgment that the other team had performed poorly.

In our studies of rural communities in Peru, we found a striking prevalence of Competitive relations of the zero-sum type. One study of rural development (Ritter, 1965) describes the situation in this way:

> The ambiguous and uncertain situation of communal lands from the legal point of view, on the other hand, and the fanatical devotion of the Indians to these lands they consider their own, give rise to interminable litigations that impoverish the villagers, holding back the development of the economy of the communities and supporting a steadily increasing number of lawyers. Thus it is said that in the last ten years the number of lawyers in Caraz has grown fivefold and in a village as small as Julí (pop. 3874), there are now thirty lawyers living off the litigation of the Indians. These court cases sometimes have their origin before the legal recognition of the indigenous community (by the Ministry of Labor and Indigenous Affairs). Thus the community of Ollantaytambo, Cuzco, has cases that have been in litigation more than forty-four years. We have paradoxical situations such as that of Recuayhuanca, district of Marcará, Ancash, one of the few communities that still has lands that are cultivated in common for the community. There the harvest of these communal lands is divided in the following manner: half to the lawyer, a quarter for the expenses of the *personero,* and a quarter divided among members of the community.

> The value of the lands in litigation generally represents only a very small fraction of the sums that are invested in these legal struggles. When the authorities of the community of Huaylas, Ancash, told us that they have been in litigation with a private citizen of the community since the official recognition of the community, the author expected to find this citizen a rich man. He was much surprised when he saw that the man's house was one of the poorest in the village and when the man himself declared that with the money he had invested in litigation over the years, he could have bought an *hacienda* near Lima. . . .

> These litigations appear to the observer like the endless competition of two villages in soccer. One year one village wins, the next year the other, in a contest that never ends. One court decides one way, other courts in another way, but the consequences are more serious than those of athletic contests, for they impoverish both contestants. (W. F. Whyte, translator; in Whyte and Williams, 1968:9-11)

While recognizing the destructive effects of this kind of competition, we must nevertheless note that it can have very powerful motivational effects on the participants, who put everything into the contest. The development strategist who decides to abandon competition altogether may be hard pressed to find a substitute that will provide an equally strong motivational force. The problem is to devise activities that are both competitive and independent in outcome: competitive in that participants are stimulated by comparing their performance with the performance of rivals; independent in that the quality of performance of A (or team A) is not dependent on the quality of performance of B (or team B), and neither party can adversely affect the performance of the other.

NEGATIVE EXCHANGE

This is the inverse of Positive Exchange: The values involved are negative, but the form is alternating. A tries to do some damage to B and later B tries to do some damage to A. This is a very common type and tends to be explicitly recognized in conversation: We often hear one person saying that he needs to "get even" with another or to "pay him back."

While each exchange participant may tell his friends how and why he is going to do something negative to the other fellow, the values involved tend to remain *implicit* in verbal interaction between A and B. That is, if A tells B about the negative action he plans for him, B immediately takes steps to protect himself and/or to strike at A—in which case the transaction transforms itself into Open Conflict.

Negative Exchange, of course, tends to develop or maintain hostile sentiments between the transactional participants. I assume that this type of transaction tends to be unstable. Either the parties break off the relationship altogether or else the damage they impose on each other become explicitly recognized and the form shifts from alternating to simultaneous—in which case the hostilities have escalated to Open Conflict.

Negative Exchange is unlikely to bring the parties any direct benefits beyond the personal satisfaction of "getting even," and the costs in time, energy, and even money can be high.

OPEN CONFLICT

As in Negative Exchange, the values received by each party are negative; but in Open Conflict the temporal form is not alternating but rather simultaneous and continuing. While Negative Exchange appears to me an unstable type, there is nothing inherent in Open Conflict that tends to bring about its transformation. Experience indicates that this type of transaction can continue indefinitely.

On a group or organizational basis, this type represents strikes or physical conflicts between groups, communities, or nations. Much as the parties damage each other, every wound inflicted seems to intensify hostile sentiments that demand even stronger attacks on the enemy. Thus from union-management conflicts to the Vietnam War, we find the parties willing to suffer enormous costs that can hardly be matched by eventual material gains.

It may seem strange that we devote so little space here to a relationship as important as Open Conflict. The brevity of the discussion derives not from the unimportance of the type but from the lack of theoretical problems in relating Open Conflict to behavior and sentiments. We certainly need not go to any great lengths to explain why it is that, when two parties are in Open Conflict with each other, the continuation of the conflict strengthens hostile sentiments between them and reduces the likelihood that they will engage in activities designed to reward the other party. The difficult theoretical and practical problems arise when we try to determine how to terminate the Open Conflict relationship and shift the parties to other types of relationships.

It seems to me that the sociological debate on the relative values of cooperation and conflict has been confused by a failure to distinguish (1) immediate from long-run outcomes, and (2) acute from chronic conflicts.

While conflict does tend to strengthen social bonds within each party, conflict also generally involves the utilization of large resources for the sole purpose of defeating the enemy. In most cases, each party would be better off *materially* if it used those resources toward some more productive outcome. However, that generalization applies only to the immediate costs and benefits of the conflict. In some cases, a group or organization may find it impossible to reach its long-run objectives without first removing the enemy from the path toward those objectives.

In that case, if party A wins the conflict, then the long-run benefits for party A clearly outweigh the costs of engaging in the conflict.

We cannot assume that all conflicts come to a clear-cut ending. Some conflicts appear to go on forever. Active hostilities may cease from time to time, but the underlying issues remain unresolved, leading to renewed clashes. Such chronic conflicts clearly yield a net negative value balance for both parties, as each party does prevent the other from reaching its objectives and each pours resources endlessly into maintaining a stalemate.

Some level of conflict is a natural and healthy state of human affairs. It is both unrealistic and undesirable to attempt to eliminate all conflict from a group or organization. For me a good organization is not one that is without conflicts but rather one that has developed the capacity to resolve acute conflicts and to avoid becoming bogged down in chronic conflicts.

17. Costs and Benefits in Complex Transactional Relationships

Elementary types can occur in pure form, not associated with any other types—though they can and do occur also in association with other types. In contrast, complex types always occur in association with one or more elementary types or with other complex types. We may visualize the complex type as providing a general framework shaping relations, within which the particular combination of other types will strongly influence outcomes in interpersonal sentiments and the creation of surpluses or deficits.

We focus here on three general types of complex relations: Authority, Joint Payoff (in which the rewards jointly sought by two or more individuals or groups are expected to be secured from the environment rather than directly from each other), and Resource Allocation/Conflict Resolution.

AUTHORITY

In the employment situation, Authority is sometimes thought of as if it were an elementary Trading relationship: The worker trades his labor for a specified financial reward. That is reasonable for a one-time transaction, agreed to and carried out in a short time.

The situation for what I call the Authority relationship is quite different. Both parties expect the relationship to continue for an extended period of time. Authority relations apply to situations where it is *formally* recognized that A has a right to give orders to B and that B is obliged to obey. It is further assumed that the boss controls the rewards offered for performance in conformity with his orders and has the right to exact penalties for nonconformity. These statements are phrased in absolute terms. We shall explore the factors that limit the ability of the boss to reward or penalize his subordinates and that limit the kinds of activities he can require of his subordinates.

The Authority relationship is universal in human societies and of special importance in complex societies where bureaucratic organizations develop. Note that I have defined authority without using the word "power." It is important to keep "power" separate from "authority" conceptually. Power is indeed involved in the Authority relationship, but it is also involved in a number of the other types discussed in this book.

Authority can be considered as two-party or multiparty relationship, but for present purposes it seems more useful to put it in the multiparty category. We expect the superior in the Authority relationship to initiate activities for the subordinate. For some purposes, we can concentrate on a single man-boss relationship, but we recognize that most organizations are structured (in part) by a chain of man-boss relationships.

THE MAN-BOSS CONTRACT

In Authority relations, the subordinate agrees to work for the superior for certain rewards and with the understanding that penalties may be expected if he does not perform in terms of the implicit or explicit contract. We think of the relationship as one in which the subordinate provides services to the superior in exchange for benefits received.

The problem in the Authority relationship is that it is never possible to specify in detail the terms of this exchange—exactly what each party will do for the other. In a U.S. industrial plant, the worker receives wages and fringe benefits specified in detail, and he agrees to work up to some minimum standard of performance. There is no problem in calculating hours worked, but there is a problem in determining what should be the minimum level of performance; and this is the source of much worker-management conflict. Even what a worker has a right to receive is rarely specified in detail beyond wages and fringe benefits. The worker assumes he has a right to get help from his supervisor in managing a difficult job and in getting the tools and materials he needs, but it is not clear what level of help is a fair exchange for the worker's services.

This lack of clarity regarding the exchange rate is not a function of modern technology. We found the same ambiguity on the traditional *hacienda* in the Peruvian sierra in the 1960s. The general terms of exchange were clearly understood, and yet their application involved many problems. According to the customs of the particular area, the peasant owed the landowner or the renter of the *hacienda* from three to five days a week on this land. A woman from his household was also required for periodic duties as a servant in the household of the *hacendado* (owner or renter). In return, the peasant got the right to farm a small plot of land, usually located in the least fertile part of the *hacienda*. For his work he also received a token daily payment of a few cents and an allotment of coca to chew upon. The peasant could also expect to get help from "his" *hacendado* in case of problems with authorities outside of the *hacienda*. In conflicts with other peasants, he could call upon the *hacendado* to resolve the dispute, but, of course, he never knew whether he or the other fellow would win. In theory, the *hacendado* was expected to be a good father to his peasants and help them out in case of illness or some other problem. In fact, we rarely heard of an *hacendado* who fully carried out this paternalistic role, and peasants seemed to have little idea of what paternalistic benefits they could expect. Of all the expectations of the parties, the most unclear involved the amount of work expected from the peasants. The number of days and the number of hours were specified, and an overseer could punish a peasant if he was obviously not working at all, but this did not establish how much diligence and skill was required.

If a contract is stated in clear and simple terms and covers in detail what is to be done and what rewards are to be transferred, the contract would be readily enforceable within the Authority relationship or in a court of law. The problem of the employment contract is that the boss often tries to interpret it as if it were such a clear and detailed instrument, whereas the application of the instrument must be worked out in the interactions of the parties. When we examine the way the Authority relationship works, we discover the other types of transactional relationships, which are often embedded within it.

When the boss is not satisfied with the performance of subordinates, what does he do? One common response is punitive: He penalizes those who fall below his standards of performance. If the penalties are levied only on a few individuals and if other workers agree with the boss's evaluation of the offenders, then the penalties provoke no new problems for the boss. Without the support of other workers, they are powerless to strike back.

Authority and Negative Exchange

If the penalties are levied more generally and if other workers are in sympathy with the offenders, then the boss faces quite a different situation. As he exacts penalties, the workers seek to "get even," and the two parties find themselves in a Negative Exchange relationship.

We often see organizational members acting as if they were engaged in a contest. The boss tries to bend subordinates to his will by levying penalties on those who do not "measure up," and the subordinates try to evade the penalties and punish the boss in ways that provide no cause for further penalties. Recognizing the covert resistance, the boss tries to devise new tactics to punish offenders, and the workers think up new ways of simulating compliance. In some plants, this struggle goes on for years. As a participant observer in such a plant, Donald Roy encountered a vivid example of such a self-perpetuating Negative Exchange relationship (Whyte, 1955:151).

The same social process prevailed on the traditional Peruvian hacienda. The peasants did as little work as they could get away with, and the administrator tried to penalize those who were most obviously causing him difficulty. The peasants retaliated with sabotage and theft.

Authority and Competitive Transactions

Within many Authority relationships, we observe a high frequency of competitive transactions as subordinates compete to win the favor of the boss or to escape his penalties. This kind of competition may serve to stimulate subordinates to perform better, but it is not only superior performance that pays off in praise from the boss and escape from his censure. In many situations work is so interdependent that it is not obvious who is responsible for success or failure. Subordinates may therefore find that the best way to escape blame from the boss is to shift the blame onto somebody else. We thus find subordinates expending much effort and ingenuity in protecting themselves against others at the same level and in pinning the blame for failure on someone else.

In one plant where Chris Argyris and I were conducting a foreman training program, we found the participants suffering under a hard-driving boss who was determined to fix personal responsibility for any deficiency. In explaining how they sought to protect themselves, the foremen frankly described their custom of "throwing the dead cat over into the other fellow's yard." Again and again they evoked the image of that airborne dead cat to symbolize their problems (see Argyris, 1952).

To the extent that productivity depends on collaboration, such competitive gaming promotes inefficiency. At the same time, this divisive leadership pattern gives the boss illusory confidence that he is exercising tight control.

In the old Peruvian *hacienda* system, it was customary for the *hacendado* to stimulate competitive relations among the peasants as a means of strengthening his control. Certain individuals and their families, considered particularly loyal to the *hacendado*, would receive more rewards and fewer penalties than did the rank and file.

Authority and Positive Exchange

If the Authority relationship only specifies the minimum terms of the man-boss exchange, the introduction of Positive Exchange transactions opens the possibility for raising worker performance—and raising the performance of superiors in relation to workers. As we interview workers about what makes a good supervisor, we find them speaking explicitly in terms of the exchange of favors. The following three quotations from waitresses expressed this evaluation of supervisors (Whyte, 1948:249).

Miss Nelson is always ready to do little favors for us when she can, so naturally we're glad to help her out.

I like Mr. Jennings a lot. He's always ready to do a favor for you if he can.

Miss Loomis was really a wonderful supervisor. She was always willing to do us a favor whenever she could. So naturally we wanted to do everything

we possibly could to help her. You know, it didn't seem like work to help
Miss Loomis. I was always glad to do anything I could for her. We didn't
want to let her down.

The waitresses were not only saying that they appreciated the favors;
they were also saying that this made them want to do more for their
superior.

We see another side of this reciprocity phenomenon when we observe
in this example what happens when the workers turn against a formerly
popular supervisor. In an earlier period, the barrel department workers
regarded Joe Walker very highly. They produced record barrel runs for
him. They had also helped him in other ways. Joe Walker was weak in
paperwork, so he often organized the job without having all of the right
instructions to go with it. Impressed by Joe Walker's interest in them
and willingness to help them out, workers had been ready to point out
his errors so as to avoid production problems. But Joe Walker changed
and lost the cooperation of the men (Whyte, 1961:142). Now they no
longer pointed out his errors. They let his mistakes get him into trouble.
The union steward explained the changes along these lines.

Earlier Walker's barrel department had made several production
records. Under pressure from management, Walker was getting after the
men to do every day what they had done on these special occasions, and
the men were getting tired. As the barrel shells rolled from one work
station to another along a long line, Walker could easily see who was
not keeping up with the work flow. He would then move in on that
worker and say, "What's the matter, are you sick? If you are sick, you
ought to go home. If you can't get out production, I'll have to take you
off here and put somebody in who can."

The steward explained that on this line some men had "easy jobs"
and some men had "hard jobs." Under pressure from Walker, the men
on the easy jobs would speed up, drawing Walker's attention to workers
on "hard jobs," who thus created apparent bottlenecks.

The steward said that Walker used "pretty rough language" on the
men. The foreman's language had changed little but its impact had
changed. When he was getting along well with the men, they would
explain, "That's just the way Joe is. It don't mean nothing." Now the
meaning had changed, and the men would complain to the steward that
Walker was "cursing them out."

Since union and management had been working well together in the past, on occasion Walker would complain to the steward that the workers were not doing their jobs well enough and ask him to do something about it. Observing the line, the steward would then conclude that the men were meeting the minimum requirements of the job so that he could not ask them to do more. He made clear the reciprocity implicit in the relationship: If Walker wanted the men to do more for him, he would have to do more for them.

Authority Relations:
Strengths and Limitations

Authority relations are of fundamental importance in any complex organization. From the standpoint of the members, Authority relations have one major strength: They provide a clear structure for the environment. While individuals differ as to their needs for structure, there is a general human need to know where you are and where you are going. Without such structure, individuals become confused, frustrated, and anxious.

On the other hand, the need for structure does not necessarily require a rigid structure or a structure imposed on people who have nothing to say about it. It is on this point that we note the difficulties that are likely to be associated with Authority relations. If people at higher levels come to count on the exercise of Authority largely or exclusively in order to get the work done, we find the organization taking on a rigid structure, where superiors are struggling to impose their will, and subordinates are resisting this imposition. The parties on both sides of the conflict then come to invest much of their energy and intelligence in a power struggle instead of concentrating on accomplishing the organization's mission.

We see the limitations of Authority relations especially when they are accompanied by Negative Exchange and zero-sum Competition relationships. Subordinates then try to settle on the minimum level of performance that will shield them from penalties, and the conflict centers around determination of this minimum level—with management being unable to stimulate subordinates to go beyond that level.

This enforcement style of management depends for its effectiveness in large measure on the absence of alternatives for subordinates. If management becomes too repressive, and workers can quit to find a good job elsewhere, even the threat of discharge will have little impact. If the worker feels that he would be unlikely to get a job if he were discharged, then management threats will have a much greater impact. Subordinates will not enjoy the threats, but they will take special pains to make sure that they keep their jobs.

A union further limits management's freedom of action in Authority relationships. The superior might still penalize the subordinate, but the worker can appeal to the union, and union officers may be able to get the penalty reduced or canceled and thus penalize the superior.

The emphasis on Negative Exchange and win-lose Competition tends also to produce severe problems of communication within Authority relationships. If people gain benefits and avoid penalties primarily by competing with each other to win the favor of the boss, then subordinates bring the boss good news quickly and try to delay the report of bad news or soften its impact. They will be quick to tell the boss things that will make their competitors look bad and make themselves look good—and make the boss look good. They will avoid telling the boss anything that will make them or the boss look bad. An Authority system that runs on these principles provides the superior with a highly distorted picture of what is going on. Because the men in the control room of the aviation gasoline plant believed they had to protect themselves from the arbitrary exercise of authority of their earlier foremen, they "boiler housed" their daily operating data reports. This led the foremen to spend innumerable hours analyzing fictitious data.

Authority relationships that are built primarily upon Negative Exchange and zero-sum Competition relations also tend to create highly rigid and legalistic organizations. This makes it difficult to link relationships that are not included within the hierarchy of authority. In many situations the production and assembly process flows through a number of departments so that each department is dependent on the others, but all the department heads are on an equal level so that no one of them can give orders to the others.

Those who build organizations on the Authority principle assume that all will go well if everyone does his or her job. Therefore the duties of all jobs must be specified in detail. Any complex organization involves a number of interdependent relations. Even when each individual works according to the job specifications, there will always be cases where it is not clear who has to do a task. It is time-consuming and inefficient to resolve cases of conflict and doubt on these boundary

problems appealed up the line until the contesting parties reach someone who has authority over both of them. When parties frequently
appeal to superior authority to resolve conflicts, we observe the following negative effects:

Delays. Especially if the first common superior of the contending
individuals is several levels up the hierarchy, it takes time to get his
attention and still more time to get a decision. Even when the first
common superior is only one level up, he may be too busy to render a
decision when it is needed.

Lack of relevant knowledge. It is a well-known maxim of management that a problem should be solved, if possible, by those closest to
the problem through their own personal experience. They are in the best
position to assess the implications of any solution considered. Through
lack of intimate knowledge of the situation out of which the dispute
arises, the organizational superior's decision may create more problems
than it resolves.

Power orientation versus task orientation. When A and B frequently
refer their disputes up the line for decision, they inevitably come to
count those decisions as victories or defeats, which affect their power
and influence in the organization. A and B come to consider themselves
as rivals for the favor of the boss, and they play the game as if they were
involved in zero-sum Competition transactions. As this pattern develops, A and B become less able to resolve problems between them
directly. And, as they concentrate on the win-lose problem, they are less
likely to find solutions that would produce surplus values for the
organization.

Negative interpersonal sentiments. This is simply another way of
stating the point above. As A and B come to see their relationship in
win-lose terms, they develop hostile feelings toward each other.

Finally, the traditional approach to Authority relations assumes that
each worker must have a single boss. If workers have two or more
bosses, it has been assumed that they will not know what to do and
confusion and conflict will result. On the other hand, in modern complex organizations, if we are looking beyond the legalistic interpretation
of organization structure, we find that any subordinate is likely to have

to respond to the initiatives of several superiors. Failure to respond as expected by these superiors can lead directly or indirectly to the imposition of penalties on the subordinate. Joan Woodward (1965:65), in her pioneering studies of technology and organization, even found a number of cases in the chemical processing industries where officially, in the organization chart, department heads reported to five different superiors, each of them being responsible for different aspects of the department's operations.

If we build our organization structure in terms of the tasks that have to be performed, then we will have something that is not as neat as the traditional line organization but is more realistic in reflecting the behavior and interrelations of people.

On the basis of the preceding discussion, the difficulties of the Authority relationship may seem insurmountable, but note that we have stressed the problems in relating Authority to Negative Exchange and win-lose Competition relationships. The leader who wishes to use Authority relations in a manner that will improve organizational performance and at the same time build human satisfaction through participation will seek to minimize the incidence of Negative Exchange and win-lose Competition and will seek to substitute Positive Exchange and Joint Payoff relations. This is another way of saying that he will seek to be responsive to subordinates as they do things for him; he will also try to work out with them a definition of goals and a sharing in the rewards of performance so that they will feel that he and they are working together on the same objectives.

JOINT PAYOFF RELATIONSHIPS

A Joint Payoff relationship is established when two or more individuals or groups agree to combine their resources and efforts, in order to gain resources from the environment. That is, they do not gain or lose directly from dealing with each other—as in Positive Exchange, Trading, Negative Exchange and Authority relations—but rather from external sources.

In Joint Payoff, each party states explicitly the resources to be committed and the resources to be gained from the environment, at least as far as extrinsic rewards are concerned. The parties may gain personal satisfactions from working with each other, and these intrinsic satisfactions may be necessary for maintaining the relationship and thus for gaining the extrinsic satisfactions; but the parties rarely spell out in advance the intrinsic satisfactions they expect to gain through their joint efforts.

Joint Payoff relationships must be rather long lasting if the rewards are to be harvested. This is true partly because the parties are not directly rewarding each other but are gaining rewards from the environment. Generally they have to invest substantially of their own resources and efforts before they are in a position to reap the rewards from the environment, whereas rewards can be gained from Positive Exchange and Trading at the moment when values are transferred from one party to the other.

Within the Joint Payoff relationship, we are especially likely to have instances of Positive Exchange as the parties do favors for each other. We may also have Trading relationships as the parties make explicit decisions about what each will do for the other. The general terms of the Joint Payoff relationship are established when the parties begin to work together, but it is never possible to anticipate all the tasks that will have to be performed and to arrive at a prior decision as to how these tasks are to be distributed. Thus as new situations arise, A may say to B, "If you can do X for me, I will take care of Y for you." If the Joint Payoff relationship is to be maintained, clearly the parties must minimize the frequency of Negative Exchange, zero-sum Competition or Open Conflict transactions.

The Joint Payoff relationships may appear in both balanced and unbalanced forms. In the balanced form, the parties invest roughly an equal amount of resources and expect to get an equal share in the gains of the enterprise. In this form, the parties expect to have roughly equal influence in decision making. In fact, generally one of the partners gains informal leadership but maintains that leadership only so long as the other partners are satisfied that their ideas and interests are being taken fully into account.

In the unbalanced form, A puts in markedly more resources than B, and he expects to get a markedly larger share of the gains of the enterprise than B. In this case, both A and B will expect A to have a greater share in decision making than B. Whether B considers the distribution of rewards and his share in decision making equitable depends on elements to be considered as we examine the conditions required for maintaining Joint Payoff relationships.

Conditions for Joint Payoff Maintenance

The maintenance of the Joint Payoff relationship depends on (1) its continuing to yield rewards to the parties, and (2) their opinion that the rewards continue to be distributed equitably.

A business partnership cannot be maintained indefinitely if it continues to lose money. The outcome of a research partnership is not so completely predictable, as the measurement of gains and losses is not so objective. Nevertheless, if two professors team up on a research project and then find, for whatever reason, that they are unable to complete the project and publish their findings, this failure is likely to lead to the dissolution of the relationship. If they do succeed in publishing, but if the publication is sharply criticized by authorities in their field, then we expect that the partnership is less likely to continue than it would be if the product were met by critical acclaim.

In examining the question of equity, we are concerned with the investment-reward ratio (IRR). As Homans would put it (Zaleznik, Christenson, and Roethlisberger, 1958), B does not necessarily require that the rewards coming out of the relationship be equally divided between himself and A. If A has been putting in more resources than B, B may well be satisfied when A gets the larger share. He is likely to be aggrieved only if he feels his rewards are not proportional to his investments. That is, if B feels that he has contributed roughly equally with A and judges that A is getting twice as much of the rewards, B will naturally be resentful. In that case we would expect him to protest to A and, if his protest did not bring about a more equitable distribution, we would expect him to terminate the Joint Payoff relationship.

I am not suggesting that the parties seek to calculate their IRRs in exact terms. Except in the case of money, no exact calculations can be made. Beyond money the parties may also seek less tangible rewards, such as increased social recognition. Nevertheless, I argue that people do make rough assessments of their investment-reward ratios and are inclined to change relationships when they see their rewards running markedly below their investments.

The maintenance of the relationship does not depend upon each party believing that he has achieved an exact IRR balance. A may feel that, in relation to the rewards he is receiving, he is putting in greater investments than B. He may nevertheless be willing to continue the relationship if (1) he feels that he is doing better within the relationship than he would if it were terminated, and (2) he feels that B is not deliberately withholding his contributions.

Joint Payoff and Authority
Relations Combined

In a business or research partnership, only a few individuals are involved, and Authority relations do not come into play—except insofar as a partner may have subordinates working under his Authority. In such partnerships, there is a relatively simple and direct relationship between the investments of individuals and the rewards they receive.

As the organization expands and grows in complexity, this simple and direct relationship breaks down, and Joint Payoff can only continue to operate as it is combined with a system of Authority relations.

Spokespersons for private companies would like to have workers believe that their company is one large Joint Payoff relationship, because without profits the company will sooner or later shut down which would leave the workers unemployed. Furthermore, a strong flow of profits enhances the ability of the company to reward its workers financially.

Few workers would reject this general argument, and yet the relationship rarely seems like Joint Payoff to workers. There are two reasons for worker refusal to accept such management logic.

First, a Joint Payoff cannot be unilaterally determined. The ground rules regarding investments and rewards must be jointly agreed on by participating individuals or by their representatives. Similarly, the participating individuals or their representatives must participate in the implementation of the program covered by these ground rules.

Second, individuals and their leaders must believe that there is a reasonably equitable balance between investments and rewards for each of the parties.

Recent history of labor relations in the Chrysler auto company illustrates this equity principle. When Lee Iacocca led the successful campaign to save the company and served as president at first for $1 a year, he was a hero to Chrysler workers. Several years later the now highly profitable company rewarded Iacocca with $23 million in a single year, which provoked a widespread sense of outrage among Chrysler workers. It also led to a successful union demand that bonuses paid to executives be linked to profit sharing for workers. At this point, even Iacocca publicly acknowledged that such a linkage was legitimate.

Organizational performance can be enhanced by the integration of Joint Payoff with Authority relations.

In one organizational form, the worker cooperative, Joint Payoff provides the main organizing principle. Control is not based on capital but on labor through the one member, one vote principle. Ideally all or nearly all workers are members. When the cooperative resorts to filling vacancies with hired labor, as has happened in many cases, then the Joint Payoff relationship does not fit the relations between members and hired labor.

The Mondragón cooperatives discussed in Chapter 12 present an impressive example of a set of organizations developed on the basis of the principle of Joint Payoff: sharing profits and losses among all members. Note, however, that establishment of this principle does not guarantee that the members will see this sharing as being administered equitably. Achieving this sense of social equity among the members has depended on systems of member participation in decision making and on the building of a unique organizational culture.

I do not assume that Joint Payoff relations can only occur when the firm is structured as a worker cooperative. In interdepartmental relations, leaders of two or more units can agree on joint objectives as a means of reducing conflict and improving the performance of each unit.

In a small single plant company, an agreement to share profits with employees can be perceived as Joint Payoff. In a large company, particularly where the firm has many plants, profit sharing generally appears too remote from any local unit to lead workers to feel that they are in a mutual sharing relationship. Furthermore, the level of profits declared is so dependent on management decisions that profit sharing (by itself) is not likely to have a strong motivational impact.

Gain sharing plans are more likely to be perceived by workers as Joint Payoff relations. Gain sharing is designed to link worker payoffs more directly to the actions of workers. The first program of this type was a social invention of Joseph Scanlon, then a local union leader in the United Steelworkers and later a professor at the Massachusetts Institute of Technology. To save a small steel company from going under, Scanlon invented what came to be known as the Scanlon Plan (Whyte, 1955).

There are two basic elements to the Scanlon Plan. The first is an accounting formula based on the plant's labor costs for a recent period together with a management commitment to share with labor (on a prenegotiated basis) the money saved through a reduction in those labor costs. The second element is a system of labor-management commit-tees in the various departments created to study operations and recom-mend changes designed to increase labor productivity; at the top of this structure is a joint labor-management screening committee designed to evaluate proposals from the departmental committees and urge man-agement to implement proposals it finds helpful. Scanlon always em-phasized that little could be expected from the accounting formula unless it was supported by an active program of worker participation.

This strategy contrasted with conventional management approaches to labor productivity and compensation. It was customary for manage-ment to use its own engineering studies to determine the required level of labor productivity. Then, finding labor always below that required level, management would consider some form of labor bonus only if and when labor reached the level of performance predetermined by management. Scanlon's social invention was a radical shift away from this management style. Instead of accepting as the benchmark manage-ment's *normative* figures, the Scanlon Plan used actual experience— generally performance for the three months prior to the introduction of the plan. (Of course, the formula had to be adjusted for technological changes affecting labor productivity.)

When the Scanlon Plan worked well, as it has in a number of cases, it yielded impressive Joint Payoffs. Management tapped a flow of worker ideas on reducing labor costs. Workers gained bonuses and increased their job security.

Since the Scanlon invention, consultants have devised other plans along the same general lines. They all use actual performance as the benchmark and provide for gain sharing with workers when that level is surpassed.

Intensified international industrial competition has led to the emer-gence of Joint Payoffs based on a different benchmark: competitive costs. Original equipment manufacturers (OEMs) generally purchase forty to sixty percent of the components of what they market. For components previously manufactured in-house, management's procure-ment department may be charged with the responsibility to look around the country and the world to find vendors who can produce that com-ponent more cheaply while meeting the company's standards of quality and delivery. When they find a lower-cost vendor, his bid then becomes the benchmark that must be met through internal cost savings if the component is to remain an in-house production item.

In Chapter 10 we have seen how Xerox and the Amalgamated Clothing and Textile Workers created an extraordinarily participative system of cost study teams (CSTs) to cope with national and international competition. Successes achieved in these CSTs yielded Joint Payoffs: for management, major increases in manufacturing efficiency and in the effectiveness of participative management; for labor, retention of jobs and enhanced learning opportunities at work. For both parties, substantial organizational learning regarding ways to build and sustain a highly participative and cooperative union-management relationship.

Social Significance

Joint Payoff makes possible the organization of cooperative efforts without determining who gives orders to whom. Two independent parties can combine voluntarily and, by pooling their efforts, achieve rewards that they could not possibly gain alone. Furthermore, if the relationship is well structured, the agreement regarding joint investments and Joint Payoffs provides for the motivation of the parties so that B does what A expects him to do—not because he is forced to do so, but because he wants to.

This relationship is important for building organizations and for establishing and maintaining collaborative relations between organizations. In principle, it may be applied not only to fully independent organizations but also to units within a given organization. Since power struggles often consume much of the energy and imagination of organizational members, strategies that facilitate coordination on a voluntary basis offer great promise for both improved performance and improved interpersonal sentiments.

Regarding the value of this type of relationship to society, we should introduce a note of caution. We are concerned here with performance in meeting the objectives of the participants, and we are not offering any judgment as to the overall value of this performance to society. For example, two Mafia chieftains might set up a Joint Payoff relationship for the management of gambling and drug sales, and the necessary police and political protection for those activities. The relationship is likely to be more profitable to them and their members than Competition or Open Conflict. I do not assume that harmony between Mafia chieftains is beneficial to society.

RESOURCE ALLOCATION/CONFLICT RESOLUTION

Relationships of this type involve the allocation of resources and do not directly increase or decrease the resources available to the parties. This does not make them unimportant. Serious disputes over resource allocation often arise within or between organizations. Unless the parties can resolve these disputes, they may be unable to use existing resources to create more resources.

Where the Authority relationship is unchallenged, those in power simply allocate the resources as they see fit. Where those in authority face an opposing organization, the opposing parties may seek to reach a decision through negotiating or bargaining.

In some markets, the prices of goods are determined, within limits, by what is commonly called bargaining but what I classify as simply a form of Trading. The vendor announces a price higher than he expects to receive and the customer counters with a price lower than he expects to pay. The vendor then lowers his price somewhat and the customer raises his bid somewhat, and this alternation continues until they reach agreement.

Although this type of relationship can be important in economic affairs, it is of little interest to students of organizational behavior. In such bargaining, either party is free to terminate the relationship, with the vendor looking for other customers and the customer seeking other vendors or abandoning the market. In the cases of interest to us, the parties are "locked into" a continuing relationship. Neither party can permanently dissolve the relationship without serious consequences to itself.

Such interorganizational bargaining (between union and management or between nations) also involves resolving more varied and complex issues than the price to be paid for a single item of merchandise.

There is a voluminous literature on collective bargaining in industry and on international negotiations (for industry, see particularly Walton and McKersie, 1965). The literature also deals with third-party involvement in dispute resolution as in mediation, arbitration, and other forms of third-party intervention. Here I limit myself simply to indicating how bargaining relates to some of the transactional relationships already discussed.

214

In bargaining, the main values involved are generally—but not always—made explicit. However, these values do not change hands in the bargaining process itself. The parties are trying to work out agreements regarding the future transfer of values. They are constantly interpreting the values expressed orally or in writing in relation to the behavior anticipated from the other party in the future.

Trading is, of course, prominently involved in the bargaining process. One party offers a concession if the other party will agree to a comparable concession.

One would think that Positive Exchange would not be involved in bargaining, because it involves implicit obligations to reciprocate rather than explicit agreements. Furthermore, bargaining involves the simultaneous action of both parties rather than a sequence of alternating actions. Nevertheless, we find instances of what we may call Positive Exchange in cases of successful bargaining. In one type of situation, one party takes the initiative by unilaterally offering a concession to the other party. At some future time, the second party may reciprocate by offering a concession to the first party. The exchange can continue on this alternating basis until some of the most severe points of tension between the two parties have been eliminated. In some cases, this Positive Exchange can take place without the parties interacting directly at the time the concessions are announced. In fact, Amitai Etzioni (1967) traced a series of reciprocating concessions between the United States and Russia that resulted in markedly reduced cold war tensions during the Kennedy administration.

When the parties have reached an impasse and do not seem to be able to reach a direct agreement, initiating Positive Exchange may be a useful way of introducing movement into the negotiations. Why make a unilateral concession? In a sense, one party is testing out the other. The party taking the initiative does not lead off with an important concession. In fact, it may concede a point in which its own members have lost interest but where this loss of interest has not yet become apparent to outside observers. The small concession is a trial balloon. If the second party does not respond favorably, then the first party does not follow with a new concession. But, even when one concession does not lead to another, the party taking the initiative has risked and lost very little. If the second party does reciprocate with its own concession, this may break an impasse. As each new concession is received, negotiators find themselves viewing their opponents more favorably and become willing to risk somewhat larger concessions. This alternating exchange may reduce the tensions to such an extent that the parties can get together to negotiate agreements on really major issues, as happened in the case of the Nuclear Test Ban Treaty.

Positive Exchange can also take place when one party takes the initiative in requesting or demanding a concession from the other party. In fact, this pattern does tend to develop where union and management negotiators are approaching reasonably harmonious relationships. When management makes no demands or requests on the union and is simply responding to union demands, then the management people inevitably feel they are in a defensive position. In this type of situation, the management people tend to see the union negotiators as enemies who must be held in check as much as possible, so management yields only when its negotiators believe that not yielding could be more costly. In contrast, if management presents a set of demands to the union, this creates the possibility of reciprocating concessions and the development of more favorable interpersonal sentiments.

Negative Exchange in its implicit form is not likely to appear frequently in bargaining relationships. In that kind of setting, the negative things parties do to each other or threaten to do are generally made quite explicit.

We find Open Conflict occurring when bargaining relationships break down. In union-management relations, Open Conflict takes the form of a strike, lockout, boycott of the sale of the company's products.

The parties are influenced not only by the conflict that takes place but also by the possibility of such conflict. Much of the talk at the bargaining table may involve discussion of the dire consequences that will be experienced by opponents if they do not agree on key issues.

Effects on Behavior

We cannot predict the impact on behavior of the bargaining relationship unless we have information about the distribution of transactional types during the process. This in turn may be strongly influenced by the way the parties conceptualize the issues and by the skill with which they handle the process. Richard Walton and Robert McKersie (1965) conceptualize the process in terms of two types of issues: *distributive* and *integrative*. Distributive issues involve dividing up the resources available to the two parties so that if one party gets more, the other party gets less. Integrative issues involve matters on which the two parties find common interests so that the agreement reached on the particular issue will be of positive value to both parties.

In few bargaining relationships would it be possible to eliminate distributive issues altogether, yet the distributive-integrative division will be important in the parties' ability to come to an agreement and in the quality of their relations. If the parties devote all or nearly all of their time to arguing distributive issues, we predict that they will have great difficulty in coming to agreement and that their relations in the period immediately following the end of bargaining will be marked by hostile feelings and an absence of jointly agreed on activities.

In union-management relations, there are a number of issues that lend themselves to an integrative approach. Safety affects the health and even the lives of workers, and management has efficiency as well as humanitarian considerations in promoting a safety program in which both parties play a role. The employee cafeteria and other employee facilities present other obvious areas where there is no necessary conflict of interests. While the extent of management's subsidy is certainly a distributive issue, there may be a variety of ways of operating the cafeteria within the range of the figures acceptable to management, and management can have a positive interest in arriving at arrangements acceptable to the employees.

Absenteeism is another potentially integrative issue. Management may find a high rate of absenteeism costly, and the union negotiators have no interest in keeping the rate high. In fact, where employees are paid on individual or group piece rates, the earnings of workers may be reduced by absenteeism and by the consequent readjustment of worker assignments caused by absenteeism. In the bargaining one year between the United Steelworkers and Inland Steel Container Company the union leaders accepted management's request for help on the absenteeism problem for another reason also: If union officers and stewards could talk to the workers about the importance of reducing absenteeism, and if absenteeism then did drop markedly, this would demonstrate to management that the leaders had support of the members and would thereby strengthen the union's position in its dealings with management. In other words, it is not only through mobilizing workers in conflict against management that union leaders can demonstrate that they truly represent the workers. There are cases where this demonstration of solidarity can be accomplished on issues that benefit both parties and thus increase their chances of coming to a mutually satisfactory agreement.

Matters of cost and level of production are usually thought of as distributive issues, but in some cases the parties have been able to agree on a system for sharing in the financial gains of increased efficiency and productivity. The setting up of such a system involves establishing Joint Payoff relationships, discussed previously.

As noted earlier, the development of Positive Exchange relationships within bargaining tends to build more favorable sentiments between the parties. Trading relationships may have the same positive effect, except where the weaker party accepts a deal that seems unfair but is "the best we could get." Increases in the frequency of Competitive, Negative Exchange, and Open Conflict relations tend to strengthen hostile sentiments between the parties.

IN CONCLUSION

The activities involved in Resource Allocation/Conflict Resolution necessarily involve costs to both parties, with little or no material payoffs while the process is going on. Those costs can be reduced if the parties have previously established a pattern of reasonably harmonious relations and if the principal negotiators are skillful, but the costs cannot be eliminated entirely. The problem for the parties is therefore one of using the negotiation processes in ways that establish bases on which they can build future relations bringing them more favorable outcomes. This can be done through developing negotiation processes shaped by other transactional relationships, especially Positive Exchange and Joint Payoff.

18. Combining Joint Payoffs with Multiobjective Planning

If it is possible to increase the value of potential payoffs without increasing the costs of the activities required to produce them, then we can make major gains in operations and also strengthen motivation and job satisfaction among the participants in those activities. Less spectacular but still substantial gains are possible if we can increase potential payoffs without increasing proportionately the costs required to produce those payoffs.

Can this be done? To understand the possibility, we must first overcome the mental obstacle involved in the economist's conception of *opportunity costs*. The principle involved holds that, in order to pursue one line of activity, persons need to forego the opportunity to pursue other lines at the same time and with the same resources. Giving up other lines of activity thus costs persons the opportunity to gain the benefits from such alternatives.

To get around this mental block, we need to distinguish objectives from the activities that may be required to reach them. Persons can and do pursue more than one objective at the same time. In fact, often we can infer from observing behavior that persons are pursuing several objectives, though they may not have made explicit even to themselves anything beyond what they regard as an especially important objective. I argue that it is socially and economically useful for persons to open their minds to the possibility of multiple objectives and to imagine what it would take to pursue several of them at the same time.

I began my exploration of the potentials for enhancing Joint Payoffs through multiobjective projects when Ulises Moreno told me the story of the Huasahuasi project. I saw in this case important theoretical and practical implications and I was puzzled by the reactions of project critics. Those I consulted agreed that the project was led by a good man and that it was a good thing for Huasahuasi, yet they saw no theoretical or practical significance in it.

Such interpretations of the project cannot be explained by frictions with the project leader, for they all considered themselves his friends. Nor could their evaluations be based on ignorance, for they were well informed. If their evaluations are mistaken, then the mistakes must be due to lack of an adequate theoretical framework for evaluating such a project. I aim to provide some of this framework, after telling the story of the project (first reported in Whyte, 1977).

INTRODUCING ULISES MORENO

Ulises Moreno was born and brought up in the Peruvian highlands town of Huasahuasi. From Huasahuasi, Moreno went down to the coastal Agricultural University and then came to Cornell where he received a doctorate in plant physiology. He wrote his dissertation on Peruvian potatoes.

Moreno may have been the first student from any developing country to return to his peasant community to report on his doctoral thesis. He presented his talk one evening in the central square of the town, projecting slides showing the various aspects of potato physiology on a scale the villagers had never seen before. Afterward, many villagers gathered around to urge Moreno to organize a project to help the small farmers of Huasahuasi.

When Moreno became a professor, his agricultural university had a contractual relationship with the Ministry of Agriculture to support technical assistance to communities. In 1973, Moreno secured a grant of $2,000 to be used primarily for his university team's travel expenses to Huasahuasi. The villagers pledged room and board for the team while

it was in that community. The national potato program made contributions of improved seed varieties. Moreno arranged for the participation
of extension agents working in the region. A Bayer company agent
provided chemical materials and agreed to demonstrate their use.

THE SETTING

The agricultural economy of Huasahuasi was based on potatoes. At
this time, the municipality was producing more than half the seed
potatoes used by coastal potato farmers. All of these seed potatoes,
however, were grown by the large farmers, the largest one having up to
7,000 hectares (1 hectare = 2.47 acres). The big farmers had been
getting up to forty tons of potatoes per hectare, while the small ones,
without improved seeds and other inputs, had been getting about ten tons
(which was nevertheless above what was then the national average).

The municipality of Huasahuasi (population approximately 10,000)
was sharply divided in economic interests and political orientations. At
the time, the government had been trying to implement a land reform
program, and the large farmers feared that their properties might be
expropriated. Their main defense was the argument that, if their lands
were divided into small family parcels, the overall production level of
potatoes would drop to ten tons per hectare. This would have a disastrous impact on the coastal potato farmers, who would no longer be able
to buy the seed potatoes they needed. As potatoes are more susceptible
to disease in lowland areas, coastal farmers had been counting on seed
potatoes from the highlands. The large farmers had been dependent on
small farmers for labor, but they had always refused to share any of their
seed potatoes with the small farmers, in order to protect their monopoly.
The large farmers had ample access to credit and technical assistance,
whereas the small farmers were not considered by agricultural bank
officials as good credit risks; and the small farmers themselves had been
hesitant even to seek credit for fear they would not be able to repay
loans and might lose their land.

Politically, the municipality was controlled by officials appointed by
the national government, and those officials were closely linked to the
families of the large farmers. Within Huasahuasi, there was also an
officially recognized peasant community, whose membership was limited to small farmers called *comuneros*. The *comuneros* elected a *junta*

comunal for its community government, with each *caserio* (hamlet) electing its delegate to the *junta*. The *junta* elected its own president and other officers.

PROJECT ORGANIZATION AND DEVELOPMENT

Beginning in August 1973, the project went through several stages. First, Moreno organized a team of five professors, four graduate students, and seven undergraduates. The professors represented plant physiology, plant pathology, entomology, agricultural extension, and sociology; the students were majors in agronomy, biology, and economics and planning. (The team was smaller in later stages, but its interdisciplinary character was maintained throughout.)

The team spent a week at the university working on plans. The two weeks the team spent in Huasahuasi were divided between exploratory discussions and observations, with team members walking the fields and talking with the villagers about their problems. On Sunday beginning the second week, the team attended a community meeting at which Moreno discussed the organization of seminars in each *caserio* throughout the following week.

These *caserio* discussions were not designed simply for instruction. While technical aspects of potato cultivation received major attention, villagers spoke about their needs for transportation to markets, credit, improved seed varieties, and for more effective cooperation among themselves. They further discussed the quality and quantity of government services.

The second team visit to Huasahuasi took place in February 1974, during the university vacation period. The community government now voted to allocate land for experimental plots, and one villager volunteered a section of his own property. The team worked out an agreement with community leaders so that the potatoes harvested from experimental plots would be distributed among the volunteers who did the work at each stage of the agricultural cycle.

The team returned to Huasahuasi in October 1974 to supervise the planting of experimental plots. All of the team members shared fully the manual labor involved in preparing the fields and planting the potatoes, and also engaged in extensive discussions with the small farmers regarding the logic of the experiments. The planting was done according to an experimental design permitting later comparison of improved seed potato varieties with the locally popular variety; there were also variations in the use of fertilizer, in the use of fertilizer with and without insecticides, and in the spacing of the rows—forty centimeters or thirty centimeters apart.

The university team returned over a weekend for the harvesting. The team worked with the villagers to dig up potatoes, leaving them along each row so that villagers could observe and compare. When each plot had been completed, the potatoes were picked up and weighed so that people could note the weight of each variety under each condition. As the work went on, Moreno discussed with the villagers the advantages of using improved varieties, fertilizers, and insecticide. He did not have to lecture, as they could draw their conclusions from their own observations.

Finally, Moreno worked with the villagers to extrapolate from each small plot the potential yield of that treatment if it had been applied to a one-hectare lot. The figures for the improved seed varieties with the optimum complementary inputs projected a yield of approximately forty tons per hectare, equal to the best records of the large farmers.

The villagers also learned of a further advantage of the new seed varieties: early maturity and increased resistance to late blight. The common local variety was late in maturing and often seriously affected by late blight.

Moreno had planned to follow through with Huasahuasi the next year to assist those who were now in a position to plant seed potatoes they had raised themselves and to promote the extension of the program to larger numbers of small farmers. He was unable to raise even the small funds necessary for this purpose. Also, he had been elected director of academic affairs for his university, which made it increasingly difficult to get away to the highlands.

Nevertheless, Moreno received reports that some of the small farmers who had participated in the first harvest had gone on to get credit to purchase the inputs needed and were achieving higher yields, and that some other small farmers had now bought seed potatoes from their fellow villagers.

Although the benefits achieved by the villagers participating in the project were beginning to spread slowly to other small farmers, the political problems precipitated by some members of the university team blocked the full utilization of the lessons of the Huasahuasi project.

While visiting farmer fields some of the students had spoken of the "exploitation" of the small farmers by the large farmers. Large farmers seized on this to brand the project as communist inspired and lobbied the agriculture ministry to block further project funding. (During the same period, leftist student leaders at the university were attacking Moreno as a reactionary and a tool of Yankee imperialism.)

Subsequent events indicate the political and economic problems that may arise to prevent the full utilization and diffusion of what has been learned in a locally successful project. The project increased the small farmers' confidence in their ability to repay loans and persuaded bank officials to open lines of credit to them. Furthermore, small farmers who had not participated in the experiment now were purchasing seed potatoes from fellow small farmers, thus breaking the large farmer's monopoly. Finally, the Huasahuasi project had received favorable publicity in Lima newspapers, providing a base for generating stronger political support for such initiatives.

THE EVALUATION PUZZLE

Since I believed in the project, I needed to sort out the reactions of critics. Among the arguments raised, I focus on the two: *global vision* and *single-objective fixation*.

On global vision, one critic said, "Such projects can't contribute much until the basic underlying problems of Peruvian agriculture are solved." When I asked what these problems were, he listed the following Peruvian needs: improved and expanded facilities for the production of seed potatoes, more efficient systems to get inputs to farmers, expanded credit for small as well as large farmers, construction of area and regional storage facilities so that farmers would not be forced to sell all of their potatoes at harvest time, a bigger and better agricultural extension program, improvement of the state purchasing program to guarantee minimum prices to the farmers and help them move their crops to market, and government price policies that provide incentives to farmers.

I asked, "How long do you suppose it will take for the government to do all these things? Ten years? Twenty years?" He nodded, whereupon I asked, "Then that means nothing should be done at the local level until these things are taken care of?" The critic refused to accept this implication, but he still had no ideas for worthwhile local projects.

The critic assumed that all limitations must be removed throughout the country before progress can be attained anywhere, and that progress must always come from the top down. Without denying the importance of changes in government policies and programs, we have learned that problems cannot be resolved solely with the top-down strategy, that top-level changes must be linked with participatory changes at local and regional levels.

The critics were evaluating Huasahuasi simply as an experiment in the plant sciences. The picture changes when we view it as a social experiment: the development of a new organizational model for intervention in peasant agriculture.

To evaluate such a project, we have to consider at least the following seven objectives:

(1) Help the small farmers of Huasahuasi to do as well in potato growing as the large farmers.

(2) Develop and test a new organizational model for research and development in agriculture.

(3) Discover the social and economic barriers to progress in a community such as Huasahuasi, thus combining social knowledge with knowledge of plant sciences.

(4) Improve the education of students and professors. Perhaps the most important lesson learned involved humility. One young woman said to Moreno, "This has been a fascinating but also a frustrating experience. I have learned so much from the farmers of Huasahuasi, and at the same time I have had to recognize that, for all my years of study of biology, plant pathology, calculus, and so on, there is very little that I have been able to contribute to them." If students can learn this kind of lesson before it is too late, then they should be able to contribute far more than those whose university education has been limited to classroom and laboratory.

(5) Stimulate interdisciplinary communication for both professors and students. University programs tend to develop in terms of specialization; rarely do professors work with those in a different specialty. Moreno had demonstrated one way of stimulating interdisciplinary communication and collaboration.

(6) Improve relations among the university, the national and international research programs, and agricultural extension. In Peru, as in many other

developing countries, the activities of these various institutions tend to proceed more or less in isolation from each other.

(7) Improve the effectiveness of agricultural extension. As extension agents participate in projects such as Moreno's, they learn how to make a more substantial contribution to agricultural development.

While the benefits to be gained from the second through seventh objectives are difficult to quantify, they nevertheless are built upon deficiencies and needs that have been widely recognized in research, development, and education in many countries.

ON LIMITING-FACTORS INTERVENTION STRATEGIES

This strategy takes advantage of the principle that it is not necessary to eliminate all limiting factors before starting an action program. Overcoming obstacles builds momentum so that the field of forces at later stages may be markedly changed from when the program was begun.

Limiting factors are not fixed elements. They vary according to the situation the change agent is trying to affect and according to the resources (including information) with which he or she has to work. Therefore, the first task is to make a diagnosis to determine whether or not, with the resources the change agent controls and might be able to mobilize in later stages of the program, initial success is probable. From past experience and observation of Huasahuasi, Moreno concluded that two limiting factors had to be overcome before any local success would be possible:

(1) The small farmers had to gain access to an initial supply of seed potatoes of the new improved varieties.

(2) The small farmers would have to acquire the information needed and the physical inputs required to ensure success in the experimental plantings.

The university team organized the project to provide the human and material resources indispensable to success.

THE THEORY OF MULTIOBJECTIVE PLANNING

Multiobjective planning translates certain ideas of economists and city and regional planners into social theory. While economists have given more attention to the analysis of scarcity, comparing objectives in terms of trade-offs and opportunity costs, they also recognize "externalities" (Samuelson, 1967); the additional valuable outcomes produced in carrying out a project aimed at one principal objective. City and regional planners necessarily must think in terms of more than one objective, but often their analysis involves estimating how much of one objective must be sacrificed to reach another or how much additional cost must be incurred to reach both objectives.

We are likely to assume that it must cost more to carry out a multiobjective project than a single-objective project. The Huasahuasi case shows that, under some circumstances, the opposite conclusion is warranted. If the project had had only a single purpose—to help small farmers of a particular community to grow more and better potatoes—then it would have been impossible to recruit team members on a volunteer basis. People would have had to be paid for their work, and the costs of the project would have been so high as to make it clear that the project could not be expanded beyond a few communities. By combining objectives, a project of major potential significance was carried out for a direct cost of as little as $2,000.

In the past sociologists backed into this problem through considering "latent functions" (Merton, 1949) and "unanticipated consequences of purposive social action" (Merton, 1936) but without drawing the action implications from such notions. Now, if sociologists are so smart in finding these latent functions and unanticipated consequences in the actions of other people, why cannot we apply this same analysis—in advance—to the actions we ourselves plan to take? In other words, why cannot we plan so as to make the latent functions explicit and to make intentional the otherwise unanticipated consequences?

It may be helpful to express these ideas in graphic form (Figure 18.1). Let us say that P, the leader of an organization, is considering the possibilities of moving simultaneously toward goals A, B, C, and D. Suppose we call the money and other material resources and human effort put into the pursuit of an objective a cost. If P wishes to reach objective A, this will require the cost represented by 1a. Similarly, let us call 1b the cost P will have to make in order to reach B. Now suppose

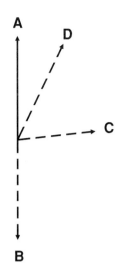

P = Person planning project
A = Principal objective
B, C, & D = Other potential objectives

Figure 18.1. Compatible and Incompatible Objectives for Multiobjective
Planning

P wishes to move at the same time toward both objectives; what cost
should he expect to incur? The obvious answer would seem to be 1a +
1b, but for this type of problem, the obvious answer is almost always
the wrong answer.

As we see in Figure 18.1, from the position P occupies, he would have
to divide his personnel and their activities so as to move in opposite
directions if he wished to proceed simultaneously toward A and B. The
cost required would be much greater than 1a + 1b.

In going for A, P maintains more or less constant distance from C.
The diagram suggests that moving toward A and C will require at least
the cost of 1a + 1c.

With objectives A and D, the situation is more favorable to a multiobjective strategy. As P moves toward A, he cannot help approaching

D, and the cost required should be far less than 1a + 1d. We may encounter situations where no additional costs are incurred for moving toward two objectives at the same time. In fact, there are cases where it is impossible for P to reach A unless he pursues a strategy of moving toward D at the same time.

To assess the compatibility or incompatibility among various objectives, we visualize the activities and interpersonal interactions required to reach objective A, those required to reach objective B, and so on. If similar activities and interactions are required, we can assume a high degree of compatibility and proceed to work out detailed plans.

The judgment regarding compatibility or incompatibility is not obvious in most cases. At one extreme, we find objectives that are incompatible regardless of how interactions and activities are structured. At the other extreme, some objectives may be so naturally compatible that it is hard to aim for one without also seeking the other. Almost all objectives will fall somewhere between these two extremes. In such cases, planners need to assess the costs versus the benefits involved in combining objectives.

We should not assume that compatibility or incompatibility is automatically determined by the way objectives present themselves to human actors. Even when two objectives appear incompatible, if we reconceptualize one or both of them, we often discover points of compatibility not previously apparent.

COMBINING FIELD RESEARCH WITH EDUCATION

To illustrate the reconceptualization of activities required in order to use a multiobjective development strategy, I draw on a case from my own experience in Peru in the 1960s. During that period I served with Lawrence K. Williams of Cornell and José Matos Mar of the Instituto de Estudios Peruanos (IEP) as codirector of a program of studies of change in rural communities.

That program had a number of objectives that were explicitly agreed on at the outset:

(1) Add to knowledge on processes of rural change and development through research and publication in English and Spanish.

(2) Strengthen the capacity of IEP, our host organization, and Cornell's Latin American Studies Program for carrying out research on rural change and development.

(3) Develop methods for integrating village surveys with more intensive social anthropological studies. (Our program carried out surveys in twenty-six villages in 1964 and followed with resurveys of twelve of these villages in 1969. The interviewing-observational studies were concentrated on the twelve villages we were able to follow closely from 1964 through 1969 and for several years thereafter.)

(4) Educate our student field-workers in methods for integrating surveys with social anthropological studies and in the behavioral science literature relevant for such a strategy.

(5) Strengthen the capacity of professors and students in departments of sociology or anthropology in five universities to carry out fieldwork integrating surveys and interviewing-observational studies. (In each area studied in 1964, we worked with and through a professor whose students were the principal field researchers.)

How can such a broad range of objectives be served through any coherent program of activities? Let us concentrate here on the problem of integrating research and student education. Although these two activities are often depicted in academic rhetoric as complementary, in American universities their relations are often sources of considerable tension, with students and other critics claiming that teaching is being neglected while professors seek to lighten their "teaching loads" so as to devote more time to research.

Our experience suggests that this tension is partly due to the conventional ways in which teaching and research have been organized. In the social sciences, students get little or no opportunity to engage in research during their four college years. In graduate school, generally they only become involved in research in their second year as they work on a master's thesis. Furthermore, as noted in Chapter 1, many students get their doctorates without doing any fieldwork at all.

In contrast, we organized teaching and learning around the field research process. At first I sought to recruit graduate students in sociology or anthropology to do the fieldwork, but I found that potential candidates were either employed by the Peruvian government or were studying abroad. The Peruvian university has a five-year undergraduate program, the first two years devoted to general studies and the last three (culminating in a thesis) concentrated in the student's major discipline.

For our first village studies (in the Chancay Valley near Lima), Dr. Matos worked with a group of students from San Marcos National University, where he was also a Professor of Anthropology. The students were in the third to fifth years of their undergraduate program, and two fifth-year students served as field supervisors. This arrangement worked so well that we continued to work with and through undergraduate students throughout our program. (For a detailed account of the IEP-Cornell program, see Whyte, 1984:129-51.)

The only formal teaching throughout these years was concentrated in a two-week workshop in the IEP for those students who had done the best work in the various surveys and preliminary anthropological studies. Instruction was concentrated on the statistical analysis of the village survey data. Julio Cotler of IEP and I participated in the discussion, which was organized and led by Cornell's research associate Oscar Alers. Each student was required to derive a hypothesis from his or her own field studies and then test the hypothesis on the area survey data.

Otherwise, the teaching and learning were organized around our meetings with students in preparation for fieldwork and in discussions with them during and after the fieldwork as we sought to make sense out of the surveys and anthropological studies.

We linked our teaching and research at Cornell closely with our field studies in Peru. For a number of years, Williams and I collaborated in a seminar based on the analysis of our Peruvian research data. Williams had the expertise in administration and analysis of surveys that I lacked, and he guided students through their own analyses of the surveys carried out in 1964 and 1969, against the background of the anthropological studies. Students who took the seminar in preparation for carrying out their own field studies in Latin America told us that this was an invaluable experience. The preliminary work in discovering what could and what could not be learned from further analysis of our Peruvian data gave them a head start in designing their own thesis surveys.

One of those students, Georgio Alberti, became a key figure in the further development of IEP. From the seminar at Cornell, he went on to design and carry out a series of community studies in the Mantaro Valley of the Peruvian highlands for his doctoral thesis.

Teaming up with Lamonde Tullis, a graduate student from another American university, Alberti recruited several students from the sociology or anthropology departments of the Central University at Huancayo to carry out studies designed by Alberti and Tullis in half a dozen rural

communities. Alberti combined the field activities with informal seminars in Huancayo, orienting students to methodologies and theories so
that they would not be simply hired hands. These informal seminars
continued during the field trips as Alberti and Tullis discussed with
students on the way out what they were going to be doing that day and
on the way home, after collecting the students from their field sites,
what they had learned that day. Of course, Alberti himself was actively
involved in the fieldwork at one or another of these communities. One
of these students later moved to Lima to become a valued staff member
of IEP.

Alberti's skillful performance in the field with these students encouraged us and Matos to find the financing to continue his involvement in
Peru, following completion of his doctoral thesis, as a key staff member
of IEP representing our Cornell program in Peru.

With the exception of our two-week seminar in survey analysis, our
teaching was limited to discussions centered around our surveys and
anthropological studies. We encouraged the students to report in writing on their own field studies so as to avoid the exploitative relationship that would have prevailed if we had simply used them to gather
data and had reserved the data analysis and report writing for project
directors.

What were the payoffs of this program? One of the most obvious
payoffs was a series of research publications both in Spanish and English. Furthermore, the authorship of these publications was not limited to the senior American and Peruvian researchers. A number of the
more promising Peruvian students got their start with IEP in research
publications.

Although Cornell had nothing to do with the creation of IEP, in its
early years the financing through our American grants became essential
to the survival of IEP. When it appeared that our Cornell financing was
coming to an end, Matos told me that this would mean the end of IEP,
and we had a bittersweet discussion regarding how mutually fruitful our
relationship had been and how sad we were that it was coming to an
end. At the eleventh hour, we received new National Institute of Mental
Health (NIMH) grants that supported the continuation of our joint
program and ensured the survival of IEP for at least another two years.
Of course, this dependence of IEP on financing from Cornell was not
healthy for IEP or Cornell, although I pointed out to Matos that we at
Cornell had become completely dependent on IEP for carrying out our
field program in Peru. By the time we decided to bring our IEP-Cornell

involvement to an end, fortunately IEP had established such a track record in research and publications that it had become completely independent of Cornell financially. At this writing, IEP remains vigorous and productive in research and publications under new Peruvian leadership—an extraordinary record of institutional survival in a very precarious political and economic environment.

We can also point to important payoffs in the development of Peruvian human resources among social scientists and historians. Of those students who participated in our field studies, one went on to gain a doctoral degree in development sociology at Cornell and another received a master's degree in the same field. Three students in our program went on to earn a doctoral degree at English universities. In no cases was the financial support for these graduate programs provided by either Cornell or IEP. The students had won fellowship support on the basis of what they had achieved in our joint program. Later they reported they had entered graduate work in America or England with a head start over native students. They began their formal graduate studies abroad, bringing with them the basic material for master's or doctoral theses and reports on these materials, written in Spanish. They simply had to translate what they had written into English and make some further adjustments in the analysis to satisfy their professors.

During this same period, the Agency for International Development (AID) contracted with North Carolina State University to develop within Peru's Agricultural University a program of teaching and research in rural sociology. This program developed along traditional lines, following the assumption that it was necessary to build the teaching program first. This required financing for salaries and for moving and living expenses for the American professors who were to design the program and teach some of the basic courses. Only after the courses and seminars had been developed and taught several times did the staff try to give students some exposure to fieldwork—and the projects undertaken seemed more like student exercises than serious research enterprises. Several of the advanced students were then granted fellowships for graduate work in the United States, supported by the AID contract.

Compared to our own program, it seemed to me that this AID-financed program had certain unfavorable characteristics. First, getting to any serious research took much longer, if it ever got done at all. Second, this program was far more costly. Third, there was no assurance that students sent to the United States for their graduate training would come back prepared to fit into Peru and to develop effective teaching and research there. Our program's students only went abroad to study after developing a firm base for research and future teaching in Peru.

Before leaving this case, I should acknowledge that we were not able to reach all the objectives set for ourselves. It soon became clear that we would not be able to follow closely over five years the twenty-six villages surveyed in 1964, so we decided to concentrate our future fieldwork and our 1964-to-1969 comparative surveys to twelve villages. That change in scale, however, only affected one of our objectives: that of strengthening the capacity of sociology and anthropology students and professors to carry out our model of integrated fieldwork. Here we suffered not only from an overly ambitious research plan but also from the internal political struggles within the various universities, which made it impossible to deal with such a far-flung set of activities along with the diplomatic problems involved in the research operations.

Even so, the five-university strategy did not turn out to be a total loss. We did get reasonably good 1964 survey data from four of the universities, providing a base for the twelve village cases that we continued to work with through 1969, with the more experienced students in IEP playing the leading roles in later research. Furthermore, several of the more promising students from the regional university in the 1964 program later joined the IEP staff for the follow-up studies. Also this program strengthened my ties with Oscar Nuñez del Prado, professor of anthropology at the University of Cuzco, who directed our 1964 research in his area. With my encouragement, he wrote up his own account of an impressive applied anthropology project he had directed in one of the villages included in our studies (Nuñez del Prado, 1973).

This case illustrates a further advantage of a multiobjective strategy. If you pursue a single objective and fail to reach it, then your project seems to you and to others a flat-out failure. If you pursue a multiobjective strategy and fail to reach one of your objectives, then your project may nevertheless seem to you and others as successful—perhaps even as a great success.

Finally, to reemphasize my initial point in introducing this case, it would not have been possible to pursue all of these objectives in the same project or program if we had attempted to strengthen teaching and research by organizing those two activities in the traditional pattern. To achieve an effective integration of teaching and research, we built the teaching into the research program, thereby showing that it was possible to do solid research with student field-workers beginning their research several years before their American counterparts in conventional American programs.

JOINT PAYOFFS AND MULTIOBJECTIVE PLANNING IN AGRICULTURE AND INDUSTRY

Here we review how these theoretical ideas apply in industry and in agricultural research and development.

In the transfer of technology model, it was assumed that the objectives of the development process should be determined by the professional experts, with little or no consideration of objectives the farmers might determine for themselves. While the experts hoped to provide benefits for the small farmers, Joint Payoffs were not involved; according to my definition, Joint Payoffs only arise when two or more parties discuss and mutually agree on an action program.

In the program of participatory action research in Guatemalan agriculture, the professionals encouraged small farmers to take an active part in discussing objectives and determining objectives. As these participatory programs developed further, the professionals added to their own objectives one shared with the small farmers: strengthening rural community organization so as to contribute to a number of other objectives beyond enhancing farm output. They found themselves working with the villagers in strengthening local leadership and increasing small farmers' abilities to develop and utilize new ideas and information.

Within both ICTA and CIP, those in leadership positions sought to structure applied research in ways that built effective interdisciplinary collaboration and advanced science in the various disciplines. In both organizations, the professionals were not focused solely on bottom-line considerations: material progress in agricultural yields or in publications demonstrating their contributions to science. They were concerned also with developing new and better ways to carry out applied research and with diffusing these methods through national and international informational and educational networks.

In industry, the Xerox-ACTWU case of participatory programs leading up to the cost study teams illustrates both Joint Payoffs and multiobjective projects. Workers and union leaders had an obvious interest in maintaining employment, and Xerox top management had committed itself to maintaining at least fifty percent of its worldwide manufacturing employment in the United States. Through the CSTs and related activities, they were learning how to make this shared objective a practical reality. At the same time, leaders of both parties were committed to the objective of maintaining and strengthening what had been for years a reasonably cooperative union-management relationship. This led them into further Joint Payoff projects organized around the objectives of building management and union training programs designed to strengthen operational efficiency, developing more effective leadership within both organizations, and building greater employment security.

In the Mondragón case, we have noted how the leaders of the cooperatives made explicit to themselves and to the members the social and economic values that established commitment to a number of objectives. Furthermore, we have observed how their decision-making processes were guided by the aim of finding an equilibrium or balance between two value-laden objectives rather than sacrificing one for the other. Clearly the whole cooperative structure is build on a Joint Payoff principle, the mutual sharing among all members of financial gains or losses. For this principle to be internalized among the rank-and-file members, a financial formula is not sufficient. Commitment to cooperative values is supported by an extraordinarily widespread participation of the members in decision making.

19. Determinants of the Meaning of Rewards and Penalties

How do persons determine what behavior is effective in gaining rewards and avoiding penalties? The answer is obvious when the question refers to dogs or pigeons, for whom Pavlov and Skinner provided immediate and tangible rewards and penalties following the action specified by their experiments. Such a linkage between stimulus and response psychologists call a conditioned reflex. In human affairs, rarely do concrete and tangible rewards or penalties occur immediately following a particular action.

In most situations, humans have to judge whether a particular line of action (usually more than a single act) advances them toward rewards or helps them to avoid penalties. How do they make those judgments?

In my view, the connecting link between such judging and subsequent action is provided by significant *symbols* (words, actions of others, or physical objects) that, in the individual's experience, come to stand for favorable or unfavorable outcomes.

How do *symbols* acquire their meaning for a person? I visualize five principal sources: well nigh universal characteristics of human nature, the personal life experience of the individual, cognitive maps that frame their meaning, cultures, and social structures. Here I summarize my interpretation of their influences, and I will then go on to illustrate with case examples.

Humans develop their capacities to make sense out of symbols through their life experience. I am not concerned with making in-depth personality studies of particular individuals but rather with discovering how numbers of individuals, sharing similar life experiences, come to interpret certain key symbols in similar ways—for example, What life experiences lead men to accept or reject unions?, a question I explore later in this chapter.

It is characteristic of human nature in general to regard a material gain as rewarding and physical pain as punishing—except for those whose values commit them to an austere way of life, and those who accept pain as necessary in the restoration of health (in surgery, for example) or whose religious commitments lead them to regard physical suffering as a means of purifying the soul. For most people most of the time, the positive or negative values of material gain or of physical pain can be taken as obvious. The harder questions to answer are those focusing on experiences that are not so obviously rewarding or punishing.

Humans do not interpret a particular symbol as if it appeared on a blank slate. They develop their own conceptual frameworks through which they interpret a given symbol. Those frameworks I call cognitive maps. I am not suggesting that this cognitive mapping process is an entirely intellectual and wholly conscious process or that the judgments made would be considered rational by a detached observer. I assume that the formation of such cognitive maps arises out of both thinking and feeling and may provide persons with either effective or ineffective guidance regarding what actions will pay off for them. The point is simply that it is useful to understand the cognitive maps of persons to the extent that we can interpret these maps from observing persons' actions and listening to how they explain themselves.

If shared by many people, especially those in leadership positions, cognitive maps are an important element in culture, but there are many other elements important in shaping behavior. Some have defined culture in such an all-encompassing way as to include all aspects of social, economic, and political life, even including "material culture"—the tools and machines people use. With this definition, we cannot study the influence of culture on anything else because there is nothing else to which to relate it. I prefer to limit the definition to widely shared patterns of behavior and beliefs regarding what activities are positively or negatively valued, and norms or standards of how members of that organization or community *should* behave.

In some cases, we can find common elements of culture shared throughout a nation, but in many cases we need to be aware of important cultural differences based on ethnic group identification or religion. Furthermore, while members of any organization will inevitably be influenced by the culture of the comnmunity where they have grown to adulthood, their organization over time will develop its own internal culture. As we have seen, the Mondragón cooperatives incorporated some elements of Basque culture, but also developed cultural elements not found elsewhere in the Basque country or anywhere else.

Social structure affects behavior, values, and beliefs in pervasive ways. The individual's position in that structure can strongly affect his or her chances for achieving success in social, economic, and political life. The rigidity or flexibility of that structure can influence the success or failure of those who wish to create new economic enterprises. I will illustrate some of the more important influences of the social structure on economic development later in this chapter.

COGNITIVE MAPS AS THEORETICAL FRAMEWORKS

I see cognitive maps as providing humans with theoretical frameworks regarding the way the world works, at least within their immediate environment.

It is a mistake to assume that only scientists have theories. It is impossible for anyone to behave in an orderly fashion without developing some kind of theoretical framework to provide a context for guiding actions in search of particular consequences.

As noted in Chapter 1, we need to distinguish among several types of theory, along the following lines:

Local theory. Max Elden has drawn attention to the importance of recognizing the local theory in use by members of organizations (Elden, 1979). Furthermore, in any organization where there are important cleavages between different levels or segments, there may be several local theories. Thus there can be one local theory held by members of management and another local theory held by workers.

Nowhere is such a local theory written out and explicitly stated. On the other hand, through observing consistent patterns of behavior and through interviewing and examining written communications, the researcher can deduce its general outlines.

Formal theory. This refers to more elaborate, systematic, general, and explicitly stated propositions. The existence of this body of theory is widely recognized. Such formal theories are often developed by powerful and/or socially elite individuals who use the theories to influence and control others. Some elements of formal theory may be based on scientific research, but others are based on unsupported assumptions. Nevertheless, formal theory gives the believer a coherent view of the way the world works—however accurate or inaccurate that view may be.

Scientifically grounded theory. We refer to a set of propositions that have their primary basis in empirical observations, measurements, and experiments. At any time, researchers may discover errors and incorrect inferences out of scientifically grounded theory, but science advances through the correction of errors and the reinterpretation of empirical data.

In this book, we hope to contribute to scientifically grounded theory. We must also deal with local theory and formal theory. We recognize that local theory in particular and also formal theory to some extent emerge out of past patterns of behavior, but they also tend to shape present behavior. We need to understand local theory in order to fit proposed innovations into the preexisting cognitive map of the members of the organization. As local theory differs from locale to locale and from organizational segment to segment, it is impossible to generalize beyond pointing out its universal existence. As formal theory is articulated and diffused so widely that we can trace its impact, we will focus on the relation of formal theory to behavior.

Formal Theory in Industry

Frederick W. Taylor is universally recognized as the father of scientific management, although he was not the first to give his formal theory that title. The title was bestowed by Judge Louis Brandeis in hearings before Congress on the Eastern rate case in 1910. The decisions in that case hinged on the question of whether increasing costs forced the railroads to increase their rates or whether increasing efficiencies could make it possible to avoid such price increases. In making the case against rate increases, Brandeis argued that F. W. Taylor's "scientific management" could be implemented so as to make such increases unnecessary.

Well before his doctrines came to the attention of Congress, Taylor was having important impacts on management ideologies, structures, and practices. Taylor did not begin his efficiency studies in scientific laboratories. He went out first to work on the machines and to observe skilled workmen. Through his observations he aimed to systematize and quantify operations and to discover modifications in methods that would yield better results. When he and his associates had determined the "one best way" to perform a particular job, they then set down detailed rules to standardize the motions of all those performing the particular job. This was designed to wrest the planning and control of work from workers and place it in the hands of managers and engineers.

Regarding Taylor's appeal to management, Hugh Aitken gives this explanation in his study of the most extensive application of Taylor's program at the Watertown Arsenal from 1908 to 1915 (Aitken, 1960:120):

> The system which Taylorism displaced had been characterized by a considerable degree of informal organization, well understood by the participants but never reduced to written formulas. In part, the officers' firm belief in the efficiency of the new system may have been due to the fact that, under Taylorism, they felt that they, and not the workman, were really managing the arsenal for the first time.

Taylor recognized that, in order for management to gain control over production,

> the management must take over and perform much of the work which is left to the men; almost every act of the workman should be preceded by one or more preparatory acts of the management. (Taylor, 1911:26)

Taylor did not hesitate to express his views directly to workers, with predictable reactions. His biographer cites one such argument (Copley, 1923:188):

Now, among the sarcastic remarks which Taylor used to toss off to his men, the one that caused them to rear and plunge the most often will appear in this statement by William A. Fannon: "I often thought Mr. Taylor would have made more rapid progress if he had been more tactful and not so willing to combat in such an intense way anyone who did not agree with him. A remark that always impressed Mr. Shartle and myself was one he sometimes used when we opposed him or discussed a proposition with him. 'You are not supposed to think,' he would say. 'There are other people paid for thinking around here.' To this Mr. Shartle adds: "I never would admit to Mr. Taylor that I was not allowed to think. We used to have some hot arguments just over that point."

Taylor recognized the need to explain his methods to what he called "the officer class," but he did not believe in discussions with workers. On dealing with the worker, he wrote,

Rarely reason with him; never match wits with him; throw him onto the defensive; take short steps one after another in quick succession without talking about them, at least until after they are taken; set object lessons for men to see. (Copley, 1923:421)

Taylor recognized from the outset that he faced serious resistance from traditionally minded management people. He once wrote,

One of the most recent developments of the experts has been that of the Science of Engineering. So recent is this development that I can remember distinctly the time when an educated scientific engineer was looked upon with profound suspicion by practically the whole manufacturing community. . . .

The Science of Engineering started only when a few experts (who were invariably despised and sneered at by the engineers of their day) made the assertion that engineering practice should be founded upon exact knowledge of facts rather than upon general experience and observation. (Copley, 1923:100-101)

How do we evaluate Taylorism today, from a scientific standpoint? Clearly "scientific management" is mainly a formal systematic theory, but it does contain certain elements of scientifically grounded theory, involving scientific observation and measurement. In his own evaluation of Taylor's work, Aitken points to some genuine scientific achievements. His experiments in the cutting of steel with various alloys speeded up the cutting process two to four times over the prevailing methods. Taylor also made important contributions to industrial accounting systems and to the analysis of work flow. He developed systematic methods of observing and measuring the workers' motions in carrying out various jobs.

Social relations at work had no place in Taylorism. Scientific management focused only on the behavior of individual workers, assuming that such behavior could and should be controlled entirely by management. To the extent that he recognized their existence, Taylor saw concerted actions by groups of workers or by unions simply as obstacles for management to overcome.

As Giorgio Alberti has pointed out (personal communication), Taylorism is also flawed in its separation of information, ideas, and planning, on the one hand, from execution, on the other. Those who follow Taylor's cognitive map thereby abandon the possibility of developing a *learning organization*. In the real world, it is not only managers and engineers who learn from experience. In the course of field research over the past half century, we have encountered innumerable cases in which workers have discovered serious technical problems in the instructions given them by management.

As a social philosophy, Taylorism is no longer praised by American managers, and it has become generally discredited around the world. A modern manager is unlikely to express his views in such elitist terms, and it would be rare indeed to find a manager who would tell a worker that he was not supposed to use his brains. This does not mean, however, that Taylorism no longer has any impact on American management. Taylor's impact is still observed in organizational structures, technologies and work-flow arrangements, the division of labor, and the managerial bureaucracies that grew up in response to this formal theory. Furthermore, Taylor himself recognized that his system was designed to take power away from workers and concentrate it in management. Most managers are still much concerned over the protection of their prerogatives. The power protection element of Taylorism thus has contributed to the formation of management beliefs and values that are still evident today.

Formal Theory in Agricultural
Research and Development

In agricultural research and development, local theory is the general framework developed by small farmers in a particular community out of their own farming experience. Until recently, professionals in this field saw no need to understand local theory, even if they were aware of its existence.

How do persons come to abandon formal theories such as Taylorism and move toward a formal theory incorporating active processes of participation? And how does behavior change along with this shift in theoretical frameworks? We will provide case illustrations of such shifts and later formulate some general conclusions.

CULTURAL INFLUENCES SHAPING
HUMAN INTERACTION

Culture exerts pervasive influences on our responses to particular symbols and therefore on behavior. Culture shapes styles of interpersonal interaction and communication. We can observe differences along these dimensions: use of physical space and touching, expression of emotions, directness of expression, and duration of interaction required for business dealings.

In the use of conversational space, we find marked differences between North Americans and Latin Americans.

In North America, the "proper" distance to stand when talking to another adult male you do not know well is about two feet, at least in a formal business conversation. (Naturally at a cocktail party, the distance shrinks, but anything under eight to ten inches is likely to provoke an apology or an attempt to back up.)

To a Latin American, with his cultural traditions and habits, a distance of two feet seems to him approximately what five feet would to us. To him, we seem distant and cold. To us, he gives an impression of pushiness.

As soon as a Latin American moves close enough for him to feel comfortable, we feel uncomfortable and edge back. We once observed a conversation between a Latin and a North American which began at one end of a forty-foot hall. At intervals we noticed them again, finally at the other end of the hall. This rather amusing displacement had been accomplished by an almost continual series of small backward steps on the part of the American, trying unconsciously to reach a comfortable talking distance, and an equal closing of the gap by the Latin American as he attempted to reach his accustomed space.

Americans in their offices in Latin America tend to keep their native acquaintances at our distance—not the Latin American's distance—by taking up a position behind a desk or typewriter. The barricade approach to communication is practiced even by old hands in Latin America who are completely unaware of its cultural significance. They know only that they are comfortable without realizing that the distance and equipment unconsciously make the Latin American uncomfortable. (Hall and Whyte, 1960:9-10)

Different cultures have different standards regarding how much emotion it is appropriate to express in casual or business communication. A common American pattern dictates that emotions should not be strongly expressed except in intimate relationships, but among the ethnic groups making up our population there are of course marked differences in this regard. In the course of my first research project, studying an Italian-American slum district in Boston, I was living with a family of immigrants who owned a restaurant. I was at first puzzled when I observed the mother and father of the family engaged in conversation with friends after the restaurant had closed for business. At times, I would be startled by the apparent vehemence with which the people expressed their views—from loud voices to what seemed to me unrestrained gestures. But then the conversational interchange would end with an outbreak of laughter. In my culture a conversation involving such high-decibel sounds and vigorous gestures indicated that people were really angry at each other; I was learning that these Italian immigrants were just enjoying the interchange.

Duration of Interaction

In your first encounter with someone with whom you hope to do business or resolve a particular problem, how long should the conversation last? In the United States, following our well-known maxim "Time is money," we take pride in getting down to business quickly, focusing directly on the problem at issue, with a minimum of social amenities.

In Latin America and also in Japan the expected pattern is quite different. People in those cultures tend to assume that those who are going to do business with each other should first establish some personal relationship. They go on the reasonable assumption that the kind of person you are is more important than what you say you want to do. Under these conditions, the American is likely to seem aggressive and insensitive and therefore perhaps unreliable, whereas he may think a Peruvian or Japanese person is confusing business and social relations.

Resolving Disagreements

Cultures also vary regarding the appropriateness of expressing disagreements directly. In the traditional American pattern, we place a high value on bringing disagreements out into the open, assuming that if we confront them directly, we can move on to a resolution.

We also feel that it is important for two parties in disagreement to work out their disagreement directly without recourse to third parties, while at the same time we recognize that the intervention of third parties may be necessary in some situations. This suggests distinguishing among styles of resolution of disagreements in terms of two dimensions: direct versus indirect expression of disagreements; and confronting versus nonconfronting. That formulation suggests the four-box framework illustrated in Figure 19.1.

Placement of the United States in box "1" indicates that our culture favors direct confrontation of problems among the interested parties. We are expected to be forthright, expressing our opinions frankly, "thrashing it out," in order to reach a common understanding and continue working together. When this process is handled with sensitivity and skill it works well, as it gets problems out in the open where they can be resolved more readily. All too often, however, the process produces bruised feelings that make it more difficult for the parties to work together in the future. Furthermore, we often find ourselves unable to resolve the problems we confront directly and therefore resort to third-party intervention—mediators and arbitrators in industrial relations, courts of law in civil disputes. (We show this in Figure 19.1 with the dotted-line arrow pointing to box 2.) We are becoming known as an increasingly litigious society. In this regard, it is interesting to note one field in which the United States far surpasses Japan: per capita we have ten times as many lawyers as the Japanese have (Vogel, 1979).

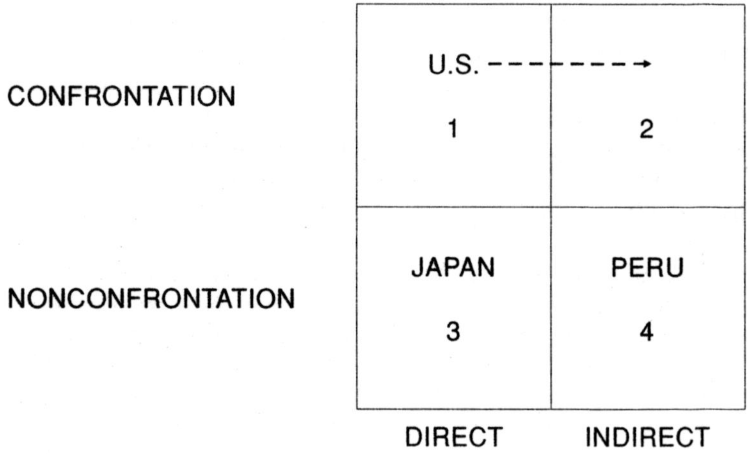

Figure 19.1. Cultural Styles for Resolving Disagreements

The Japanese have their confrontations in mass demonstrations, but in small-scale discussions and negotiations confrontations are avoided. In the initial stages of discussion the Japanese avoid flat statements of opinion. One who thinks he has an important idea will nevertheless express it very tentatively as if it were a mere casual thought and only begin to elaborate on the idea if he perceives that he is getting a positive response. If that response is not forthcoming, the Japanese backs off from his initial approach and seeks to draw out his discussion partners to discover what others are thinking and feeling so as to modify his original idea or find a different way of expressing it. Language itself seems to facilitate this feeling-out process for the Japanese. While English lends itself readily to precise and unambiguous statements, Japanese is more suited to the communication of feelings than of precise cognitive meanings. This induces the Japanese to recognize that understanding each other often requires an extended feeling-out process in discussion.

This cultural difference often leads Americans to be impatient with the time it takes Japanese to come out of a discussion with a decision. American-style discussion and decision making proceeds more rapidly, but, when it comes to implementing decisions, the Japanese appear to have a clear advantage. All those who will play major roles in implementation will have been involved in the discussion and will have fully explored the action implications of the decision, so many potential problems are worked out in advance.

While Americans and Japanese seek to resolve disagreements directly, Peruvians tend to avoid either the United States style of confrontation or the Japanese style of feeling their way around differences. In an earlier writing we expressed the U.S.-Peruvian contrast in this way (Whyte and Braun, 1968:135-36):

> Peruvians have no such idea of the value of personal confrontation. In their culture, the emphasis is on avoiding direct expressions of interpersonal conflict. This same tendency to avoid open disagreement is found in cases when one Peruvian asks another to do something for him. It somehow does not seem appropriate to refuse outright. The appropriate response is one or another form of "yes," but then often the thing does not get done.
>
> In Peru the word is used so seldom that we are startled when we hear someone say "no." One attuned to the culture learns not to take "yes" seriously. You cannot judge by the words alone; you must learn to listen for the melody. In other words, you look and listen for cues surrounding the word "yes" in the current situation and in the past behavior of the speaker in order to predict what he is likely to do. While a well-attuned Peruvian is far better at divining the meaning of "yes" than an outsider, even Peruvians have a hard time judging what a man will do on the basis of what he says. In part, this grows out of the cultural inhibition against saying "no." If a man cannot say "no," then the word "yes" loses its meaning. Under these circumstances the predictability that is so important for organizational life is difficult to achieve.

This unpredictability might be reduced if Peruvians adopted a more Japanese style of discussion in which outright expressions of disagreement are avoided and yet people reach out beyond the words expressed to feel their way to a common understanding of their mutual problems. Peruvian culture avoids both confrontation and this feeling-out process. As differences of opinion and interests arise in practice, Peruvians have difficulty resolving them in face-to-face discussion. If they must continue to work together in an organization, they refer disputes to higher authority for resolution.

Interpersonal Trust

Cultures also differ in interpersonal trust or faith in people. Surveys carried out in the 1960s by Lawrence K. Williams, Graciela Flores, and

I show marked differences between Peru and the United States in this regard. Earlier the Cornell Values Study of 2,975 students in eleven colleges showed that eighty percent of the respondents picked the high-faith alternative on the item "Some people say that you can trust most people. Other people say that you can't be too careful in your relations with other people." Our survey of 1,833 male high school seniors in public and private schools in Lima and several provincial cities showed only thirty-one percent choosing this same alternative. The same item applied to 202 white-collar workers in a Peruvian public utility yielded a thirty-seven percent trusting response. Perhaps the best comparison is that between a U.S. Sears, Roebuck and Company unit (n = 176) and a Peruvian Sears unit (n = 164). This also showed U.S. employees giving the more trusting response—and by a wide margin, ninety-three percent to forty-seven percent.

In international comparative surveys (Almond and Verba, 1963), we also find the United States markedly higher in interpersonal trust than England, West Germany, Italy, and Mexico. Unfortunately I do not as yet have survey data from Japan on these same trust items. However, everything else we know about Japan suggests that Japan is a high-trust culture.

Interpersonal trust is a critical variable affecting managerial leadership style and the way people work together in organizations. If you do not trust people, you hesitate to delegate authority and responsibility— how do you know that subordinates will really do the job and not undermine your position? If you do not trust people, you will find it difficult to handle negotiations and other relationships where no direct exercise of authority is involved. How can you count on the other fellow to do what he says if you have no control over him?

Individualism Versus Group Solidarity

On this dimension, there appears to be a sharp distinction between Japan, on the one hand, and the United States and Peru, on the other— with Japan emphasizing group solidarity and organizational loyalty and American and Peruvian cultures strongly emphasizing individualism. As we look at Peru and the United States more closely, we see an important difference. The typical Peruvian pattern of relations between the individual and the organization places the Peruvian in a position of either rebelling against the organization or withdrawing from it, with the necessary qualification that where rebellion is out of the question, submission is required. Peruvians typically do not see much possibility in individual initiative to change organizations.

The American pattern differs in that the individual is expected to exercise initiative within the organization and to strive to make it function better—or at least function so as to better satisfy the desires of the individual. There is a widespread belief that organizations can be changed by individual initiative, and it is generally assumed that the individual exercises initiative not simply by him or herself but rather by mobilizing other individuals to bring pressure on the organization. This pattern was confirmed in the international comparative studies of Almond and Verba, where American respondents showed a much greater tendency toward activism to change organizations than was manifested by respondents in other countries.

To a much greater degree in the United States than in Japan, the organization is believed to be led and dominated by outstanding individuals—industrial leaders are culture heroes. In Japan, while such individual leaders are well known and respected, the prevailing pattern is to conceptualize the organization in terms of integrated groups and departments working together with strong bonds of overall organizational loyalty. This organizational loyalty has been supported in the past by much stronger organizational commitments to employment security for all employees than we find in the United States or Peru. Loyalty to the total organization is much stronger in Japan than in our other two nations. The United States has long been characterized by more active movement of workers and of staff people and managers from one firm to another than is the case in Japan; and feelings of organizational loyalty seem to have diminished in the United States in recent years as merger and takeover activities have become more prominent. Today even management people who previously would have had very secure positions cannot be sure that, even if they do a good job, they will be promoted or even continued in that position. From one day to the next, a raiding organization might take control of the firm and replace key people with a new team.

Culture and Career Choices

Culture influences career choices by establishing distinctions from highly honored to low prestige occupations and professions.

If the culture places low value on industrial entrepreneurship, this will diminish the supply of individuals striking out to create their own firms, and in fact we may find entrepreneurs only among those not fully integrated into that culture.

This has been the case in Peru, and Peru in this regard seems to mirror what has been reported for a number of other Latin American countries. With very few exceptions, Peruvian successful industrial entrepreneurs have been immigrants or sons of immigrants. By the time the next generation after the immigrant grandparents comes along, those Peruvians seem to be sufficiently integrated into the culture that entrepreneurial careers do not interest them.

To understand this cultural influence, I began reading children's history books, looking for the role models who might serve to stimulate Peruvian children and socialize them into the values of their culture. I found no industrial entrepreneurs featured as role models. The greatest heroes in the history books all gained fame in the way that they lost battles and their lives in the war of the Pacific, in which Peru suffered a catastrophic defeat at the hands of Chile. For example, General Alfonso Ugarte won his place in history during his command of a division in a battle on the coast. In the course of this losing battle, he saw that the Peruvian flag of one of his battalions was about to fall into the hands of the enemy. Spurring his horse forward, he grabbed the flag as he plunged off the cliff, "preferring to bury himself in the sea rather than see it soiled by the enemy." The battle was already lost when Ugarte made his charge, and his heroic self-sacrifice accomplished no concrete result. The other heroes also won their places in history through the gallant way in which they died rather than through any concrete achievements. In traditional Peruvian culture, style was more important than substance.

In the 1960s, the most prominent Peruvian entrepreneurs were Luis Banchero, Alfredo D'Onofrio, and Oscar Ferrand. Son of an Italian immigrant, Banchero had to struggle to support himself while getting an education, at one time working in an automotive service station. Later he got into the fish-meal business and built the largest and most successful firm exploiting the resources of the sea. D'Onofrio arrived in Peru from Italy when he was one year old, bringing his family with him. He got his start on a pushcart, selling ice cream and candy. From that small beginning he went on to build the largest firm in this line of business. Oscar Ferrand was the son of a French immigrant who ran a small grocery store. The son then struck out for himself, establishing a successful company in the glass industry while at the same time building up the largest Ford Motor Company agency in Peru.

In an article published in English (Whyte, 1963) I included descriptions of the humble origins of these Peruvian entrepreneurs. When that article was to be printed in Spanish, jointly authored with research assistant Graciela Flores, she pleaded with me to omit reference to those humble origins.

I asked her, "Why leave that out? Aren't the facts well known in Peru?"

She replied, "Of course, but the children and grandchildren of the entrepreneurs would be embarrassed by accounts of humble origins of the original entrepreneurs."

In the United States, children and grandchildren of the entrepreneur who progressed "from rags to riches" take pride in those achievements. In Peru, the descendants of the successful entrepreneur strive to maintain the fiction that their family has always been well off and socially prominent.

This interpretation was reinforced for me as I followed the Lima newspapers over several years. Those Peruvian entrepreneurs received coverage in the press in the business section of the newspapers, and only when their firm had something important to report. Notably absent were any human interest stories regarding the struggles and personal successes of the entrepreneurs as they rose from those humble beginnings. Such feature stories, of course, are frequently found in the United States press.

In traditional Latin America, the high-prestige occupations have been in law and medicine, along with the ownership of large landed estates. In recent decades, the profession of engineering has been gaining ground. That trend is, of course, favorable to industrial development, but Peruvians have in the past looked on engineering as a profession that one practiced in an industrial organization or in government rather than as a base from which to launch one's own enterprise.

CULTURE, ENTREPRENEURSHIP, AND INDUSTRIAL DEVELOPMENT

In our cross-national comparisons, we begin with the question, Is creating a business a privilege or a right? In our culture, it does not occur to us to ask the question because we take the answer for granted: Anyone willing to risk personal efforts and capital has the right to start a firm. In earlier centuries in many countries a permit to start a firm was a privilege granted or withheld by the crown. Such privileges thus supported the patronage system through which the ruling family rewarded loyal and influential subjects. In some countries the administrative bureaucracies have maintained such systems of patronage long after the monarchs have passed from the scene.

Consider, for example, the case of Spain under the Franco dictatorship (1939-1975) as we trace the earliest steps in creating the Mondragón cooperatives. Five young Basques applied for a permit to create a foundry. They never even received an answer from government. As one of them wrote later,

> In 1955, authorizations for permits to establish a factory were subject to rigorous control, and those who had the authorizations looked upon them as if they were made of gold. (Whyte and Whyte, 1988:34)

Only through a combination of luck and the founders' alertness was it possible to launch Ulgor, the first worker cooperative.

> The first break came toward the end of 1955 when the five men learned that a private firm in Vitoria had gone bankrupt. The founders were less interested in the building and equipment than in the firm's license, which was extraordinarily broad in scope. The firm was authorized to produce a line of electrical and mechanical products for home use. By buying the firm, the founders gained rights that would have been inaccessible through any other channel. (Whyte and Whyte, 1988:34)

If the founders of the Mondragón cooperatives had not been able to find this rare loophole in government controls, the most dynamic and prosperous industrial complex in the Basque provinces today might never have come into existence.

In Peruvian government bureaucracies today we still see elements of the business control system established during the Spanish colonial era. During my years of research in Peru (1961-1976) I often heard statements on the difficulty of going through official channels to create a new business, but at the time I did not study this problem. Recently the problems facing the potential entrepreneur have been impressively documented through an experiment conducted by the Peruvian economist Hernando de Soto (1986). In seeking a permit for a small firm, his associates followed the official procedures and only offered bribes on two occasions when it became evident that otherwise it would be impossible to get the permit. It took the group 289 days and $1,231 in lost wages and bribes to get official recognition of the experimental firm. In the United States or Japan, completing the necessary procedures would ordinarily not require more than several hours.

This does not mean that no Peruvian firms are created except by those with money and political influence. It does mean that entrepreneurial activity has been largely concentrated in what is known as "the informal sector," consisting of illegal businesses whose precarious survival depends on escaping government attention or paying off the authorities. Such clandestine firms naturally have great difficulties in securing the technical assistance and bank financing necessary for survival and growth.

This case indicates that a cultural shift toward high values on entrepreneurial careers would not be sufficient to unleash a surge of entrepreneurship. Even if that very difficult cultural change could be accomplished, it would only increase the number of frustrated entrepreneurs—unless it were accompanied by elimination of the bureaucratic barriers. Such elimination could only be accomplished by a powerful political movement, which one day may come to pass in Peru and other developing countries facing the same problem.

SOCIAL CLASS AND INTERCLASS RELATIONS

Social class position tends to shape the way people regard those in markedly lower or higher positions than themselves. While such attitudes may be modified by abstract egalitarian beliefs, there is a general tendency to underestimate the intelligence and abilities of those occupying class positions markedly lower than one's own.

In any complex society, power has become increasingly built on higher education and professionalization. Professionalization requires not only learning certain skills and knowledge but also gaining organizational and public recognition so that only those with professional training have the right to lead others. This orientation leads to a sharp separation of professionally gained knowledge from knowledge gained by experience. Furthermore, this leads people in privileged positions, who have enjoyed high levels of education, to equate education with intelligence. This confusion can occur even among people who profess strong sympathies for the poor and oppressed. For example, the leaders of what they called "the Revolutionary Government of the Armed Forces" that took power in 1968 proclaimed that they were acting in the interests of the great masses of poor Peruvians. I had no reason to doubt their sincerity, but I was struck by the way the general who headed the council of advisers to the president expressed this commitment:

> We must work in this direction, to make the people understand that we are not going to achieve in a day the changes we hope for. We must recognize with sufficient clarity the cultural level of the worker in the lowest stratum of our society. For this reason I call this society ignorant, and therefore the greatest obstacle that the revolution faces is ignorance, because the clear needs of society cannot be understood by our people and they are not to blame for not having had the opportunity to educate themselves. (Whyte, 1975:37)

As we pursue our studies of cases where participatory processes have developed, again and again we encounter management people or agricultural professionals who tell us about their great revelation: the discovery that low-status people can actually think—and can even tell their superiors what they need to know if a given change project is to succeed. It will be an important sign of progress when this discovery no longer comes as a surprise to those in power positions.

PART IV

Integrating
Theory and Practice

20. Theory and Practice in Agriculture and Industry

I had planned to write chapters on theory and then on practice, but I found it did not make sense to put them in separate compartments. As various authorities have said in various ways, there is nothing so practical as a good theory. If that maxim is valid, then the best way of demonstrating the value of a theory is to show how it has been (or can be) applied in practical affairs.

First I need to state what I mean by theory. I do not start with the aim of erecting a structure of tested hypotheses that fit together, more or less, into some grand theory. I aim at something more modest but also more useful for guiding both research and practice.

For my theoretical stance, I hark back to a course in "Concrete Sociology" taught in 1937 by Harvard's Lawrence J. Henderson, an eminent biochemist whose interest in the work of Vilfredo Pareto had led him into this invasion of the social sciences. This background of scientific research and intellectual interests suggested to Henderson a parallel between sociology and medicine.

> The sociologist, like the physician, should have first, intimate, habitual, intuitive familiarity with things; secondly, systematic knowledge of things; and thirdly, an effective way of thinking about things.

With some modifications, I would accept that formulation today. To be sure, most physicians do not do research, but those who are engaged in research do not draw the sharp dividing line between basic and applied research that prevails in mainstream sociology. Furthermore, practicing physicians are expected to follow the research literature and attend research conferences in order to learn the latest methods of diagnosis and treatment. As sociology is not yet supplied with many researchers whose findings are designed for practical application, those of us who want to do applied sociology have to provide the linkages between research and practice ourselves.

I cannot provide readers with the "intuitive familiarity with things" that comes only from personal experience with those "things," but I have sought to provide "systematic knowledge of things" in agricultural research and development and in industrial relations. Here I proceed to lay out my view of "an effective way of thinking about things," which I take to mean establishing a firm base for both theory and practice. This general framework provides a way of viewing and defining problems, and ways of selecting relevant data and linking those data together analytically.

In this chapter I concentrate on linking theory and practice for participatory systems in the two types of organizations. In the final chapter, I discuss the implications of this applied research strategy for social research methods and for the further development of social theory.

CONCEPTUAL REQUIREMENTS FOR ORGANIZATIONAL LEADERSHIP

Moving from traditional organizational systems to participatory systems depends on a vision of the nature of participatory systems and some sense of direction to guide the change process. Ideally this means that the vision and sense of direction should exist among the leaders of the change process. By vision, I do not mean a clearly thought out and articulated statement of how the organization should function when participatory systems have been effectively established. Movement from one organizational state to another can be accompanied by a trial-and-error process through which failures or partial failures are abandoned or reshaped into new moves. Leaders should then seek to project to organization members the vision of a learning organization, capable of learning from its own experience. Learning, however, has practical meaning only insofar as it leads toward reaching certain objectives. Therefore, it is important for leaders to be able to articulate to organization members the objectives of progressing toward participatory systems. They need to be able to reflect on—and help organization members to reflect on—the relationship between current practices and the state of organizational systems toward which they aim to move.

Leaders should find it useful to think in terms of the three types of social theory discussed in Chapter 1. They need to recognize that organization members develop an implicit local theory, and, in any large organization, there will be somewhat different local theories being acted out in practice. Such local theories influence behavior, so it is important for leaders to recognize the common assumptions and shared attitudes and values that support prevailing ways of working.

Leaders also need to recognize the formal theories that have developed in their fields of action and that may continue to shape their own thoughts and actions. In industry, such formal theories have come to be known as "scientific management," a doctrine popularized in the early years of this century. While practitioners today generally have rejected this doctrine as a set of guiding principles, earlier practitioners shaped their organizational structures and work processes in accordance with the teaching of F.W. Taylor and his associates. In many cases, those structures and processes remain in practice even as the formal theory supporting them has been abandoned. As they try to move their organizations toward some approximation of a scientifically grounded theory shaping their practice, leaders need to be able to relate this theory-practice objective to the prevailing local theories and formal theory.

As we have noted, in agriculture no fully articulated formal theory (comparable to scientific management) has been created, yet we have identified some of its main elements underlying traditional ways of organizing agricultural research and development. They involve the assumptions that, for any agricultural problem, there must be a strictly technical "fix"; that the professionally and scientifically trained people know all that has been learned about agriculture; and that the peasants or small farmers are locked into their traditional ways. If the problem is resistance to change, the solution therefore is to devise a system to transfer technologies developed by the professional experts in ways that overcome this resistance. For leaders aiming to move their organizations toward participatory systems, it is important to recognize the constraints imposed by the formal theory and then to find a sense of direction toward participatory systems for themselves and others.

To meet the needs of participatory systems, leaders must shift the mix of transactional relationships away from the traditional pattern, which relied heavily on Authority. (See Chapters 16 and 17 for a discussion of Authority and other key concepts.) That does not mean abandoning Authority relationships, because we cannot assume that disagreements in participatory systems can readily and efficiently be resolved through discussions leading to consensus. A conceptual shift from control to commitment calls for less reliance on Authority and more reliance on Positive Exchange and especially on Joint Payoff relations.

In industry, we see increasing use of gain-sharing projects, and, of course, worker cooperatives are built on the Joint Payoff principle. In agriculture, farmer cooperatives build on the same principle and the various R&D projects we described exemplify it also, as we have seen in the socio-technical innovations increasing farmers' crop yields and in professionals' and technicians' acceptance of new methods that have enhanced reputations and led to organizational advancement.

Emphasis on Joint Payoffs also stimulates the development of multi-objective project and program planning. Often the creation of Joint Payoffs can only be accomplished if party A and party B get together to pursue an objective of party A and a different objective of party B. In that case, the project will advance more efficiently if both parties commit themselves to both objectives. In the Xerox case, for example, employment maintenance was the chief objective of the union leaders, but the management people dealing with the union also became strongly committed to that objective. Similarly, establishing or maintaining the economic viability of a department or plant was the chief objective of management, and that objective gained strong union commitment. This is reflected when we hear union officials talking about "what we have accomplished" through the economic recovery of a company. This indicates that the single-minded pursuit of the bottom line is a poor business strategy, even from a purely financial point of view.

In agricultural R&D, especially through the experience of CIP, we see among farmers, professionals, and program administrators a shift from pursuit of the narrow objective of increasing crop yields toward the related objectives of organizational learning.

Leaders also need to learn—and help others to learn—to think in terms of developing socio-technical systems. In both industry and agriculture, we have seen that purely technical fixes simply did not work. Obviously, a purely social fix will not work either. For those who recognize the need for such learning, much can be picked up from experience; but some formal training may be required. We will discuss the nature of such training as we follow the trail from social invention to organizational learning.

FROM SOCIAL INVENTION TO ORGANIZATIONAL LEARNING

There is some truth in the old adage "Necessity is the mother of invention." That appears to be one key to social inventions in both agriculture and industry.

In agriculture, the early achievements of "the green revolution" delayed recognition of the need to develop better ways of working with small farmers. As students of agriculture began to learn that the benefits of these achievements were not reaching small farmers dependent on rainfall, the special needs of small farmers began receiving more professional and political attention. This was fueled by not only humanistic concerns. In the developing world, radical political parties were making land reform their battle cry, and many liberals were supporting this general objective. In countries where a large percentage of arable land is owned by a relatively small number of rich families, transferring any sizable part of those holdings to poor farmers involves enormous political and economic problems. It may appear that such a transfer can only be accomplished through a revolution. Most governments are therefore more inclined to look for ways of helping small farmers to do better with their existing holdings.

There were also macroeconomic reasons in Mexico and Guatemala for giving special attention to small farmers. In both countries, most of the maize was being grown by small farmers, and the productivity of their farms was not keeping pace with population growth and increasing consumer demands. Unless the small farmers could increase their output of maize and other crops, consumer needs would have to be met through imports—a major problem for nations short of foreign exchange.

In industry, different countries faced different needs but all these needs seemed to move them in the same general direction. In Norway, it was the need for change to make the shipping industry more competitive with fleets attached to low-wage nations. For Volvo, in Sweden, it was the need to change the nature of work so as to recruit and retain more Swedish workers. In Japan, the devastation of losing a war produced a general search for new and better ways of working, and postwar union-management conflicts impelled industry leaders to search for new ways of involving workers in a cooperative process with management. In the United States, it was the growing threat of Japanese competition that motivated industry leaders to reach out to try to learn and apply Japanese methods of worker participation.

Experience and research in the United States indicated that the adaptation of quality control circles did not meet the need that had given rise to the growing interest in worker participation. As international competition made increasingly significant inroads into American manufacturing, it became clear that worker discussion groups, strictly limited to immediate shop-floor problems, were not the answer. This led to the development of distinctively American social inventions, such as Xerox's cost study teams. Such social inventions fit into an emerging pattern of involving the union in strategic decision making with management and integrating employee involvement with collective bargaining.

Going from a social invention to organizational learning involves advancing from a pilot model to generalized practice. The social invention is usually tried out first on a small scale. Then, if it shows promise, its promoters seek to expand that scale. Such expansion must be supported and guided by changes in organizational structure, in budgetary allocations and policies, and in other social processes.

In agricultural R&D, the first problem was to discover how professionals could work participatively with small farmers. We have followed this process of social invention first in ICTA in Guatemala and also with the International Potato Center (CIP). Then the problem became how to fit this new way of working into the existing structures of agricultural experiment stations and extension programs, or how to adjust existing structures and practices to support this new element.

To accommodate this shift toward farmer participation, many complementary changes were required. While maintaining their experiment stations, administrators had to shift some material and human resources into on-farm research. But the shift in location alone did not solve the problem, for a professional researcher could direct on-farm projects, treating small farmers as hired labor. As participative methods were developed they also influenced a strategic change in the direction of research programs. Because nearly all small farmers raised a variety of crops, often in association with animals, the location and methods shifts also involved developing a new focus on farming systems research. Here we see a major new line of social and biological research arising out of a farmer-level participatory program.

The emergence of on-farm client-oriented research (OFCOR) then naturally posed the question of its relation to on-station research (OSR). OFCOR did not eliminate the need for continuing specialized experiments on individual crops under tightly controlled conditions, but it did provoke some rethinking among research planners who now had to figure out how to utilize research involving many more variables under much more loosely controlled conditions.

OFCOR also required major changes in budgetary allocations and policies. As the professionals would no longer be working constantly at the same location, they needed vehicles to get them out to the farmers as well as general travel expense support. Then, when administrators decided that it would be valuable to both OSR and OFCOR researchers to spend some of their time participating in the other program, many OSR people resisted. This reluctance was not simply based on a psychological tendency to resist change or a desire to avoid involvement in a lower-status program—though those factors may have been involved. If the OSR people were to participate in the field, they would need travel funds not currently allocated to support such fieldwork. Could that be done by reallocating funds within the existing OSR budget? That would mean curtailing certain current activities, to which staff people were currently committed, in order to support their participation in OFCOR projects in a situation where, OSR researchers might assume, their participation would not win them professional recognition or advancement. Furthermore, many governmental budgets are so rigidly structured as to make such internal reallocations extremely difficult. OSR participation in OFCOR projects might require an increase in the overall budget for OSR. If the national director of research expresses verbal support for such OSR field participation, is he just mouthing a currently popular doctrine, or will he back up the words with financial support?

As we have seen with ICTA, a successful OFCOR program inevitably leads staff people onto the turf traditionally allocated to the extension organization. As the professionals learn to work participatively with small farmers, they come to appreciate the intelligence and resourcefulness of their new associates and also to recognize the value of their potential leadership positions in their areas. This suggests expanding the research unit with paraprofessionals. This involves changes in budgets and in compensation policies, but it does not necessarily mean spending more money on a given program. In fact, because the paraprofessionals are paid substantially less than the professionals and do not receive hardship pay for living where they already want to live, it can be much more cost efficient to expand OFCOR with paraprofessionals rather than professionals. In any case, of course, the hiring of paraprofessionals requires the development of new policies and procedures governing the relations between professionals and paraprofessionals.

Scaling up from a pilot project also involves fitting new activities into regionally based organizations. This means that the top leadership must understand and support the new activities and consult with regional directors regarding how to integrate them into their programs. This dimension of structural change involves all the familiar issues of centralization versus decentralization.

As OFCOR researchers recognize that successful local projects lead to diffusion from farmer to farmer of the new methods or materials, they realize that they are, in effect, engaging in extension activities. This naturally leads them to question the conventional extension methods and strategies, and such questioning may reach the top of agricultural ministries.

Can research and extension work more effectively together?

To answer that question, it is important for practitioners as well as researchers to recognize that the formal theory supporting conventional extension programs does not fit with new participative research strategies. As we have seen in Guatemala, DIGESA and BANDESA followed the technology transfer strategy, seeking to control the farmers' work program through supervised credit, until DIGESA's leaders recognized the need to abandon their formal theory and make the appropriate structural and policy adjustments. Perhaps the development of PROGETTAPS, bringing extension and research people together, may pave the way to a more integrated overall relationship between ICTA and DIGESA.

In industry, through Xerox and related cases, we have seen the progression from early adaptation of quality control circles to the social invention of strategies such as cost saving teams. As decision makers came to appreciate workers' intellectual contributions, and as managements became increasingly concerned over ballooning overhead costs, companies began to thin out supervisory and middle management ranks and to rely more heavily on teams of workers. This in turn led to changes in the recruitment and training of management people, as planners had to reshape their thinking in response to the continuing revolution in manufacturing and administrative methods.

As new technical systems such as an emphasis on statistical process control (SPC) for total quality programs and just-in-time (JIT) systems came into the production plants, managers had to learn how these drastic changes could be integrated with employee involvement (EI). Probably more often than not, managers had to learn first from the mistakes of trying to introduce new systems without any careful planning of how they could be fit into the preexisting socio-technical systems of the plant.

In Chapter 11 on "Coping with the New Manufacturing Organization" I described a case in which a new total quality program cascaded down from top management until it reached the production workers, at which point the union leaders blew the whistle and temporarily derailed the program. Management learned from this social process failure. When management decided to introduce a JIT system, local union leaders and plant personnel people worked closely with technical specialists so as to integrate JIT with employee involvement and the total quality program. Review of such developments illustrates the importance of thinking and planning within a socio-technical framework.

Grappling with these major changes has also led to the creation of a distinctively American social invention: the internal company and union *facilitator.* So far as we know, this role does not exist in either Europe or Japan. The external consultant who comes in to consult with management on organizational changes is well known in various industrialized countries, but the facilitator role focused on here involves internal personnel, engaged full time in working with management and union and workers to guide and stimulate the socio-technical change processes. In the three American auto companies, as well as in Xerox and various other companies, the facilitation staff is made up fifty-fifty of management and union personnel. In Xerox, we have traced how facilitators first were involved solely in shop-floor changes but have been expanding the scope of their operations to guide and shape the integration of new technical systems with EI.

This overview underscores the complexity of socio-technical change processes in both agriculture and industry. It also suggests, however, that many of the change problems can be anticipated and planned for, thus reducing the human and financial costs of change. If the planners start their thinking within a socio-technical framework, then they can ask questions whose answers will enable them to anticipate problems likely to arise in reaction to any planned change. If we start with a technical change, then we need to ask, "How will this change affect the social system? And how will this change affect existing technical systems?" Then we need to ask, "How will this change affect the work activities of those directly or indirectly involved in producing the industrial or farm output?" The importance of this last question is most clearly reflected in our review of the problems of integrating on-station research (OSR) with on-farm client-oriented research (OFCOR) and with integrating research with extension. If top management people reach agreement on new patterns of work activity without helping those responsible in the field to reorganize their existing work patterns, then the new policies are not likely to get much beyond the paper on which they are written. This is probably one of the most common bureaucratic errors: adding new work assignments without prior study of how they might be fit into existing patterns of work activities and of which existing work requirements could be eliminated or simplified in order to make time and energy available for new activities.

Finally, planners need to figure out what changes in structure, social processes, and budgetary policies and procedures need to be implemented to support new ways of working. This involves not only the problem of scaling up from pilot projects to large continuing programs, but also rethinking and reshaping the relations among the various technical specialties involved in managing the work processes. One major aspect of this change involves moving from technocratically managed operations toward socio-technical management, which necessarily means broadening the disciplinary base to include elements of the social sciences. This requires, of course, not only that techologically trained managers be open to social sciences but also that social scientists be willing to change their traditional ways of working so as to meet the needs of the organization they serve.

TRAINING FOR PARTICIPATORY SYSTEMS

A shift from previous patterns to participatory systems requires major changes in behavior, thinking, attitudes, and values, so organizational leaders must be willing to support this shift through major investments of human and material resources in new training programs. To some extent, different programs need to be developed for people at different organizational levels and levels of previous formal education. I have done no research focused particularly on such training programs, but studies of the change processes in agriculture and industry have yielded some illustrative cases.

In agriculture, the ICTA ten-month program for new professional employees is impressive for its demonstration of a very strong commitment to training and also for its linkage of experiential learning with classroom instruction. I can imagine no better way of convincing young professionals that they need to learn from the small farmers than requiring them to manage and work a small farm lot through a full agricultural cycle under conditions similar to those facing small farmers in the same area. The realism of the experience is reinforced by the ground rules that penalize or reward the trainee, according to the financial results of his or her plot.

Participatory systems also involve training of small farmers but of quite a different nature from that common in conventional systems. The old style placed major emphasis on the demonstration project, which was exhibited on field days to which local farmers were invited. In this style, the professional expert was telling small farmers how to farm more successfully and using the field day to provide evidence of the value of the recommendations offered them. In the new model, teaching and learning are structured participatively. Professionals, paraprofessionals, and small farmers learn from each other and from the process of planning field experiments and then observing their results.

In industry, American companies have been increasing their investments in training but are still far behind the Japanese in percentage of company income devoted to such activities. Managers generally recognize that, if workers are to assume more responsibility for making decisions on the way they work and on the results of work, then they need additional technical training. Professionally educated managers would like to assume that it is just other people who need training, but experience and research indicates that the training needs are different yet equally great at these levels. Especially if their higher education has been in engineering, accounting, or finance, they will need help in dealing with the social side of socio-technical systems. If they have learned to manage within autocratic systems that reward individual decision making, they will need help in learning how to participate in group discussions. They need to aim toward a delicate balance between throwing all decision making responsibility to the group and making all the decisions themselves without prior involvement of the group. As fewer supervisors assume responsibility for more subordinates, it is obvious that they can no longer supervise as closely as before, but the nature of the supervisory role is no longer clear. Do supervisors become "resource persons"? What does that mean in practice? Then, also, what happens to supervisors who are no longer needed? Many executives believe it is not only inhumane but also wasteful of valuable human resources simply to lay off supervisors and staff people whose jobs have been eliminated. It is better policy to develop retraining programs to help them to prepare for newly emerging jobs.

Local union leaders also need training to help them to participate in joint programs with management. To some extent, they need the same sort of training as managers in dealing with new technical systems such as JIT and SPC. In some cases (Xerox and ACTWU, for example), this has led to joint training programs. This approach enables the parties to gain the additional payoffs of multiobjective projects. As managers and union leaders go through the same training experience, they are not only learning the new technical systems but also developing interpersonal relationships that will help them to work together on the job.

The introduction of new technical systems creates new training needs for internal management and union facilitators. Their role was much simpler when they were limited to dealing with shop-floor problems. As Xerox prepared to implement a system of just-in-time manufacturing and inventory control, the facilitators assumed leading roles in guiding JIT by trying to integrate it with a total quality program and employee involvement. They took on this responsibility only after several months of training and study. As the implementation proceeded, they also assumed responsibility for training managers and union leaders in the social and technical integration of new systems with already established systems. In effect, they were becoming consultant-facilitators for a wide range of problems reaching well beyond the shop floor.

21. Theory and Practice in Applied Social Research Methods

In this final chapter, I explore the theoretical and practical implications of the studies reported in this book. I seek to answer the question, What research methods are required in order to advance both theory and practice?

GOING WHERE THE ACTION IS

For those who are trying the help an organization through a major change process, it is important to go out into the field, where the action is. Surveys are, of course, fieldwork, but we should not rely on surveys as our only data-gathering method. Surveys are especially useful for the systematic measurement of attitudes, beliefs, and values across a sample of the population under study. They provide an unreliable guide to understanding human actions. As I have argued elsewhere (Whyte, 1984; Whyte and Alberti, 1976), for understanding actions, surveys are most effective when integrated with field interviewing and observation.

Actions proceed through time, so it is not sufficient to document actions taking place at any single point in time. We need to track and study sequences of actions. We see the importance of the time dimension especially as we seek to trace events from an initial social invention to the diffusion of that innovation to other parts of the organization within which it arose and then to other organizations. Such a research focus leads us to a study of organizational learning. In a given field of action, as we learn how practitioners learn from each other—and from social researchers—we become more effective in supporting and strengthening the organizational learning process.

From Thinking to Writing—and Rewriting

Writing is not usually considered a component of research methods, yet it seems to me an indispensable part of the analysis process. Often I think I have a good idea figured out in my head only to have it fall apart as I undertake to put it into writing. But that does not mean that the thinking has been wasted. As I go back and forth from writing to thinking, that process enables me to clarify my thoughts so as to reshape the original idea or to abandon it in favor of a better idea.

What do I think about? I find myself going back and forth between concrete cases and the theoretical framework I am trying to build. For this purpose, it is useful to have in mind cases that are thoroughly familiar to us because that makes it more likely that we will think of data that do not readily fit into our framework and thereby challenge us to rethink our analysis. Furthermore, if we are thoroughly familiar with these cases, our minds are likely to deal with them more resourcefully than if we are trying to generalize across a large number of cases we know only superficially. I assume that some of my best ideas emerge out of my unconscious or semiconscious mind, when I am not at my desk but out weeding the garden or doing some other unrelated activity.

Polishing up a single idea, of course, does not end the analysis process. We need to connect a series of ideas together. That may be done best after we have written down each idea as we go along, which clearly indicates the need for rewriting in order to fit them together.

Then there are major questions of the organization of the writing, which also then involve rethinking as well as rewriting. For example, in the first draft of this book, I began by presenting some of the ideas now in Part III: Theoretical Foundations, in Part I, preceding the case materials in agriculture and industry. Upon reading this draft, Davydd

Greenwood found the agriculture and industry stories strong and convincing, but thought the book would be improved by beginning with the cases and then following with whatever theoretical analysis was necessary to bring out their general significance.

As I pondered this criticism, I realized that in the first draft I had yielded to the urge to get into print once again some theoretical ideas that I thought had not received the attention they deserved from my colleagues when I had published them earlier. Clearly that was no justification for laying them out so early and in such detail in this book.

For the second draft, after the introductory chapter, I started with Part I, Participation in Agriculture and then Part II: Participation in Industry. Then, after reviewing those materials, I extracted from the first draft only those theoretical elements that seemed essential to frame the analysis from social invention to diffusion and to organizational learning.

In the first draft, I had written separate chapters on theoretical implications of the agriculture cases and on their practical implications, then following with separate chapters for theoretical and practical implications for industry. When I reached this point in rewriting, I realized that such separation did not make sense. I found I could not make sense out of theoretical statements without considering practical implications, nor could I make sense out of practical implications without considering their theoretical underpinnings. I therefore decided to deal with both theory and practice in the same chapter. Then, as I had been claiming from the outset that I had found important elements in participatory systems in both agriculture and industry, I decided to put those common elements together in a single chapter. Such decisions, of course, required considerable rethinking and rewriting. They have yielded a book that I find much more satisfying than the first draft. The value of the final project must be judged ultimately by its readers.

TYPES OF APPLIED SOCIAL RESEARCH

A commitment to doing applied social research (ASR) tells us little about how such research should be done. There are various ways of defining and categorizing types of applied social research. My definition is based solely on *the relations of the researcher to the subjects of research*. In Chapter 1, I distinguished three types of research in terms of this definition:

(1) The professional expert model, in which the researcher makes a study and recommends a course of action to decision makers in the organization studied;

(2) action research controlled by the researcher, in which the researcher aims to be a principal change agent as well as controlling the research process; and

(3) participatory action research (PAR), in which the researcher seeks to involve some members of the organization studied as active participants in all stages of the research/action process.

Significant work has been done with the first and second types, but they are familiar models to those interested in applied social research. Therefore, I will concentrate on the third type, which is less familiar and also seems to me to offer some strengths not provided in the first and second types.

THE RATIONALE FOR PAR

The standard model of social research is an elitist or top-down model. It is commonly assumed that, in order to meet the exacting standards of science, the professional researcher should exercise maximum control over the research process, from the initial design to the conclusions and recommendations emerging from the study.

Participatory action research challenges this standard model. In presenting this challenge, I will review and reinterpret some case material presented earlier and add additional case information.

As I noted in Chapter 1, I began my research career following the purist doctrine that I must keep my actions separate from the research. In some cases I became involved in what I call *participatory research,* in the sense that I involved key informants in helping me gather and interpret data, but those projects did not directly involve any planned actions.

When I became committed to applied social research, I was unconsciously committed to the *action research controlled by the researcher* model. I tended to evaluate my success or failure by the extent to which

I was able to persuade decision makers to follow my recommendations. Perhaps it was fortunate that I had few successes with this model as that fact may have encouraged me to consider the possibilities of other models.

In PAR some of the practitioners in the organization under study participate actively through the research-action process, from project design through data gathering, analysis, and report writing, on to the implementation of conclusions emerging from the research. I illustrated the nature of PAR through three cases described earlier, with emphasis on the practical outcomes. After briefly reviewing those practical outcomes, I focus on the social research process and its implications for methodology and theory.

In the Norwegian shipping case, the principal actors were Einar Thorsrud and his associates in the Work Research Institutes, shipping company executives, top union leaders, and government officials. As we have seen, these projects achieved enormous changes in the sociotechnical systems of Norwegian shipping companies.

In the case of Xerox and ACTWU, PAR arose out of a shift from conventional quality of work life (QWL) programs to the development and establishment of cost study teams. The principal actors were Peter Lazes, the consultant-facilitator; leaders of management and the union; the people involved in the formal structures of participation that were established; and the members of the cost study teams themselves. The practical outcomes were dollars and jobs saved, employment security clauses in labor contracts, and, perhaps most important, the establishment of a methodology for studying and resolving future cost competitiveness problems.

In the FAGOR case, the principal actors were social anthropologist Davydd J. Greenwood; José Luis González, director of personnel; and the study team composed mainly of members of the FAGOR and individual cooperatives' personnel departments.

The practical results in the FAGOR project are difficult to measure but nevertheless appear to have been substantial. We noted a major innovation in FAGOR's personnel program, with the commitment to PAR as a regular component of future projects, along with the initial undertaking of several mini-PAR projects. Of perhaps greater importance have been changes in concepts and orientations among members of the study team, which included leading figures in FAGOR's personnel programs. The shift from assuming low member participation was due to apathy to attributing it to problems in formal structures and processes of participation involved abandoning a diagnosis that pointed to no practical solutions in favor a diagnosis that opened the way to new action options. Making explicit the study team members' conceptions of organizational culture should also open the way to more reflective and effective practice.

In the field of agricultural research and development, we have been following a broadening stream of intellectual exploration. We traced the course of organizational learning as professionals came to recognize that the customary ways of organizing agricultural research were primarily benefitting large commercial farmers and were providing little assistance to small farmers, except where they had access to good irrigation. This led policy planners and some researchers to look for new and better ways of involving small farmers in the research and development process.

In reviewing what had been learned from the Puebla Project, some of the researchers came to recognize that a top-down strategy of simply demonstrating to small farmers what they should do in order to become more prosperous would not be effective. The discovery that the professional researchers had much to learn from the small farmers led to an exploration for improved ways to encourage small-farmer participation.

Working with small farmers, the professional researchers learned that the crop specialization model that produced rich rewards for large commercial farmers simply would not work for small farmers who cultivated a variety of crops and generally also raised animals. This recognition led some of the agricultural professionals to shift their frame of reference from crop specialization toward the study of farming systems. Since small farmers had the experience and therefore the expertise in farming systems that the experiment station scientists lacked, this naturally shifted the focus of research toward learning from the small farmers.

The shift in the research focus also had important consequences for research strategies and project designs. The experiments could not be so tightly controlled as on the experiment station. The shift also meant that the experiments necessarily dealt with many more variables. When the experiments were done at experiment stations on particular commodities (maize, rice, wheat, potatoes, or other crops) the experimenter could focus on a relatively small number of variables: comparison of the performance of different varieties under the same standard conditions of irrigation, fertilization, and plant protection measures, or experimentation with the same variety under different conditions of fertilization, irrigation, and plant protection measures. When experiments are done on farming systems including two or more crops and animals, the number of variables and the number of interactions among variables are enormously increased. This means that the classic simplicity of the experiment is no longer possible. While this leads to conceptual and turf problems between station researchers and on-farm researchers, the movement to farming systems research brings the agricultural sciences much more into realistic alignment with the actual farming conditions of a major part of the farming population.

THE CASES COMPARED

That the cases discussed differ so widely in fields of operation and the objectives sought by the researchers and practitioners indicates a wide range of uses for PAR.

In Xerox, the practitioners and the consultant-facilitator began focusing on a narrow economic problem of the cost competitiveness of one department, but the process then led them to work through major social and economic implications of their cost-saving studies. In the Norwegian case, the parties began with a broad economic focus with major emphasis on the social and organizational changes needed. In FAGOR, economic factors were not a major focus of study. The focus was on exploring organizational culture and the role of personnel departments within that culture.

In the agricultural R&D projects, the main objective was always to find ways to enhance the economic and social welfare of the small farmers, but the economic targets could not be nearly so specific as in the Xerox case, where the parties had to cope with a precise figure of cost reduction. In agriculture, secondary but equally important objectives involved discovering new and better ways to structure the research and development process. We thus see equally far-reaching changes in social organization and work roles as we observed in the industrial cases.

In industry, the chief practitioners involved were leaders of industry and labor. In agriculture, there was necessarily a broader range of practitioner participants, beginning with small farmers but also including agricultural researchers, extensionists, and input suppliers.

DIVISON OF LABOR IN PAR PROJECTS

In all of these PAR projects, the social processes were structured and guided by research professionals. In the industrial cases this role was played by social psychologists Einar Thorsrud and Peter Lazes and by social anthropologist Davydd J. Greenwood. That does not mean, however, that the projects were controlled by the professional researchers. They shared control with key practitioners in the organizations being studied. In agriculture, because the chief clients for PAR are toward the bottom of the rural structure, the small farmers cannot be expected to play as prominent a role in structuring the PAR process as do workers in the industrial cases. Nevertheless, we have observed strong efforts on the part of the social and plant science professionals to include the small farmers as active participants in the R&D process.

In industry, the general idea of having such a study can originate with the professional researchers (as in the shipping and Xerox cases) or with a practitioner (as in the FAGOR case). In either case, the research design is a joint product of discussions between the professional researchers and the involved practitioners. Furthermore, the practitioners carry a major responsibility for gathering and evaluating data and serve as the professional experts on technical matters such as technology, ship architecture, engineering, and cost accounting. The professional researchers assume responsibility particularly for helping the practitioners to integrate the social aspects with the technical elements so as to develop a socio-technical model of the change process. They also provide the practitioners with some guidance through bringing in information and ideas from cases they have previously studied and from the research literature.

This means that a PAR project cannot be developed in situations where professional researchers have a strong interest in a study topic and a particular research design but where key practitioners are just willing to open the doors to the research and then await the results. This does not mean that the professional researchers and the key practitioners must see eye to eye on all important points at the outset or that the professional researchers simply agree with the practitioners in order to secure their participation. In all three industry cases, the projects began only after vigorous discussion during which the professional researchers felt free to express their ideas and opinions and encouraged the practitioners to do likewise.

For a PAR project to appear viable and important to practitioners it must meet two conditions: The problem must seem important to key members of the organization studied, and the research methods and the types of data to be studied must appear credible to the participating practitioners. Practitioners generally will not be willing to accept what professional researchers would consider sloppy research methods. We have found their demands in this regard to be very exacting because they expect the PAR project to have important consequences for them and their organizations. Nevertheless, their standards are necessarily different from the standards of rigorous research in the mainstream of the behavioral sciences. If the professional researcher is not interested in the problem proposed by the practitioners or believes that the research methods proposed are not scientifically acceptable, then he or she has two options: Abandon the project, or engage in further discussion to explore the possibility of redefining the problem and reshaping the proposed research methods to see if a mutually satisfactory resolution can be reached.

If the state of theoretical development and substantive knowledge has reached the point where the next step calls for the testing of a critical hypothesis or set of hypotheses, then PAR is certainly not appropriate, simply because it does not lend itself to such tight researcher control. When and where have researchers encountered a situation that points so clearly to the next logical line of attack to reach the greatest scientific payoff? In my experience over more than half a century I cannot think of a single case of this nature. We commonly face situations where the current state of knowledge seems confusing. There is no shortage of hypotheses to test, but it is not at all clear how to determine which hypothesis is most likely to lead to an important theoretical advance.

ADVANCES IN SUBSTANTIVE KNOWLEDGE
AND THEORY THROUGH PAR

When we describe the cases reported on here, we have no problem demonstrating that PAR can produce important practical results. But those committed to familiar and scientifically legitimated methodologies naturally raise the question, Can it be scientific? That means, can it also produce advances in theory? To answer that question I present brief examples of theoretical contributions achieved through the PAR methodologies.

The Work Research Institutes Norwegian shipping program is an impressive demonstration of the scientific and practical values of the socio-technical systems theoretical framework developed by Eric Trist and his associates in the United Kingdom and elsewhere. (For a discussion of the evolution of socio-technical thinking, see Trist, 1981.) The socio-technical framework is based on a simple yet basic idea: For both theoretical and practical purposes, organizational research must integrate data and ideas from both the social system and the technical or technological system. As the social system shapes ways in which technology is developed and applied, and the technological system shapes and channels social relations, analyses that focus on only one of these two systems are bound to be theoretically misleading and of limited practical value.

As I reflect upon my early research in industry beginning in 1942, I recognize that I was studying social systems. I was implicitly guided by the maxim that Burleigh B. Gardner expressed somewhat later in the first textbook on *Human Relations in Industry* (Gardner, 1946): "A factory is a social system." To be sure, I recognized that technology was important; but I was at a loss as to how to deal with it, beyond simply providing brief background descriptions. Many of my colleagues in what was then called the human relations movement seem to me to have been stuck in that limited social systems framework. Eric Trist led the way to a more useful and scientifically valid framework, and Einar Thorsrud provided probably the best case for the practical and scientific value of that socio-technical systems framework.

The theoretical advances gained through PAR in the Xerox case can be summarized briefly as follows. (A more detailed argument is laid out in Whyte, 1989, and Whyte et al., 1989.) The Xerox case led us to a radical reconceptualization of one of the most frequently studied problems in organizational behavior: the relationship between worker participation and productivity. Long before our involvement in PAR, we had been aware of the general research findings: There appears to be a moderate positive correlation between participation and worker job satisfaction, but no such positive correlation has been consistently shown for the participation-productivity relationship. (See, for a research review, Locke and Schweiger, 1977.)

In the face of such a general pattern of findings, how can it be that the CST form of participation in Xerox yielded cost savings of from twenty-five to forty percent? To be sure, the dependent variables were different in the comparison cases, and yet costs and productivity appear to be just two sides of the same coin.

This apparent paradox suggested that there might be basic flaws in the prevailing paradigm for the study of the participation-productivity relationship and led us to rethink the conceptualization of the independent variable (participation) and the dependent variable (productivity).

What is called participation in the academic literature comes in a wide variety of structures and social processes guided and practiced with varying degrees of skill or incompetence. Is it not naive to assume that there should be a positive correlation between such a miscellaneous set of activities and productivity? If we are to understand the impact of activities called participation, we have to get behind that label in order to describe systematically the nature of the human interactions and activities studied.

Regarding the dependent variable, we asked ourselves, Why are we focusing on the productivity of direct labor—the production and maintenance workers—whereas the output of the organization is the joint product of all of the people in that organization and the material resources used?

Suppose, instead, that we call our dependent variable *total factor productivity*. To achieve a more holistic measure of organizational performance, we suggest focusing on costs that are attached to the use of all of the organization's human and material resources rather than simply measuring worker productivity.

We can readily link this holistic conception of costs to productivity. For any operational unit, the relationship between the total costs charged to that unit and the value of its output can be considered a measure of the productivity of that unit. Changes in that relationship over time then reflect changes in what economists call total factor productivity.

In the Xerox case, we can describe in detail the structure and social processes of worker participation represented by cost study teams, and we can also show how immense gains in total factor productivity arose in direct response to the CSTs. We do not claim that our analysis of a single case is sufficient to prove the superior value of our framework, but this does lead us to suggest that others try out this framework on future participation-productivity research.

This shift in framework seems particularly appropriate in a period when many manufacturing plants are achieving increases in total factor productivity in part by reducing personnel in line management and staff positions through delegating greater responsibilities for production and quality to workers. To illustrate with a hypothetical example (which represents many actual cases), suppose in factory X over a period of time the same number of workers produces the same total output while staff and line management personnel have been reduced by half. Under those conditions, does it make sense to state that worker productivity has not changed?

The Xerox case also led us to a theoretical advance in the study of the allocation of costs to particular components or products in factories producing a range of different items. In following the CSTs, we became aware that this social invention forced management to allocate costs in a manner quite different from what had been customary practice. As we had no educational background or experience in industrial cost accounting, at first we did not know what to make of this observation. Then, thanks to a suggestion from Chris Argyris, we began examining the path-breaking research in industrial accounting by Robert Kaplan and his associates at the Harvard Business School and Carnegie Mellon University.

According to these researchers, the basic problem is that management has been using accounting methods devised for tax purposes and for supplying overall company financial information to stockholders.

How have the indirect costs of products been allocated in the past? One common method has been simply to allocate them in the same proportion as direct labor costs. According to Cooper and Kaplan (1988:96),

> Allocating indirect costs, such as factory and corporate overhead, by burden rates on direct labor introduced few problems for narrow-product-line, early 20th century organizations. . . .
>
> Today, direct labor has shrunk to a minor fraction of corporate costs; the costs of factory support resources, marketing and distribution activities, engineering services, and general corporate overhead have exploded. These large overhead and support costs, however, are either still allocated to products by the diminishing direct labor base or, as in the case of marketing and distribution costs, not allocated at all.

If indirect costs are allocated in proportion to direct labor—or if some of them are not allocated to products at all—these accounting formulas can have important practical and scientific significance. On the practical side, such formulas may lead management to continue production of unprofitable items under the illusion that they are profitable and to phase out jobs and production of profitable items under the illusion that they are unprofitable. On the scientific side, this line of analysis opens up a new area of basic research on how executives actually do make important production decisions and on the possible consequences for management and labor of the accounting formulas with which they justify those decisions.

This line of reasoning put the Xerox cases in a new context. We now recognize that the CSTs pushed management to set aside its customary system of allocating indirect costs to products and to develop a system that appears to be similar to that advocated by Kaplan and his associates: tracing (at least to a first approximation) the percentage of each item of indirect cost that can reasonably be attributed to a particular product.

On rethinking the participation-productivity relationship, we claim some credit for originality. For ideas on the accounting-production relationship, we are happy to credit Robert Kaplan and his associates, along with our further reflections on the Xerox case.

The issue here is not simply the question of originality but rather of how one learns to integrate ideas and concepts across disciplines previously isolated from each other. We still do not claim to be able to do our own cost analyses in industry, but now we know enough to ask management the first critical question: "In estimating the costs to the company of a particular product, on what basis do you allocate indirect costs?"

For the FAGOR project, the contributions are more difficult to document because the changes occurred at the conceptual level and as yet we have no concrete evidence to prove their value. Perhaps the best way to assess progress is to focus on one central aspect of the PAR project, the study of the culture of the cooperatives. As the FAGOR team went to work on this problem, I turned my interests in the same direction. I recognized that company culture had suddenly emerged as the latest fad in the field of management development. There is now a growing recognition in the business world, as well as in academia, that organizations do develop distinctive cultures and that the organizational culture does *somehow* shape the behavior of its members. The key word in that sentence is "somehow" because most of the literature is notably lacking on specification of how particular elements of culture influence particular behaviors. It is as if culture were some free-floating force that affected behavior in mystical ways.

If well-informed members of an organization whose culture we study are in basic disagreement with the interpretation of the professional researcher, we must at least admit the possibility that there is something wrong with the researcher's interpretation. If two well-qualified researchers arrive at very similar interpretations of the culture of a community or organization, we may believe we are coming closer to the true picture. But suppose those two well-qualified researchers arrive at sharply conflicting interpretations, as has happened in several well-known cases (see, for example, Lewis, 1951, versus Redfield, 1930; and Freeman, 1983, versus Mead, 1973). If the members find themselves close to general agreement with the researcher's interpretation, then it seems to me that readers should have more confidence in that interpretation than if it had been written without any feedback for criticism and support from the practitioners. Of course, the value of our interpretation will not be determined by this argument but rather will depend ultimately on the judgment of academic students of organizational culture following reading the interpretations presented in our two books (Whyte and Whyte, 1988; and Greenwood and Gonzalez, 1990).

THE SCIENTIFIC CASE FOR
PARTICIPATORY ACTION RESEARCH

Having provided examples of theoretical and substantive advances achieved through participatory action research, let me now close with the general argument that a PAR strategy is more likely to lead to such breakthroughs than are standard research models in sociology.

In the complex field of modern industrial organizations, there are very few problems that can be resolved through the use of any single academic discipline. The problems we study can only be resolved by sociologists if we are able to integrate concepts and methods of analysis from other disciplines. And here I do not mean interdisciplinary collaboration among sociologists, social anthropologists, and social psychologists, or even simply extending this mix to include economists. In industry we need to integrate ideas and methods of analysis from engineering, accounting, and business administration in general. In agriculture, this means integrating ideas and methods of analysis from the plant, animal, and soil sciences as well as agricultural engineering.

How can this be done? For those interested in interdisciplinary integration, the conventional strategy has been to try to get together a team of professors and students representing the various disciplines that appear to be required. This strategy is unlikely to be either cost effective or scientifically productive. Immersed in the culture of academia, professors and students are concerned primarily with research that leads to articles in refereed journals in their own disciplines. Our practitioner collaborators do not feel such pressure to get their contributions in journals and may even feel that working with us offers them a stimulating learning experience. If professional researchers pursue the PAR strategy, reaching out for technical knowledge and analytical skills among practitioners in fields of action different from our own disciplinary bases, we find mutually profitable ways of combining intellectual forces.

PAR offers possibilities of researcher initiative in introducing major organizational changes that would not occur without PAR. They are not true experiments in the classic sense of tight control of variables, but such experiments are very difficult to carry out in complex modern industry. We believe the possibilities of studying important changes that would not otherwise occur far outweigh the potential disadvantages of researcher bias through personal involvement in the change process.

According to the conventional wisdom, no other research strategy can match the standard model for rigor. Whether this is true depends on how we define rigor. In the first place, rigor depends on getting the facts straight. In evaluating research reports on projects conducted in the standard manner, readers generally start with the assumption that, unless the description of data-gathering methods reveals clear deficiencies, the facts in the case are as reported by the researcher. The critic then goes on to evaluate whether the analysis is sound in terms of logic and science. If there are basic errors in the facts presented, then the most elegant theoretical analysis will be worse than useless because it may persuade readers to accept conclusions that are not supportable by the facts.

How are readers to know whether the facts are as reported? Here I am not concerned with the rare cases of fraud. There is a much more general problem, where honest researchers have simply made mistakes in data gathering and where those mistakes would be serious enough to undermine their conclusions.

In the standard model, the subjects of our studies have little or no opportunity to check facts or to offer alternative explanations. If we circulate our research reports and publications among members of the organization we studied, they often argue that we have made serious errors in facts and in interpretations. If the standard social researcher hears such criticism, he or she can shrug it off, telling colleagues that the subjects are just being defensive—defensiveness apparently being a characteristic of subjects but not of social scientists themselves.

PAR provides a critical safeguard against self-delusion by the researcher and unintentional misleading of colleagues through a rigorous process of fact checking by those with firsthand knowledge, before any reports are written. In the Xerox case, the cost saving figures developed by the CSTs were rigorously checked by higher management because decisions based on them involved millions of dollars.

In the case of our book on Mondragón (Whyte and Whyte, 1988), the evolution of this writing project demonstrates the value of PAR in getting the facts straight and recognizing important alternative explanations. When the book project was still the exclusive personal property of the authors, following our visit to Mondragón in 1983, I got my notes translated and sent to eight key informants with a request that they respond with suggestions and criticisms. That initiative yielded only one response—and that was from a woman who had become a close personal friend. As draft chapters of the Mondragón book and my essay on the culture of the cooperatives were incorporated into the PAR project directed by Greenwood and González, the relationship between researchers and informants radically changed. Our book now became a project jointly owned by some of the key informants in FAGOR and elsewhere in the Mondragón complex. The active involvement of Mondragón people in this cross-checking process ensured a far higher standard of factual accuracy than could have been achieved by standard social research methods. In the process of translating the book into Spanish, we achieved a still higher standard of accuracy. A team from the personnel group in FAGOR reviewed the translation, sentence by sentence, checking for factual accuracy. No censorship was involved in this process, but it did bring out several errors of fact that had escaped our earlier consultations with FAGOR people that we could correct in the Spanish version. If we now go on to a revised English edition, those errors will be eliminated. While it is embarassing to authors to have such errors pointed out, the experience does underline the value of PAR for publication as well as for the research process itself.

PAR in agriculture has the same strengths as in industry. Furthermore, we should note here the PAR impact in redefining a whole field of research.

PAR has been the driving force carrying agricultural research beyond the narrow confines of the experiment station and changing the frame of reference for judging progress in agricultural research. Before on-farm research became recognized as a new field of activity, the demonstrated improvement in yield on the experiment station was thought to be a success in itself. Integrating the small farmers into the research process as active participants opened up a whole new field of research on farming systems. Thus we can say that participatory action research led to a major expansion of the scope of scientific research in agriculture.

ON GETTING OUT OF THE ACADEMIC RUT

To arrive at a judgment of PAR, we should avoid comparing it with an idealized model of the way research proceeds in sociology's mainstream. As I see it, that idealized model is based on the following assumptions:

- There is a stream of validated knowledge available in the academic literature in our discipline. Therefore, the first requirement is to study the literature in our discipline.
- At the most advanced area in this stream, there are points for which the evidence is conflicting or uncertain. Therefore, the researcher should concentrate the research design on these points.
- To move beyond these points, within some framework of theory, the researcher should state one or more hypotheses to test.
- The researcher then designs a project suitable for this test. That means, in effect, predicting the conclusions of the analysis.
- The researcher then goes out to gather the data—or turns that task over to research assistants.

- If the hypotheses are confirmed at an acceptable level of significance, then the researcher has made a contribution that advances the stream of knowledge at least a bit farther. If the hypotheses are not confirmed, then the researcher goes back to the drawing board to devise a new set of hypotheses and/or a different research design.
- As this process continues over the years, the accumulation of tested hypotheses provides the building blocks for the construction of more scientifically powerful theories, which eventually may even be useful for achieving important practical objectives.

Mainstream sociologists and other behavioral scientists have been trying to follow that model for some decades, so by now the fruits of that strategy should be apparent. If I am correct in assuming that my model of the mainstream of social research has brought us to where we are today, and, if the various critics of our discipline cited in Chapter 1 are correct in characterizing our current location in the quest for knowledge, then we need to reexamine the standard research strategy.

I am not suggesting that we disregard the literature; rather, I am raising the question, What literature do we follow? In studying the transformation under way in American manufacturing, I am learning at least as much from reading the books and papers of industrial engineers and accountants as I have learned from the writings of sociologists and professors in the interdisciplinary field of organizational behavior. We learn also from discussions with practitioners who are technically knowledgeable in disciplines different from our own.

Can we really place ourselves in a stream of knowledge whose clear direction can be mapped intellectually? Or should we visualize ourselves in a swamp, trying to discover a sense of direction?

If we are in a swamp, then the mere accumulation of tested hypotheses will not extricate us. If we need a new sense of direction, then, like other human beings in other fields of activity, we need to expose ourselves to new social experiences. Instead of assuming that we should be able to devise critical hypotheses and also predict what the data will reveal, we should open our world of experience to creative surprises. We do not downgrade the importance of the discovery of penicillin because Sir Alexander Fleming was not guided to this breakthrough by any theory or set of hypotheses. We can rekindle the intellectual excitement in our field if we are willing to leave the mainstream to involve ourselves with practitioners and struggle with them to solve important practical problems—which may also have important theoretical implications.

In the process, we may persuade ourselves that the current stagnation in our academic field is due in part to the sharp separation between the academic world and the world of practice. Participatory action research provides one pathway toward intellectual revitalization.

References

Aitken, Hugh G.J. (1960) *Taylorism at Watertown Arsenal: Scientific Management in Action, 1880-1915.* Cambridge, MA: Harvard University Press.

Aldrich, Howard E. (1979) *Organizations and Environment.* Englewood Cliffs, NJ: Prentice-Hall.

Allaire, Paul A. and Norman E. Richard (1989) "Quality and Participation at Xerox." *Journal of Quality and Participation* 12,1: 24-26.

Almond, Gabriel and Sidney Verba (1963) *The Civic Culture: Political Attitudes and Culture in Five Nations.* Princeton, NJ: Princeton University Press.

Arensberg, Conrad (1951) "Behavior and Organization: Industrial Studies," in Muzafer Sherif, ed., *Social Psychology at the Crossroads.* New York: Harper & Bros.

Argyris, Chris (1952) *The Impact of Budgets on People.* Ithaca, NY: Cornell University School of Business and Public Administration.

Berk, Richard A. (1988) "How Applied Sociology Can Save Basic Sociology," pp. 57-72 in Zolgar F. Borgatta and Karen S. Cook, eds., *The Future of Sociology.* Newbury Park, CA: Sage.

Blau, Peter (1955) *The Dynamics of Bureaucracy.* Chicago: University of Chicago Press.

Chapple, Eliot D. and C. S. Coon (1942) *Principles of Anthropology.* New York: Henry Holt.

Chapple, Eliot D. in collaboration with Conrad Arensberg (1940) Measuring Human Relations: An Introduction to the Study of Interaction of Individuals. Genetic Psychology Monograph #22. Provincetown, MA: The Journal Press.

CIMMYT (International Maize and Wheat Improvement Center) (1975) *The Puebla Project: Seven Years of Experience, 1967-1973.* El Batan, Mexico: Author.

CIP (International Potato Center) (1984) *Potatoes for the Developing World.* Lima, Peru: Author.

Coates, Ken and Tony Topham (1968) *Workers' Control.* London: Panther Books.

Cole, Robert E. (1989) *Strategies for Learning: Small Group Activities in American, Japanese and Swedish Industry.* Berkeley: University of California Press.

Collinson, M.P. (1972) *Farm Management in Peasant Agriculture: A Handbook for Rural Development Planning in Africa.* New York: Praeger.

Cooper, Robin and Robert S. Kaplan (1988) "Measure Costs Right: Make the Right Decisions." *Harvard Business Review* (September-October): 96-103.

Copley, Frank Barkley (1923) *Frederick W. Taylor: Father of Scientific Management.* New York: Harper & Row.

De Soto, Hernando (1986) *El Otro Sendero.* Lima: Editorial el Barranco. English edition, (1989) *The Other Path: The Invisible Revolution in the Third World.* New York: Harper & Row.

Elden, Max (1979) "Three Generations of Worker Democracy Research in Norway," pp. 226-257 in C.L. Cooper and E. Mumford, eds., *The Quality of Work Life in Europe.* London: Associated Business Press.

Erickson, Clark L. (1988) "Raised Field Agriculture in the Lake Titicaca Basin: Putting Ancient Agriculture Back to Work." *Expedition* 30, 3: 8-16.

Erickson, Clark L. and Kay L. Candler (1989) "Raised Fields and Sustainable Agriculture in the Lake Titicaca Basin," pp. 230-248 in John Browder, ed., *Fragile Lands of Latin America: Strategies for Sustainable Development.* Boulder, CO: Westview.

Erickson, Kai (1989) "Review of Smelser, *Handbook of Sociology.*" *Contemporary Sociology* 18, 4: 511-513.

Etzioni, Amitai (1967) *The Hard Way to Peace: A New Strategy.* New York: Crowell-Collier.

Etzioni, Amitai (1988) *The Moral Dimension.* New York: The Free Press.

Faris, R.E.L. (1964) *Handbook of Modern Sociology.* Chicago: Rand McNally.

Fernow, K.H. and O. Garcés (1949) "Producción de Semilla Certificada de Papa." Universidad de Bogotá, *Revista de la Facultad Nacional de Agronomia* 10 (December): 257-295.

Freeman, D. (1983) *Margaret Mead and Samoa: The Making and Unmaking of an Anthropological Myth.* Cambridge, MA: Harvard University Press.

Gardner, Burleigh B. (1946) *Human Relations in Industry.* Homewood, IL: Richard D. Irwin.

Gostyla, Lynn and W.F. Whyte (1980) *ICTA in Guatemala: The Evolution of a New Model for Agricultural Research and Development.* Ithaca, NY: Rural Development Committee, Cornell University.

Gouldner, Alvin (1960) "The Norm of Reciprocity." *American Sociological Review* 25, 2: 161-178.

Gow, D.D., E.R. Morss, D.R. Jackson, D.S. Humpal, C.R. Sweet, A.H. Barclay, Jr., D.R. Mickelwaait, R.E. Hagan, and R. Zenger (1979) *Local Organizations and Rural Development: A Comparative Reappraisal, Vol 2: Case Studies.* Washington, DC: Development Alternatives.

Greenwood, D.J. and Jose Luis González (1990) *Culturas de Fagor: Estudio Antropológico de las Cooperativas de Mondragón.* San Sebastian, Spain: Editorial Txertoa.

Guest, Robert H. (1987) "Industrial Sociology: The Competitive Edge." *Footnotes,* American Sociological Association (January): 7.

Hall, E.T. and W.F. Whyte (1960) "Intercultural Communication: A Guide to Men of Action." *Human Organization* 19, 1: 5-12.

Hall, Richard H. (1982) *Organizations: Structure and Process.* Englewood Cliffs, NJ: Prentice-Hall.

Harwood, R.R. (1979) *Small Farm Development: Understanding and Improving Farming Systems in the Humid Tropics.* Boulder, CO: Westview.

Hayes, R.H., S.C. Wheelwright, and K.B. Clark (1988) *Dynamic Manufacturing: Creating the Learning Organization.* New York: The Free Press.

Heckscher, C.C. (1988) *The New Unionism: Employee Involvement in the Changing Corporation.* New York: Basic Books.

Herrick, Neal (1990) *Joint Management and Employee Participation: Labor and Management at the Crossroads.* San Francisco: Jossey-Bass.

HEW (Department of Health, Education and Welfare) (1973) *Work in America.* Washington, DC: Author.

Holtback, Roger (1988) "A Conversation with Roger Holtback." U.S. Department of Labor, *Labor Relations Today* (May-June): 4-5.

Homans, G.C. (1950) *The Human Group.* New York: Harcourt Brace Jovanovich.

Homans, George C. (1961) *Social Behavior: Its Elementary Forms.* New York: Harcourt Brace Jovanovich.

Horton, D.E. (1984) *Social Scientists in Agricultural Research: Lessons from the Mantaro Valley Project, Peru.* Ottawa: IDRC.

Horton, D.E. (1988) "Assessing Impact: The General Framework," pp. 331-346 in CIP (International Potato Center), *The Social Sciences at CIP.* Lima: CIP.

Horton, D.E. (1990) "Social Scientists in International Agricultural Research: Ensuring Relevance and Contributing to the Knowledge Base," pp. 218-236 in W.F. Whyte, ed., *Participatory Action Research.* Newbury Park, CA: Sage.

Inkeles, Alex (1986) "Advances in Sociology: A Critique," pp. 15-30 in W. Deutsch, Andrei S. Markovits, and John Platt, eds., *Advances in the Social Sciences, 1900-1980.* Lanham, MD: University Press of America.

ISNAR (International Service for National Agricultural Research) (1990) "Trustees Get a First-Hand Look at Costa Rica's Research System." *Newsletter* 13 (April): 7, 10.

Kaplan Robert S. (1988) "One Cost System Isn't Enough." *Harvard Business Review* (January-February): 61-66.

Klein, Janice A. (1989) "The Human Costs of Manufacturing Reform." *Harvard Business Review* (March-April): 60-66.

Klingel, Sally and Ann Martin, eds. (1988) *A Fighting Chance: New Strategies to Save Jobs and Reduce Costs.* Ithaca, NY: ILR Press.

Kochan, T.A., H.C. Katz, and R.B. McKersie (1986) *The Transformation of American Industrial Relations.* New York: Basic Books.

Lawrence, Paul R. and J.W. Lorsch (1967) *Organizations and Environment.* Cambridge, MA: Harvard University Press.

Lewis, Oscar (1951) *Life in a Mexican Village: Tepoztlan Revisited.* Urbana: University of Illinois Press.

Locke, E.A. and D.M. Schweiger (1977) "Participation in Decision Making: One More Look," pp. 265-339 in B.M. Shaw, ed., *Research in Organizational Behavior (Vol. 1).* Greenwich, CT: JAI Press.

Mauss, Marcel (1954) *The Gift.* Glencoe, IL: The Free Press. (English translation.)

Mead, Margaret (1973) *Coming of Age in Samoa.* New York: Morrow. (Originally published in 1928.)

Merton, Robert K. (1936) "Unanticipated Consequences of Purposive Social Actions." *American Sociological Review* 1(February): 894-904.

Merton, Robert K. (1949) *Social Theory and Social Structure*. Glencoe, IL: The Free Press.

Miller, Neal (1989) "The Chimaltenango Program." Ithaca, NY: Rural Development Commitee, Center for International Studies, Cornell University.

Morita, Akio (1987) "How—and Why—U.S. Business Has to Shape Up." *The New York Times* (June 6).

Norman, D.W. (1973) *Methodology and Problems of Small Farm Management Investigations: Experiences from Northern Nigeria*. East Lansing: Department of Agricultural Economics, Michigan State University.

Norman, D.W. (1980) *The Farming Systems Approach: Relevancy for Small Farmers*. East Lansing: Department of Agricultural Economics, Michigan State University.

Nuñez del Prado, Oscar (1973) *Kuyo Chico: Applied Anthropology in an Indian Community*. Chicago: University of Chicago Press.

Obermiller, Tim (1990) "Harvest from the Past." *University of Chicago Magazine* 82, 3: 26-33.

ODI (Overseas Development Institute) (1989) *340 Abstracts on Farmer Participatory Research*. London: Author.

Ortiz, R. (1990) "A Joint Venture in Technology Transfer to Increase Adoption Rates," pp. 179-189 in W.F. Whyte, ed., *Participatory Action Research*. Newbury Park, CA: Sage.

Parker, Mike and Jane Slaughter (1988) *Choosing Sides: Unions and The Team Concept*. Detroit: Labor Notes/South End Press.

Parker, Mike and Jane Slaughter (1988) "Managing by Stress: The Dark Side of the Team Concept." *ILR Report* (Fall).

Port, Otis (1987) "The Push for Quality." *Business Week*, June 18.

"Quality of Work Life: Catching On: (1981) *Business Week*, September 21.

Rankin, Tom and Jacquie Mansell (1986) "Integrating Collective Bargaining and New Forms of Work Organization." *National Productivity Review* (August): 338-347.

Redfield, Robert (1930) *Tepoztlan: A Mexican Village*. Chicago: University of Chicago Press.

Rhoades, R.E. and R.H. Booth (1982) "Farmer-Back-To-Farmer: A Model for Generating Acceptable Agricultural Technology." *Agricultural Administration* 11.

Ritter, Ulrich Peter (1965) *Comunidades Indigenas y Cooperativismo en el Peru*. Bilbao, Spain: Ediciones Deusto.

Roethlisberger, F.J. and W.J. Dickson (1939) *Management and the Worker*. Cambridge, MA: Harvard University Press.

Roethlisberger, F.J (1977) *The Elusive Phenomena*. Cambridge, MA: Harvard University Press.

Ross, Timothy L., Larry Hatcher, and Ruth Ann Ross (1989) "The Incentive Switch: From Piecework to Company Wide Gainsharing." *Management Review* (May).

Ruano, Sergio and Astolfo Fumagalli (1988) *Guatemala: Organización y Manejo de la Investigación en Finca en el Instituto de Ciencia y Tecnología Arícolas (ICTA)*. The Hague: International Service for National Agricultural Research (ISNAR).

Samuelson, Paul (1967) *Foundations of Economic Analysis*. New York: Athaneum.

Sayles, Leonard (1964) *Managerial Behavior*. New York: McGraw-Hill.

Sayles, Leonard and George Strauss (1953) *The Local Union: Its Place in the Industrial Plant.* New York: Harper & Row.

Schön, Donald A. (1983a) *The Reflective Practitioner: How Professionals Think in Action.* New York: Basic Books.

Schön, Donald A. (1983b) "Organizational Learning," pp. 114-128 in Gareth Morgan, ed., *Beyond Method.* Beverly Hills, CA: Sage.

Schonberger, R.J (1982) *Japanese Manufacturing Tehniques: Nine Hidden Lessons in Simplicity.* New York: The Free Press.

Servan-Schreiber, J.J. (1968) *The American Challenge.* New York: Harper & Row.

Short, James (1989) "Review of Smelser, Handbook of Sociology." *Contemporary Sociology* 18, 4: 500-504.

Simmons, John and William Mares (1983) *Working Together.* New York: Knopf.

Skinner, B.F. (1971) *Beyond Freedom and Dignity.* New York: Knopf.

Smelser, Neil (1988) *Handbook of Sociology.* Newbury Park, CA: Sage.

Suzaki, Kiyoshi (1987) *The Manufacturing Challenge: Techniques for Continuous Improvement.* New York: The Free Press.

Taylor, Frederick W. (1911) *Scientific Management.* New York: Harper & Row.

Thorsrud, Einar (1977) "Democracy at Work: Norwegian Expeience with Non-Bureaucratic Forms of Organization." *Applied Behavioral Science* 13, 3: 410-421.

Trist, Eric (1981) *The Evolution of Socio-Technical Systems: A Conceptual Framework and Action Research Program.* Toronto: Ontario Ministry of Labour.

Turrent, Antonio (1978) "El Sistema Agrícola: Un Marco de Referencia Necesaria para la Investigaciôn Agrícola en México." Unpublished.

Vogel, Ezra (1979) *Japan as Number One.* Cambridge, MA: Harvard University Press.

Walker, Charles R. (1957) *Toward the Automatic Factory.* New York: Harper & Row.

Walker, Charles and Robert Guest (1952) *The Man on the Assembly Line.* Cambridge, MA: Harvard University Press.

Walker, Charles, Robert Guest, and Arthur Turner (1956) *The Foreman on the Assembly Line.* Cambridge, MA: Harvard University Press.

Walton, Richard and Robert McKersie (1965) *A Behavioral Theory of Labor Negotiations.* New York: McGraw-Hill.

Walton, R.E. (1985) "From Control to Commitment in the Workplace." U.S. Department of Labor, Bureau of Labor-Management Relations and Cooperative Programs, September brief. Reprinted from *Harvard Business Review* (March-April): 76-84.

Walton, R.E. with C. Allen and M. Gaffney (1987) *Innovating to Compete: Lessons for Diffusing and Managing Change in the Workplace.* San Francisco: Jossey-Bass.

Walton, R.E. and M.E. Gaffney (1989) "Research, Action and Participation: The Merchant Shipping Case." *American Behavioral Scientist* 32, 5: 582-611.

Whyte, William F. (1943) *Street Corner Society.* Chicago: University of Chicago Press.

Whyte, William F. (1948) *Human Relations in the Restaurant Industry.* New York: McGraw-Hill.

Whyte, William F. (1955) *Money and Motivation.* New York: Harper & Row.

Whyte, William F. (1959) *Man and Organization: Three Problems in Human Relations in Industry.* Homewood, IL: Richard D. Irwin.

Whyte, William F. (1960-1961) "The Card Shuffling Method of Graduate Education." *Human Organization* 19, 4: 169.

Whyte, William F. (1961) *Men at Work.* Homewood, IL: Richard D. Irwin.

Whyte, William F. (1963) "Culture, Industrial Relations, and Economic Development: The Case of Peru." *Industrial and Labor Relations Review* 16, 4: 583-594.

Whyte, William F. (1969) *Organizational Behavior: Theory and Application.* Homewood, IL: Richard D. Irwin/Dorsey Press.

Whyte, William F. (1972) "Pigeons, Persons and Piece Rates." *Psychology Today* (July): 67-68, 96-99.

Whyte, William F. (1975) *Organizing for Agricultural Development.* Rutgers, NJ: Transaction Books.

Whyte, William F. (1977) "Potatoes, Peasants, and Professors: A Development Strategy for Peru." *Sociological Practice* 2, 1: 7-23.

Whyte, William F. (1978) "Review of The Elusive Phenomena." *Human Organization* 37, 4: 412-420.

Whyte, William F. (1981) *Participatory Approaches to Agricultural Research and Development.* Ithaca, NY: Cornell University Rural Development Committee.

Whyte, William F. (1982) "Social Inventions for Solving Human Problems." *American Sociological Review* 47, 1: 1-13.

Whyte, William F. (1984) *Learning from the Field.* Beverly Hills, CA: Sage.

Whyte, William F. (1989) "Advancing Scientific Knowledge Through Participatory Action Research." *Sociological Forum* 4, 3: 367-385.

Whyte, William F. ed. (1990) *Participatory Action Research.* Newbury Park, CA: Sage.

Whyte, William F. and Giorgio Alberti (1976) *Power, Politics and Progress: Social Change in Rural Peru.* New York: Elsevier.

Whyte, William F. and Damon Boynton, eds. (1983) *Higher Yielding Human Systems for Agriculture.* Ithaca, NY: Cornell University Press.

Whyte, William F. and Robert R. Braun (1968) "On Language and Culture," in H. Becker et al., eds., *Institutions and the Person.* Chicago: Aldine.

Whyte, William F. and Sidney Garfield (1950/51) "The Collective Bargaining Process: A Human Relations Analysis." *Human Organization* (Winter-Autumn).

Whyte, William F., D.J. Greenwood, and Peter Lazes (1989) "Participatory Action Research: Through Practice to Science in Social Research." *American Behavioral Scientist* 32, 5: 513-551.

Whyte, William F. and Kathleen King Whyte (1988) *Making Mondragón: The Growth and Dynamics of the Worker Cooperative Complex.* Ithaca, NY: ILR Press.

Whyte, William F. and L.K. Williams (1968) *Toward an Integrated Theory of Development: Economic and Non-Economic Variables in Rural Development.* Ithaca, NY: New York State School of Industrial and Labor Relations, Cornell University.

Woodward, Joan (1965) *Industrial Organization: Theory and Practice.* London: Oxford University Press.

Worthy, James C. (1950) "Organization Structure and Employee Morale." *American Sociological Review* 15, 2: 169-179.

Worthy, James C. (1984) *Shaping an American Institution: Robert E. Wood and Sears, Roebuck.* Urbana: University of Illinois Press.

Zaleznik, A., C.R. Christensen, F.J. Roethlisberger, with the assistance of G.C. Homans (1958) *The Motivation, Productivity, and Satisfaction of Workers: A Prediction Study.* Boston: Harvard Graduate School of Business Administration.

Zandstra, Hubert, Kenneth Swanberg, Carlos Zulberti, and Barry Nestel (1979) *Caqueza: Living Rural Development.* Ottawa: International Development Research Centre (IRDC).

Index

About the Author

In this book, William Foote Whyte distills out of more than fifty years of field exploration what he has learned regarding processes of participation and organizational learning in agriculture and industry. Working with others or alone, Whyte has always reached out to hear from workers, supervisors, managers, farmers, agricultural researchers, and extension agents how they view their work world. He presents that view in a framework of analysis that is both theoretically significant and practically useful. In the course of this social exploration, Whyte develops novel and productive field research methods.

Whyte received his Ph.D. in sociology from the University of Chicago. Since 1949 he has been at Cornell University's New York State School of Industrial and Labor Relations, where he is now Research Director of Programs for Employment and Workplace Systems, a consulting and applied research organization.

He has been President of the Society for Applied Anthropology, the Industrial Relations Research Association, and the American Sociological Association.

His best known book, *Street Corner Society,* first published in 1943, has come to be considered a sociological classic and is still widely used in teaching. It has been translated into Spanish, Italian, Chinese, and Japanese, and a German edition will be published in 1991. His most recent books are *Learning from the Field* and the edited volume *Participatory Action Research.*

NOTES

NOTES

NOTES